MANAGEMENT
Responsibility for Performance

McGraw-Hill Series in Management

Consulting Editors
Fred Luthans
Keith Davis

The string quartet pictured on the front cover is in many ways a metaphor for the organization of the 1990s. Like the string quartet, today's organization requires the specialized skills of each of its members. Yet it also requires the kind of shared purpose that can only come when every member plays from the same piece of music. As with the string quartet, today's organization requires harmony and teamwork to reinforce and celebrate the contributions of each of its members. And it may require the members of the organization to provide their own leadership, as often happens with a string quartet. Finally, the organization of the 1990s shares with the string quartet the challenging goal of excellence in its performance. The only difference is that in the organization, management is the responsibility for achieving that goal.

MANAGEMENT
Responsibility for Performance

Peter Hess
Julie Siciliano
Western New England College

McGraw-Hill, Inc.

New York   St. Louis   San Francisco   Auckland   Bogotá   Caracas
Lisbon   London   Madrid   Mexico City   Milan   Montreal   New Delhi
San Juan   Singapore   Sydney   Tokyo   Toronto

McGraw-Hill

A Division of The **McGraw·Hill** Companies

MANAGEMENT
Responsibility for Performance

This book is printed on acid-free paper.

4 5 6 7 8 9 0   DOC   DOC   9 0 9 8 7

ISBN 0-07-028457-1

This book was set in Palatino by Ruttle, Shaw & Wetherill, Inc.
The editors were Lynn Richardson, Dan Alpert, and Ira C. Roberts;
the designer was Amy Becker;
the production supervisor was Kathryn Porzio.
The photo editor was Kathy Bendo;
the photo researcher was Debra P. Hershkowitz.
R. R. Donnelley & Sons Company was printer and binder.

Library of Congress Cataloging-in-Publication Data

Hess, Peter (Peter William), (date).
    Management: responsibility for performance / Peter Hess, Julie
Siciliano.
        p.   cm.—(McGraw-Hill series in management)
    Includes bibliographical references and index.
    ISBN 0-07-028457-1
    1. Management.   I. Siciliano, Julie, (date).   II. Title.
III. Series.
    HD31.H474   1996
    658—dc20   95-16946

INTERNATIONAL EDITION
Copyright 1996. Exclusive rights by The McGraw-Hill Companies, Inc. for manufacture and export. This book cannot be re-exported from the country to which it is consigned by McGraw-Hill. The International Edition is not available in North America.

When ordering this title, use ISBN 0-07-114310-6.

2 3 4 5 6 7 8 9 0   DOC/DOC   9 9 8 7 6

PHOTO, ILLUSTRATION, AND TEXT CREDITS

PHOTOS

Section I FPG, International.

Section II Comstock.

Section III FPG, International.

Section IV FPG, International.

Section V Lou Jones/The Image Bank.

Section VI FPG, International.

Chapter 2 Figure 2-6: *Left,* The Smithsonian Institution; *Center,* GMI Marketing Association; *Right,* Baker Library, Fogg Museum.

TEXT AND ILLUSTRATIONS

Chapter 1 Figure 1-3: "Ten Roles of the Manager" from *The Nature of Managerial Work* by Henry Mintzberg. Copyright © 1973 by Henry Mintzberg. Reprinted by permission of HarperCollins Publishers, Inc. **Figure 1-6:** Reprinted from June 28, 1993 issue of *Business Week* by special permission, copyright © 1993 by McGraw-Hill, Inc. **Figure 1-7:** Reprinted from March 14, 1994 issue of *Business Week* by special permission, copyright © 1994 by McGraw-Hill, Inc.

Chapter 3 Figure 3-2: Adapted from Charles Garfield, *Second to None: How Our Smartest Companies Put People First,* Richard D. Irwin, Inc. © 1992, 333–340. **Figure 3-4:** Reprinted from March 8, 1993 issue of *Business Week* by special permission, copyright © 1993 by McGraw-Hill, Inc.

Chapter 5 Figure 5-6: Irving L. Janis, *Groupthink,* Second Edition. Copyright © 1982 by Houghton Mifflin Company. Reprinted with permission.

Chapter 6 Figure 6-2: Courtesy of Ben & Jerry's. **Figure 6-3:** Courtesy of Johnson & Johnson. **Pages 147–149:** Adapted with the permission of The Free Press, a Division of Simon & Schuster Inc. from *Competitive Advantage: Creating and Sustaining Superior Performance* by Michael E. Porter. Copyright © 1985 by Michael E. Porter.

Chapter 7 Figure 7-4: *Fortune,* © 1994 Time Inc. All rights reserved.

Chapter 9 Management Exercise, pages 218–220: This exercise was developed by William P. Ferris and was presented at the Eastern Academy of Management, Baltimore, MD, 1992. The sections of the Job Diagnostic Survey are used with permission from J. Richard Hackman and Greg R. Oldham, *Work Redesign,* © 1980 by Addison-Wesley Publishing Co., Inc. **From the Manager's E-Mail, pages 221–223:** David R. Hampton, *Management,* 3/e, pp. 286–289, © 1986 by McGraw-Hill, Inc. All rights reserved.

Chapter 10 Figure 10-1: Reprinted from May 9, 1994 issue of *Business Week* by special permission, copyright © 1994 by McGraw-Hill, Inc. **Figure 10-8:** Reprinted with permission from "Leadership, The Art of Empowering Others," by J. A. Conger, *Academy of Management Executive,* 1989, pp. 17–24. **Figure 10–11:** Courtesy of Lincoln Electric.

Chapter 11 Figure 11-2: Douglas McGregor, The Human Side of Enterprise, 1960, McGraw-Hill. Reproduced with permission. **Figure 11-4:** The Leadership Grid Figure for *Leadership Dilemmas—Grid Solutions,* by Robert R. Blake and Anne Adams McCanse. (Formerly the Managerial Grid figure by Robert R. Blake and Jane S. Mouton) Houston: Gulf Publishing Company, page 29. Copyright 1991 by Scientific Methods, Inc. Reproduced by permission of the owners. **Figure 11-5:** Hersey/Blanchard, *Management of Organizational Behavior: Utilizing Human Resources,* 6/e © 1993, p. 186. Adopted by permission of Prentice-Hall, Inc., Englewood Cliffs, NJ. Also, reprinted with permission from Hersey, Paul, (1984). *The Situational Leader,* p. 63, Escondido, California: The Center for Leadership Studies. All rights reserved. **Figure 11-6:** Reprinted with permission of Fred E. Fiedler. **Figure 11-8:** Kouzes, James M. and Posner, Barry Z. *The Leadership Challenge: How to Get Extraordinary Things Done in Organizations,* Copyright 1987 by Jossey-Bass, Inc., pp. 279–280.

Chapter 12 Figure 12-3: Certo, Samuel C./Graf, *Modern Management: Diversity, Quality, Ethics & the Global Environment,* 6/e, © 1994, p. 563. Adopted by permission of Prentice-Hall, Inc., Englewood Cliffs, NJ. **Figure 12-8:** *Fortune,* © 1993 Time, Inc. All rights reserved.

Chapter 13 Figure 13-4: Reprinted by permission of *Harvard Business Review.* An exhibit from "Choosing Strategies for Change," (March-April 1979). Copyright © 1979 by the President and Fellows of Harvard College; all rights reserved. **Management Exercise, page 320:** From *Organizational Behavior,* 5th Edition by Richard M. Steers and J. Stewart Black. Copyright © 1994 by HarperCollins College Publishers. Reprinted by permission.

To Mary, Simon, Erika, and Andrew
P. H.

To Bob, Andrea, John, and Irene
J. S.

CONTENTS

PREFACE

The field of management is complex and dynamic. Given this complexity, we've always found it a challenge to integrate and synthesize for our students the broad and evolving range of theories and principles that define this discipline. In teaching the introductory management course, we have searched for years for a book that was simpler and more focused and less concerned with providing an encyclopedia of every element of the field. Recently, several texts promised a more focused approach; however, these appear to be scaled-down versions of what were originally larger texts. This book is our effort to create a learning tool that supports the focus on integration and synthesis that we feel is essential to our students' learning and understanding.

A DIFFERENT APPROACH

We feel that there are three elements that distinguish our approach in this book:

1. A single theme runs throughout the book to support our goal of greater integration. Management is defined as responsibility for performance, and every chapters examines management concepts and issues from the perspective of how to improve organizational performance.

2. We organize the material into thirteen chapters, rather than the much larger number of chapters typical of most introductory management textbooks—consistent with our goal of greater synthesis. We also feel this smaller number of chapters is more realistic given the time-frame of the typical quarter or semester.

3. Each chapter maintains a simpler and more clearly-defined story line, by focusing on the key ideas and developments within each chapter, and by minimizing potentially distracting boxes and other special features.

Consistent theme, right-size in terms of the number of chapters, greater focus within each chapter, and expanded opportunity for alternative learning activities. These are the important elements that we feel distinguish our approach. In addition to these distinguishing elements, the book also includes a number of features designed to enhance student learning.

KEY FEATURES

- The book includes complete coverage of the full range of topics and issues currently defining the field of management. Each of the traditional responsibilities of management are covered, including goal setting, decision making, and the management functions. In addition, reflecting the most current trends in management thinking, we also include coverage of such topics as quality and continuous improvement, teamwork, diversity, ethics and social responsibility, the global dimension, and information technology and change. Each of these current issues is introduced in the opening chapters and revisited either as a chapter focus or as part of the discussion of related issues in other chapters.

- A second key feature is the simplicity that characterizes the book's design. We have attempted to minimize the number of boxes and other special features in the text that at times can draw the student's eye and attention away from the key points of the chapter. Instead we have fully integrated within the chapter narrative the current examples that are so effective in illustrating the concepts and challenges of management.

- The third key feature of our book is the opportunity for students to apply the ideas they are learning in the course. The end-of-chapter discussion questions in many cases require students to apply management concepts to their own experience. Each chapter also includes a management mini-case or experiential exercise that involves students directly in management decisions and organizational problems. Finally, our Manager's E-Mail feature at the end of each section engages students in a variety of complex management issues such as reengineering, pay for performance, the challenges of teams and social responsibility. In this feature the student assumes the role of manager and receives competing opinions on these issues in the form of E-mail memos from the manager's superiors, colleagues, and subordinates. The student is required to make decisions using the available data just as the manager would in comparable situations.

These key features and the distinguishing elements discussed earlier reflect our goal of greater focus, integration, and synthesis in the introductory management course. Given the complexity and diversity of this field, this goal represents a significant challenge. We hope that other instructors will view this book as a solid first step in the direction of providing our students with a more effective tool for learning about and understanding the dynamic field of management.

ACKNOWLEDGMENTS

Credit for making this book a reality goes first to Lynn Richardson, Senior Editor at McGraw Hill. Without her vision and commitment to a right-size text for the introductory management course, we would never have had the opportunity to pursue the development of this project. Our thanks go also to the other fine professionals on the McGraw Hill team. To Michael Fried for his guidance and support when we were preparing the initial proposal; to Dan Alpert for carefully shepherding us through the various stages of the book's development; and to Ira Roberts for his valuable insights and thoughtful attention in editing our manuscript.

We also wish to acknowledge the valuable insights and suggestions of our manuscript reviewers: Henry J. Coleman, Jr., St. Mary's College of California; Eugene Garaventa, College of Staten Island; Jean M. Hanebury, Texas A&M-Corpus Christi; Donna Leonowich, Middlesex County Tech College; Lucia C. Rohrer Murphy, Ursinus College; Alison Pittman, Brevard Community College; and Craig Tunwall, Ithaca College.

This book also reflects the continuing support we receive from our colleagues at Western New England College. The Management Department in the School of Business has in many ways been a support group for us not only on this project but in our professional careers. We extend special thanks to the MAN 101 team. In particular to Frederick Brown, who was an important catalyst in creating the early versions of this text; to Henry Bazan, our mentor and role model in emphasizing the needs of students in the introductory management course; and to Angelo Teixeira for his feedback on exercises and early versions of the book. Genuine enthusiasm for our ideas and continuing interest in our progress came also from David Bowman, Anthony Chelte, Russell Fanelli, William Ferris, Harvey Shrage and Ned Schwartz.

For supporting our efforts and providing important access to the College's technical resources, we thank Stanley Kowalski, Dean of the School of Business. Our appreciation goes also to Lucia Spahr for her assistance with earlier versions of the project and to Donna Utter and Janet Condon for their invaluable computer assistance. In addition, our special thanks are extended to Jack Greeley for his timely assistance in developing the Instructor's Manual.

Peter Hess
Julie Siciliano

MANAGEMENT
Responsibility for Performance

SECTION

I

Introduction to Management

This book presents the concepts, practices, and challenges that make up the dynamic and critical discipline of management. While our focus is the management of business organizations, the ideas discussed here are also applicable to the management of schools, hospitals, government units, community service agencies, and volunteer groups—every kind of organization that depends upon effective management for the achievement of its goals.

The first section introduces you to the concept of management, its history, and the social, information technology, and global issues faced by management today.

Chapter 1 is a survey of the dimensions of the management challenge. It explains what we mean by management; discusses how management impacts the numerous stakeholders of an organization; and describes the emerging challenges that confront management in terms of a changing environment, a changing workplace, and changing performance standards for every kind of organization.

Chapter 2 traces the development of management as an evolving field of concepts, theories, issues, and practices. The central management question is how to improve the performance of organizations. This chapter reviews and explores the range of answers to that question that have emerged from the Industrial Revolution to the Information Age.

Chapter 3 considers three prominent issues for organizations as they approach the twenty-first century. The first is social responsibility: the steadily growing expectation that organizations not only must do well economically, but also must "do good" by responding to social issues and problems. The second is the impact of computers and other information technology on how work is done in organizations, and on the people doing that work. The third issue is global markets. With competition now international in virtually every industry, there is strong incentive for organizations to perform successfully in global markets.

CHAPTER 1
The Management Challenge

LEARNING OBJECTIVES

After studying this chapter, you should be able to:

- *Define the concepts of organization and management, and explain the view that management is shared responsibility for performance of organizations.*

- *Discuss why effective management is essential in modern societies.*

- *Identify the stakeholders that rely on an organization's success.*

- *Describe how the changing environment has made the task of management much more difficult.*

- *Explain what is meant by the changing workplace and the kind of challenge to management that the workplace now represents.*

- *Discuss the changing performance standards of quality, speed, flexibility, innovation, and sustainable growth.*

I t has been suggested that no force in the twentieth century has done as much as management to improve the quality of life in societies around the world.[1] More than anything else, it is management that has fundamentally changed the living conditions of the ordinary person. Management has moved the common worker from behind the loom and the ox-drawn plow and away from the shovel and pick to the more skilled and often more satisfying work required to build computers and supersonic jets, and to operate modern businesses and complex organizations.

Prior to the emergence of management, the norm in almost every corner of the world for thousands of years had been hard work for bare survival. For all but the elite in every society, life consisted of endless days of backbreaking work either in the fields or as a common laborer. With the emergence of management, all of this began to change.

The impact of management was first felt with the Industrial Revolution and the rise of the factory system in Europe two hundred years ago. For the first time, craftsmen were drawn from their cottages and brought together under a single roof to take advantage of advances in technology such as mechanical looms and steam and water power. These new centers of production were called *manufactories*. The process of making these manufactories productive became known as "management."

The Industrial Revolution spread across Europe in the nineteenth century and on to the United States and to Japan. Today it is transforming the economies of Mexico and South America, and of countries along the Pacific Rim such as Taiwan, Hong Kong, South Korea, Singapore, and Malaysia. In all of these societies the pattern is the same: Poor farmers and manual laborers who once struggled just for survival now perform the skilled tasks that yield prosperity not only for their families but for the nations in which they live as well. The reason is management.

DEFINING ORGANIZATIONS AND MANAGEMENT

To understand the concept of management, it is necessary first to understand the concept of organization. An *organization* is a group of people working together to achieve a common purpose. Organizations exist to achieve goals that individuals can't achieve on their own. Besides the family, which is a special case, hunting parties were perhaps the earliest form of organizations. They were formed to track and kill animals that were too large or too fast to be brought down by a single individual. Today organizations exist to produce products or services that can't be produced by individuals working alone.

As shown in Figure 1-1, the traditional definition of management is *the coordination of human, material, technological, and financial resources needed for an organization to achieve its goals*. Management gathers the resources—the people, the financing, the technology—required to make work and workers more productive. Management designs the tasks and organizes the work to be done. It ensures the skills and the coordination necessary for the kind of cooperative effort that is the essence of organizations. Finally, it provides the sense of direction and purpose that can unify diverse people in a productive enterprise.

In this book, we will use a kind of shorthand for this larger definition of management: Management is responsibility for performance. Management is responsibility for the organization's achieving its goals. The goals may vary depending on whether the organization is a business, nonprofit, government, or volunteer group. But management is always the same: responsibility for the organization's achieving its goals; responsibility for performance.

In sum, organizations exist to perform tasks that can only be performed through cooperative effort, and management is responsibility for the performance and success of organizations.

Understanding Management

Seventy-five years ago, a French engineer named Henri Fayol provided a kind of "job description" for managers. He suggested there are five functions that define the manager's job,[2] as shown in Figure 1-2.

Fayol's definition of the functions of the manager were so clear and so concise that they have served almost as a definition of management itself for most of this century. According to Fayol, for organizations to achieve their goals management must perform the five key functions of planning, organizing, commanding, coordinating, and controlling.

More recently (1975), management researcher Henry Mintzberg provided a slightly different point of view of management.[3] After carefully observing what executive managers actually do with their time, Mintzberg suggested that management might be more effectively defined in terms of the roles that managers perform in the course of managing. Mintzberg identified the ten key managerial roles shown in Figure 1-3.

Together, Fayol's and Mintzberg's models provide an important understanding of the wide variety of functions and roles that managers are called upon to perform. However, even in the relatively short period of time since Mintzberg's research, our understanding of management has shifted. Perhaps the most significant change is the fact that managers no longer are the only ones engaged in the tasks, functions, and roles of management.

Organization	Any group of people working together to achieve a common purpose or goals that could not be attained by individuals working separately.
Management	• The coordination of human, material, technological, and financial resources needed for the organization to achieve its goals.
	• Responsibility for performance.

Figure 1-1 Organization and Management Defined

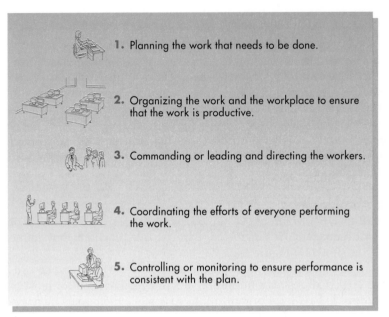

Figure 1-2 Functions of Management According to Fayol

Management as Shared Responsibility

Over the past ten to fifteen years, there has been a growing recognition that organizations have become too complex to be managed by managers alone. Organizations have discovered that performance is often better when management is the responsibility not only of managers, but of performance teams as well.

Consider the case of Chesapeake Packaging, a subsidiary of Chesapeake Corporation based in Richmond, Virginia. At Chesapeake Packaging, each department is operated like a mini-company.[4] Like an actual company, each department is responsible for selecting its own leaders, hiring its own personnel, and developing its own work processes. Teams within each department handle budgets, production schedules, and quality levels, and deal with their own internal and external customers. In short, these teams and departments perform for themselves many of the managerial tasks that used to be performed by the company's top managers.

This shift from management by managers to self-managing teams can be seen in organizations as different as Xerox, Bloomingdale's, and the U.S. Air Force, in companies as large as Ford Motor Company and as small as a local advertising agency. Management is increasingly a responsibility shared among team leaders, self-managing work groups, and all of the professionals involved in the performance of the organization.

It is important to remember that our understanding of management is true for management in every context: as true for executive managers as it is for the members of self-managing work units like those at Chesapeake Packaging; as true

1. Figurehead — representing the organization at events and ceremonies.

2. Leader — exercising influence with people and events.

3. Liaison — interacting with other organizations.

4. Monitor — receiving information critical for performance.

5. Disseminator — sharing information within the organization.

6. Spokesperson — presenting information outside the organization.

7. Entrepreneur — initiating change to improve performance.

8. Disturbance handler — dealing with issues and crises inside and outside of the organization.

9. Resource allocator — determining where the organization's human and financial resources and technology will be used.

10. Negotiator — bargaining to arrive at agreements with groups and individuals both within and outside the organization.

Figure 1-3 Mintzberg's Ten Key Managerial Roles

for store managers as it is for teachers in a classroom, or for volunteer board members in a community organization. All of these individuals and groups are engaged in management; each shares in the responsibility for the performance of their organizations.

THE IMPORTANCE OF MANAGEMENT

As we pointed out at the beginning of this chapter, management has achieved unprecedented success during the past two hundred years in transforming the economies of whole nations and, over time, the quality of life of the people living in them. As a result, societies have come to rely on their organizations more than ever before, and on management to make their organizations perform.

We Are a Society of Organizations

Peter Drucker points out that modern industrialized nations consist largely of organizations.[5] In many ways, the story of the twentieth century in America has been one of moving from smaller, more personal interactions to satisfy our needs to relying on organizations for almost everything.

Today we are born and treated in health care organizations. We rely on public school systems and colleges and universities for our education. The food on our table often comes to us from huge agricultural companies, through complex transportation systems and supermarket chains. For housing and clothing, for employment, for transportation, for communication, recreation, and entertainment—for the satisfaction of virtually every one of our individual needs, we rely on some kind of organization, large or small. This makes the task of management critical.

And it is not just a case of organizations meeting the needs of individuals. Organizations must also meet the needs of society in general. In industrialized societies all around the world, it is management that must ensure that educational systems provide children with the knowledge and skills to become productive, contributing members of society. It is management's responsibility to ensure that health care organizations promote, maintain, and, where necessary, restore health. Effective management ensures that governments provide needed services at a cost society can afford. It ensures that businesses provide quality products and services at competitive prices. And it is management's responsibility to see that organizations provide jobs for a steadily increasing portion of the world's population. We are indeed a society of organizations, and it is management's responsibility to ensure that they succeed at their many different tasks.

Organizations Are Interconnected

Further raising the stakes for management is the fact that society's organizations do not exist separately and independently from one another. They are interconnected and woven into the very fabric of society. In our society of organizations, when one organization falters or fails, others are almost always threatened. When our schools have difficulty educating our youth, our business organizations eventually suffer for lack of the skilled workers they need to compete, and lose their own ability to generate jobs. When our health care organizations aren't operated efficiently, our government is forced into debt to pay for health care for the elderly and the poor. When our businesses are not well managed, the communities where they are located suffer unemployment and social problems.

Consider the case of Sears, the company that virtually created the catalog sales business one hundred years ago. As competition from Spiegel, L. L. Bean, and other companies became more intense, Sears found itself unable to compete, and in 1993 it decided to eliminate its catalog sales operations. The impact on the thousands of Sears employees who lost their jobs in this move is obvious. Less apparent are the shock waves felt in businesses large and small outside of Sears.[6] For example:

- The company that photographed home furnishings for Sears lost $400,000 a year and was forced to lay off four of its workers.

- The company that provided cut flowers for the photography company lost $8,000 a year in revenues.

- The drugstore that sold the film for the Sears photography lost $10,000 in film sales.

- The company that built the sets for the pictures lost $25,000 in business.

- The Chicago company that printed the Sears catalog eliminated eight hundred jobs.

- The company that processed the Sears film lost $16,000 in sales.

- The U.S. Postal Service estimated it would lose $90 million to $100 million in yearly revenues from mailing Sears catalogs.

And this is only a partial list. Think of the thousands of jobs lost in all of the companies that manufactured products sold primarily through the Sears catalog.

The impact of the failure of a smaller organization—a small business, for example—would obviously be less widespread than the impact of problems at a giant like Sears. Still, whenever even a small organization fails, there are customers and employees who are affected, creditors and suppliers who don't get paid. The restaurants and stores where the employees used to spend their money feel the loss. And the morale and spirit of a community invariably suffer whenever one of its organizations fails to succeed.

The Concept of Stakeholders

One way to consider the interconnectedness of organizations to other organizations and individuals around them is through the concept of stakeholders. Figure 1-4 shows the numerous organizations, groups, and individuals who have an interest or stake in the performance and success of an organization.

The point of thinking in terms of stakeholders is this: In a society such as ours, the effects of an organization's management are felt far beyond the organization's own four walls. When an organization falters or fails in achieving its goals—whether it is a business or a school system—it not only fails to satisfy the needs of its customers and employees, it threatens all of the organizations around

Figure 1-4 Stakeholders of an Organization

it that depend on its success. This is another reason why effective management has never been more important.

MANAGEMENT IN A CHANGING WORLD

The management challenge has never been easy to meet. It has never been a simple task to combine and coordinate human, technological, and financial resources to achieve organizational goals. Organizations by their nature are complex and therefore difficult to manage. Still, as long as society, the economy, and technology remained somewhat stable or changed only slowly, management had time to make the adjustments necessary to maintain and improve performance.

During the past twenty years, however, that stability has disappeared. Gradual change has been replaced by rapid change. Today the world of the manager looks very little like the manager's world of even just twenty years ago. There is a whole new set of conditions in the environment in which management must operate. The workplace that management must coordinate is vastly different. There is an entirely different thrust to the performance standards that every management must now achieve. In short, as shown in Figure 1-5, the manager's world is a world of change.

The Changing Environment

An organization's *environment* is the set of conditions in the world outside the organization. This includes the competition and outside stakeholders, as well as political, economic, technological, and social conditions in the world beyond the organization's four walls. In recent years, these outside factors have begun to demand new attention and emphasis. Consider a few of the more significant changes.

The New Competition

Discussions of competition tend to focus on the tremendous increase in global competition as the major change. There is no question that the field of competing nations has grown significantly in recent years. For most of this century competition in trading was primarily between the United States and European nations, with Japan entering the field in earnest in the 1970s. Ten years ago, the Pacific Rim

CHANGING ENVIRONMENT	CHANGING WORKPLACE	CHANGING PERFORMANCE STANDARDS
• New competition	• Workforce diversity	• Quality
• Global markets	• Performance teams	• Speed and flexibility
• Ethical standards	• Information technology	• Innovation
• Social responsibility		• Sustainable growth

Figure 1-5 The Changing World of Management

countries—Taiwan, Hong Kong, Korea, Malaysia, and others—entered the competition. Now China appears ready to compete, with Brazil not far behind.[7]

Change has occurred, however, not just in the number of competitors but also in the nature of the competition itself. Competition for customers has become much more adversarial. It is not the foreignness of competition alone that characterizes what Tom Peters has termed "the new competition"; it is the nature and intensity of that competition. Here is Peters's picture of what the new competition is all about:

> . . . No organization can take anything in its market for granted. Suppose you are considering next year's strategy for a maturing product. Here's what you might well find:
>
> ● a new Korean competitor
>
> ● an old Japanese competitor continuing to reduce costs and improve quality
>
> ● a dozen domestic start-ups, each headed by talented people claiming a technology breakthrough
>
> ● one old-line domestic competitor that has slashed overhead costs by 60 percent and is de-integrating via global sourcing as fast as it can.
>
> ● another old-line domestic competitor that has just . . . sold off the division that competes with you to another strong competitor with a great distribution system
>
> ● a competitor that has just introduced an electronics-based distribution system that wires it to each of its 2,500 principal distributors, slashing the time required to fill orders by 75 percent.[8]

And as Peters points out, with only minor changes this scenario is as true for hospitals, colleges, and community organizations as it is for businesses. This is the new competition: a competition for customers that is both more crowded and more intense than ever before.

Global Markets

In the economically developed nations of Europe, America, and Asia, business organizations have largely satisfied the demand for most goods and many services. Also, the populations in these nations are not growing very rapidly. If businesses in these countries are to continue to grow, they will have to do it by entering foreign markets. In other words, not only must organizations learn to succeed against the new competition, they also must learn to compete in markets around the world.

Competing in foreign markets represents both a change and a challenge for most organizations. It means developing products and services that match the tastes and demands of consumers in other cultures. It means learning how to market and sell in ways that are consistent with cultural differences. It means learning how to "do business" from thousands of miles away. It was certainly easier doing business only in America, selling American goods to American customers. But with little opportunity for growth at home, and with 95 percent of the world's population outside the United States, the shift to a global marketplace is a challenge that management must answer.

Ethical Standards

Ethical behavior is behavior that is consistent with society's standards about what is morally acceptable. Evidence continues to mount that organizations of all kinds have a long way to go before they are consistently meeting society's standards of ethical behavior. Society expects organizations to conduct themselves in a way that is honest in terms of telling the truth, and fair in terms of how they treat their customers, their shareholders, their employees, and society in general. Too often, this is not happening. Consider the following examples of ethics violations that came to light during a six-month period in 1992:

- Sears Tire and Auto Centers in California were charged with systematically overcharging customers or performing unnecessary repairs so that managers could meet performance targets.

- Ernst & Young, one of the country's most prestigious public accounting firms, agreed to pay a $400 million fine for accounting practices that contributed to the national savings and loans failures that cost U.S. taxpayers billions of dollars.

- Dow Corning was charged by the Food and Drug Administration with withholding research findings on Dow's silicone breast implants.

Problems with ethical behavior are not recent or new in organizations. To realize how long these problems have been with us, one need only consider the child labor practices in nineteenth-century England, or the controversial entrepreneurs whose business practices between the Civil War and the early twentieth century gave them the nickname "robber barons." It might be suggested that more violations are now coming to light because the media is more aggressive in investigating them, or that the environment of intense competition is pressuring organizations to "cheat" more than ever before. Complicating this issue even further is the fact that other nations have different standards of what is fair and honest. For example, providing a payment to a company in return for being awarded a contract or for receiving an order would be considered bribery by U.S. standards, yet in the Middle East and elsewhere such payments are a normal part of the business transaction.

For these reasons, issues relating to ethics can be difficult under the present circumstances. Still, there is no question that management is increasingly expected to operate in ways consistent with society's standards of fairness and honesty.

Social Responsibility

Social responsibility means that organizations are expected not only to provide society with goods and services, but also to contribute to the social well-being of the communities where they operate. Increasingly, business organizations are expected to balance concerns for profit with considerations of what is good for society.

Examples of social responsibility are everywhere, and are appearing at an ever-increasing rate. In the 1980s McDonald's switched from plastic to paper packaging; and since 1990, it has spent over $500 million on recycled products ranging from paper napkins to building insulation and roofing materials. Wal-Mart is experimenting with a "green" (environmentally sensitive) store design that uses skylights to reduce the amount of electricity needed for lighting; its air conditioning doesn't use ozone-depleting chlorofluorocarbons and its buildings are made of recycled building materials.[9]

Socially responsible organizations also support service programs in the communities in which they operate. Monsanto, for example, runs training programs for local public school science teachers. And as a community member, General Electric was cited for a program that sends employees out in groups to renovate community buildings like Boys and Girls Clubs and YMCAs.[10]

In some cases, however, social responsibility has been mandated by the government to ensure that organizations treat employees, consumers, and the public responsibly. Even Monsanto, mentioned above for its service to the community, has been required by law to reduce the amount of pollution emitted from its production facilities. Today there are more than sixty-five government agencies to which organizations and their managements are accountable. The 1970s alone saw the creation of government agencies like the Equal Employment Opportunity Commission, the Environmental Protection Agency, the Occupational Safety and Health Administration, and the Consumer Protection Agency.

Critics argue that high expectations of social responsibility reduce corporations' ability to compete against businesses from countries where there are fewer or no such expectations.[11] They question how a U.S. company operating under the constraints of social responsibility can compete with a company from Mexico, for example, where there is no minimum wage, few safety regulations, and little in the way of pollution controls. Proponents respond that demanding social responsibility of our corporations is a price that developed nations must be willing to pay to ensure the safety and fair treatment of workers and customers, clean air and water, and an overall improved quality of life in our communities.[12] It is to achieve these societal goals that management is increasingly expected to transform corporations into both focused competitors and socially responsible agents.

The Changing Workplace

As much as the environment outside the organization has changed over the past twenty years, what is happening inside the organization may have changed even more. Management must now exercise its responsibility through a workforce it would not recognize from a generation earlier, using work designs and information technology that simply did not exist, and at a rate of change that could not previously have been conceived. This is the changing workplace.

Workforce Diversity

Not that long ago the "typical" American worker was white and male, and so was management. Recent studies of the effect of demographics on the workforce, however, suggest that a steadily increasing percentage of the workers entering the workforce during the next fifteen years will be women and minorities. This trend is shown in Figure 1-6.[13]

The workforce is also becoming older as members of the huge Baby Boom generation move through their forties and into their fifties. In addition, the Americans with Disabilities Act passed in 1990 seeks to remove many of the barriers that formerly prevented individuals with physical disabilities from joining the workforce. The net effect of all of these changes is that the American workforce is now and will continue to become increasingly diverse in terms of gender, race, age, and physical abilities.

While the coordination of human resources has never been easy, this growing diversity in the workplace represents a special challenge for management. The greater the differences that people bring with them to the workplace, the greater the management effort needed to blend these differences and to unify efforts in a single direction. Levi-Strauss provides an excellent example of the kinds of efforts organizations are now undertaking to make the diverse workforce productive.

> Levi spends $5 million a year on its "Valuing Diversity" training program for employees. And that's just the beginning: Ads for openings "strongly encourage" minorities to apply. It supports in-house networking groups of blacks, Hispanics, lesbians and gay men. A Diversity Council, made up of two members of every group, regularly meets with Levi's executives. Part of each manager's bonus is even tied to meeting the goals in its "Aspirations Statement," which demands that employees aspire to appreciate diversity.[14]

As difficult as this challenge may be, many organizations feel that this growing diversity also presents a special opportunity. The increasing diversity of the workforce reflects the increasing diversity of the American population in general. The more the workforce inside an organization mirrors the diversity of the customers outside, the more likely it is that the organization will satisfy the needs of those diverse customers. As one manager from Levi-Strauss noted, "It's tough to design and develop products for markets you don't understand."

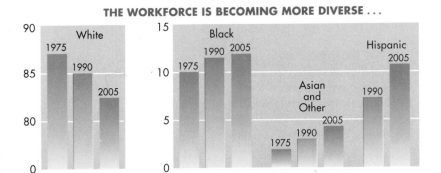

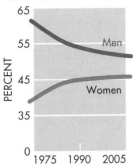

Figure 1-6 Workforce Demographics (*Source:* Business Week, *June 28, 1993*)

The workforce diversity challenge for management is to create a climate that will attract and empower the most able and talented workers of all ages, races, genders, and physical capabilities. It is a difficult but important challenge.

Performance Teams

Just as the composition of the workforce has changed, so too has the way the workforce is organized. As recently as the early 1980s, work was still primarily an individual activity. Even in the largest organizations, the work—whether it was a product or a bill, an order or an insurance claim—passed from individual to individual as it moved toward completion. There was talk of the group problem-solving approach that is part of Japanese management, but there was very little true teamwork in U.S. organizations.

During the 1980s, however, reports began to surface of team-based successes. The IBM PC, the Apple Macintosh, the Ford Taurus, and the GM Saturn were all successes attributed to a team-based approach. Soon the power of teams was being hailed from organizations as diverse as 3M, Bloomingdale's, General Electric, and the U.S. Air Force. And it wasn't just about project teams. Teamwork was applied to production, to customer service, and to eliminating administrative backlogs. In many cases, the results have been promising. Consider this example from Bell Atlantic:

> Bell Atlantic found that an order (for long-distance telephone lines) passed through 28 hands before it was filled. All those steps added costs, slowed the order down, and introduced opportunities for errors. To speed things up, the company . . . eliminated less relevant duties and assigned teams to follow a single order through to completion. Today, it can fill in hours some orders that once took 15 to 25 days.[15]

Recent research, however, suggests that teams may not be the answer in every situation. In a study of over 584 companies in the United States, Canada, Japan, and Germany, while teams were found to be most effective in identifying and solving problems, they appeared to lose their value once performance had improved.[16] In other words, while teamwork is a key element of the changing workplace, it may not be effective in every situation, and rarely is it easily implemented. Still, creating effective teamwork is clearly part of management's challenge in the changing workplace of the 1990s.

Information Technology

In organizations today, through the use of information technology, the same scanner that is used to check in an order of new parts or equipment also immediately adjusts the inventory records. The same scanner that records a sale also reorders the item if it is needed. The performance of employees can be monitored through the computer terminals they use to do their work. Meetings are held by E-mail with participants not even leaving their work station. New designs are fully tested through the use of computer simulation without a model or prototype ever being built. Every one of these applications of information technology is becoming increasingly common in the changing workplace.

However, merely adding information technology to an organization does not guarantee improved performance. General Motors spent billions on computers and robots in the 1980s, yet its real performance breakthrough in the Saturn automobile project was more a triumph of teamwork than of information technology.[17]

The challenge for management now is to find the right mix between information and an organization's resources, and to use information to enhance the performance of capital, people, and technology.

The Changing Performance Standards

During most of the thirty years immediately following the end of World War II, the primary pressure on organizations was for "more": more automobiles, more schools, more houses, more television sets, more everything. Families were producing the largest generation in this country's history, and to satisfy the exploding demand for just about everything, organizations—whatever "business" they were in—were expected to produce more. While there was always a concern for developing innovative, quality products, "more" was the standard that organizations and management had to meet to succeed.

All of that has changed over the past twenty years. As a result primarily of the new competition, "more" is not enough. Now there is an ever-increasing number of competitors trying to satisfy customers' needs. As a result, the capacity to produce goods and services exceeds the demand for them. In addition, customers will not accept products that are average in terms of quality and innovation. Today's standards place a whole new level of emphasis on quality, speed, flexibility, innovation, and sustainable growth.

Quality

If the old demand was always for "more," one of the new, essential requirements is "better." When volume was the key concern, making a product that was "good enough" was acceptable. However, because the customer now has choices, only "better" is good enough. The key to success has clearly become quality. If the prices of competing products or services are roughly comparable, the customer almost always will choose the one which he or she perceives to be of better quality.

During the 1980s, the problem for U.S. businesses was that people around the world rated the best of American products as only as good as the worst of the products produced by international competitors. For example, when asked whether "Made in America" meant quality, only 6 percent of West Germans agreed.[18] Even in America, the automobiles rated highest in quality tend to be Japanese or German rather than American.

During the 1990s, as shown in Figure 1-7, there has been improvement, but the standards of quality are rising as quickly as the rate of improvement. The pressure is on to compete globally, yet in the crucial area of quality, U.S. organizations began from well behind. And the quality problem does not just exist in the area of global competition. The demand for quality is just as clear in education, health care, and social and government services. To compete, organizations must deliver quality, and management in the United States has begun to accept this challenge.

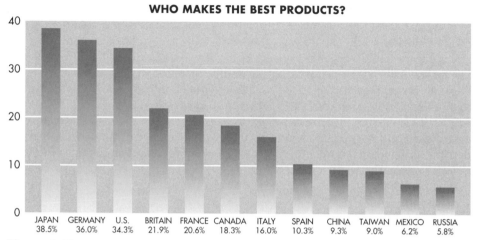

Figure 1-7 Quality Ratings of Manufacturers (*Source:* Business Week, *March 14, 1994, p. 8*)

Speed and Flexibility

As important as quality is, it is not the total answer. One executive put it this way: "Quality is your ticket into the stadium. You can't even come to the game unless you have a quality product and process in place. [But] you have to compete on other dimensions today."[19] These dimensions include speed and flexibility. As quality has rapidly become just a "ticket into the stadium," speed and flexibility have become more and more important as a way to move ahead once the competition begins.

Consider the case of Wausau Paper Mills Co. in Wisconsin. Wausau couldn't afford the high-volume equipment it would have needed to beat its competitors on price, so it decided to compete on the basis of speed. Today, some 95 percent of Wausau's orders are filled in less than twenty-four hours, instead of several days or weeks, eliminating customers' need to carry expensive inventory. "It adds a whole new dimension to competition," says CEO Arnold M. Nemirow. "It provides a way of competing that offsets our disadvantages."[20]

Speed can also save money by saving time, as was shown in the Bell Atlantic example earlier, and speed in getting new products or services to the market has become a competitive advantage. The more rapidly an organization can move from the idea stage through the developmental process to actually introducing the new product or service, the less likely it is that a competitor will beat them there.

It has been known for some time that one of the real keys to speed in a runner is flexibility. In a sprinter or a hurdler, for example, flexibility is a fundamental requirement for running at truly high speeds. The same is true, it turns out, for organizations. Organizations that are too large to be flexible, or too rigid in terms of their policies and practices, are unable to take advantage of the opportunities that appear so quickly in the world in which we live.

Consider the case of German automobile maker BMW. Once known for its luxury vehicles, BMW saw its U.S. car sales slip from a peak of 96,000 in 1986 to a low of 53,300 in 1991. As its manufacturing costs soared and Japanese rivals claimed greater market share with the Lexus and Infiniti, BMW's stodgy culture and rigid formality prevented quick action. It wasn't until the new CEO, Bernd Pischetsrieder, encouraged greater flexibility in decision making that changes began to occur. New, lower-priced models have been introduced. Recent moves to manufacture more of the company's parts outside of Germany, and building a factory in the United States, are expected to help cut costs.[21] This responsiveness to new ideas and the speed with which plans are developed and implemented are new performance standards not only for BMW but for all organizations operating in today's changing environment.

Innovation

No matter how successful an organization is, someone somewhere in the world is developing a product or service that is different or better. Providing different or better products and services or finding a better way to deliver them is what we mean by *innovation*. The need for organizations to innovate is essential in the 1990s. During the past ten years alone, General Motors, IBM, Sears, network TV, the neighborhood pharmacist, and market leaders in virtually every industry all lost leadership positions to challengers who were more innovative.

For example, the innovative use of computer systems to track and reorder inventory allowed Wal-Mart to pull even with and move ahead of industry leader Sears. Innovative programming such as CNN and MTV has permitted cable TV to challenge the more established networks. And creative mass marketing and distribution systems have enabled CVS stores to all but eliminate independently owned neighborhood pharmacies in some regions of the country. Sears, the networks, and the corner pharmacist have all become acutely aware of the fact that the combination of change and competition demands innovation.

The challenge for management is this: Organizations must learn how to give full attention to the business they are presently in, while at the same time devoting full attention to what they should do better or differently.

Sustainable Growth

The final performance standard is of a different type than quality, speed, flexibility, and innovation. It is, in a sense, the context for the others. The standard of sustainable growth is the requirement that organizations no longer seek to be as large as they can be, nor to grow as quickly as they possibly can. *Sustainable growth* is the concept that organizations should only grow at a rate, and to a size that can be maintained over the long term.[22] The 1990s have taught many of our largest organizations that bigger is not necessarily better. Growing as fast as you can in one period may result in serious problems as time goes on. The economic hardships caused by being too large to be flexible, and the emotional hardship of having to lay off loyal but no longer needed employees, have combined to teach organizations an important lesson: The right target is sustainable growth, growth at a rate and to a size that will serve the organization well regardless of the conditions.

The changing performance standards are clear: Increased emphasis on quality, speed, flexibility, innovation, and sustainable growth. Management will be judged by these standards. Successful organizations, whether business, education, health care, or government, are already pursuing them.

SUMMARY

In this chapter we define organizations as groups of people working together to accomplish what they could not accomplish individually. We describe management as responsibility for the performance of an organization, responsibility for the organization's achieving its goals.

This chapter emphasizes how important management is in a society of organizations such as ours, which relies so extensively on organizations for everything from automobiles to health care, from food and clothing to entertainment and education. Management, we have said, is responsible for ensuring that through these organizations society is socially satisfied and economically stable and prosperous. We also point out that organizations do not exist as separate units; they are interconnected. They are an integral part of a network of stakeholders, and whenever an organization fails to meet its performance goals, this entire network is threatened. For these reasons, management has never been more important.

The second half of this chapter focuses on the fact that management has become more challenging as we approach the twenty-first century. The changing environment, the world which surrounds our organizations, is marked by a new variety and intensity of competition, markets that are global, and heightened attention to ethical behavior and social responsibility.

There is now also a radically changing workplace, one that is diverse on many dimensions. In addition, work increasingly is team based and is being continuously transformed by information technology. Finally, added to management's challenges are changing performance standards. These include a new emphasis on quality, speed, flexibility, and innovation, all within the limits of sustainable growth. For all these reasons, the task of management has never been more challenging.

Before considering each dimension of the management challenge in greater detail, we will first review the course of the development of management thinking. Chapter 2 will trace the roots of management thinking back two hundred years or more to understand where the journey began, and present the more contemporary management ideas that are the bridge between that earlier thinking and where we are today.

QUESTIONS TO CHALLENGE YOUR UNDERSTANDING OF THE CHAPTER

1. Describe how the view that "management is responsibility for the performance of organizations" differs from Fayol's and Mintzberg's views about management.

2. Explain why management and the successful performance of organizations is so important in a society such as ours.

3. Identify a company that competes globally. What is different about the management challenge in this kind of company?

4. Describe the two ways in which the new competition is different from the competition that traditionally existed for U.S. organizations.

5. Describe some of the advantages of ethical performance by organizations. Are there any potential disadvantages?

6. Which do you think is the more difficult performance challenge: getting people to work in teams rather than independently, or getting people to accept diversity in the workplace?

7. In your opinion, why should it not be surprising that General Motors' multibillion-dollar investment in technology (robots, computers, etc.) did not in itself result in improved performance?

8. In what order or priority would you place the changing performance standards? Explain your rankings.

MANAGEMENT EXERCISE

Planning for Diversity

You and your partner started a computer systems sales and service business right after you both finished graduate school twelve years ago. You were both working for a larger firm at the time, but you decided you wanted the challenge of managing your own business. You've grown the business carefully and you now employ seventeen technical and sales people besides yourselves.

Most of your strategies have paid off over the years, but one aspect of your business continues to be a stubborn problem. You have had difficulties attracting and retaining female and minority employees. To make matters worse, most of those who have come to work for you have left after a year or two, often for similar positions with your competitors. When you spoke with these individuals at exit interviews, most did not express any specific dissatisfaction with working for your company, and there appears to be no active hostility toward women and minorities among your longer-term employees. However, the individuals you interviewed indicated they never felt fully accepted by others in the organization.

You are concerned that your company may be getting a negative reputation in the community because of this problem. You are convinced that this kind of reputation could mean that some of the best potential candidates for positions with your company won't even apply. You also know that an increasing number of the potential customers in your market are women and minorities.

Finally, you personally don't like the idea of your company developing that kind of reputation. You have always been a strong believer in equal opportunity in every aspect, from education to employment. You always thought this situation would eventually resolve itself. Now you know it won't, and you're ready to take action.

1. Imagine yourself as an individual who is unlike almost all of the other individuals where you work. Make a list of all of the reasons you might be uncomfortable in that situation, all of the reasons you might leave. Be as specific as you can.

2. Now make a list of the kinds of things that management could do to eliminate these sources of discomfort and make you more comfortable in that situation. What specific actions might management take not only to make you more likely to remain with the firm, but to get you to encourage others like you to join the firm as well?

3. What do you think some of the barriers might be to management's implementing such a plan and taking the steps you've described?

4. What could management do to eliminate these barriers?

REFERENCES

1. P. F. Drucker, *Management: Tasks, Responsibilities, Practices* (New York: Harper & Row, 1974).

2. H. Fayol, *General and Industrial Administration* (New York: Pitman Publishing Corp., 1949).

3. H. A. Mintzberg, *The Nature of Managerial Work* (Englewood Cliffs, N.J.: Prentice-Hall, 1980), 92–93.

4. J. Case, "A Company of Businesspeople," *INC.*, April 1993, 79–93.

5. Drucker, *Management: Tasks, Responsibilities, Practices.*

6. J. Valente and C. Duff, "Demise of the Catalog Hurts Small Businesses That Counted on Sears," *Wall Street Journal*, March 2, 1993, A1.

7. S. Baker, G. Smith, and E. Weiner, "The Mexican Worker," *Business Week*, April 19, 1993, 84–92.

8. T. Peters, *Thriving on Chaos* (New York: Alfred A. Knopf, 1987), 13–14.

9. B. Ortega, "Wal-Mart Store Comes in Colors, But Is All Green," *Wall Street Journal*, June 11, 1993.

10. A. Bennett, "Organization Cites Acts of Doing Well While Doing Good," *Wall Street Journal*, September 22, 1991.

11. G. A. Steiner and J. F. Steiner, *Business, Government, and Society*, 7th ed. (New York: McGraw-Hill, 1994), 374–375.

12. K. Davis, "The Case for and against Business Assumption of Social Responsibility," *Academy of Management Journal* 16 (June 1973): 36.

13. "The Work Force Is Becoming More Diverse," *Business Week*, June 28, 1993, 82.

14. A. Cuneo, "Diverse by Design," *Business Week/Renewing America*, 1992, 72.

15. J. A. Byrne, "Paradigms for Postmodern Managers," *Business Week/Renewing America*, October 23, 1992, 63.

16. G. Fuchsberg, " 'Total Quality' Is Termed Only Partial Success," *Wall Street Journal*, October 1, 1992.

17. J. B. Treece, "Here Comes GM's Saturn," *Business Week*, April 9, 1990, 58.

18. "Harper's Index," *Harper's*, March 1987, 15.

19. Byrne, "Paradigms for Postmodern Managers," 63.

20. Byrne, "Paradigms for Postmodern Managers," 63.

21. J. Templeman and J. B. Treece, "BMW's Comeback," *Business Week*, February 14, 1994, 42–44.

22. C. Garfield, *Second to None* (Homewood, Ill.: Business One Irwin, 1992), 22.

CHAPTER 2
The Development of Management

LEARNING OBJECTIVES

After studying this chapter, you should be able to:

- *Describe the nineteenth-century contributions to the development of management thinking of Adam Smith, J. B. Say, and Robert Owen.*

- *Discuss the key elements of Frederick Taylor's "scientific management" approach to improving performance.*

- *Describe Henri Fayol's elements and principles of management, and, more generally, how Fayol advanced the development of management thinking.*

- *Define the "Hawthorne effect," and how Elton Mayo and the Hawthorne studies expanded our understanding of management.*

- *Describe the contributions of decision sciences, systems theory, and contingency theory to the development of management thinking.*

- *Discuss the Japanese management and quality improvement approaches to improving organizational performance.*

While organizations and management have been systematically studied only for about one hundred years, organization has been with us since before the dawn of civilization. As we said in Chapter 1, organization has been necessary for as long as there have been tasks that one person could not complete alone. Tracking and hunting large game required the kind of planning, coordination, and leadership that we now call management.

Actually, even the management of large-scale organizations goes back to ancient times. The great pyramids of Egypt, for example, were the result of the efforts of numerous architects, engineers, and tens of thousands of laborers working together for fifteen or twenty years at a time. They were built from hundreds of thousands of stone blocks, each weighing two to three tons, which were quarried miles away, cut to size within fractions of an inch, and transported to the construction site on river barges.[1] The planning and direction required for these kinds of projects can only be called management, and this is only one example. The Roman Empire built roads and fortifications, waged wars, imposed laws, and collected taxes on three continents, all before the birth of Christ. The Chinese constructed the Great Wall spanning thousands of miles to defend against invaders almost a thousand years ago. There are great cities and monuments from the Mayan civilization of the same period that could only be the product of what we would call management. The Catholic Church coordinated and controlled religious practices in communities on five continents by the year 1500.

So while it was not called "management" per se, the responsibility for organized performance has been part of human society essentially from the beginning. But it was only about two hundred years ago that the ideas that formed the basis for what we now call "management thinking" began to emerge.

In this chapter we will trace the evolution of management thinking. More specifically, we will consider the interesting range of answers that have been offered to what might be viewed as the key question of management: How do you improve the performance of organizations? We will begin with some of the early answers to this question.

SOME EARLY IDEAS

Adam Smith: Task Specialization

One of the early answers to the question of performance was provided by Adam Smith, author of *The Wealth of Nations*, originally published in 1776.[2] Smith was among the first to comment on the impact on performance of something called the *division of labor*, or *task specialization*. In an example that has become famous, Smith pointed out how a single craftsman working alone could produce no more than twenty pins in an entire day's work. He compared this level of performance with a "manufactory" where ten men each did only one of the "specialized tasks" necessary to create a pin, one drawing the wire, one straightening it, one setting the head, and so on. Organized in this way, the group of workers in the manufactory could produce not the equivalent of twenty pins per man in a day, but an unprecedented twelve *pounds* of pins in a day.

Without setting out to do so, with this example Adam Smith provided one of the early answers to the question of how to improve performance. Smith's answer: Specialize the tasks. Take every large task and break it down into smaller steps or activities, and have each worker become a specialist, an expert at one specific activity or step.

There will be further discussion of task specialization in later chapters. The point here is that through his example of task specialization, Adam Smith clearly established that management makes a difference. Smith never mentioned the term "management," but it was not the workers themselves who organized the work into specialized tasks. It was management.

J. B. Say and the Concept of the "Entrepreneur"

A fundamentally different response to the question of how to improve performance came in the early 1800s from the French economic philosopher J. B. Say. Essentially, Say suggested that improved performance was the result of better ideas. In fact, Say created a term to describe people with ideas for better uses for existing technology; he called these people "entrepreneurs."[3]

Eli Whitney, inventor of the cotton gin, is an example of what Say would call an entrepreneur. Interestingly, Whitney's contribution to management thinking had nothing to do with the cotton gin. Whitney's contribution had to do with firearms. In Whitney's day—also the early 1800s—every pistol and rifle was meticulously handcrafted. Each piece of each weapon was custom machined and fitted to the weapon by highly skilled craftsmen. As a result, whenever the weapon jammed or broke, it had to be repaired by a craftsman who would recraft any part that needed to be repaired or replaced. This was a very time-consuming process, and a serious problem, especially in the heat of battle.

Whitney's "better idea" was a process whereby weapons would be assembled from interchangeable parts. This meant that every part on a given model of a weapon would be manufactured to be as nearly identical as possible to that same part of every other weapon of that model. The trigger mechanisms, for example, would not be handcrafted separately for each weapon. Instead, thousands of exactly the same trigger mechanisms would be manufactured for each model of a weapon, and so on for the stocks and the barrels and every other part of the weapon.[4]

As a result of Whitney's idea, skilled craftsmen were no longer needed for the manufacture and repair of weapons. Weapons could now be rapidly assembled and easily repaired by trained laborers working with interchangeable parts. The manufacturing process became faster and—because trained workers were used rather than skilled craftsmen—much less expensive. And the repair problems were all but eliminated. All because Whitney had a better idea about how to use existing resources.

J. B. Say's point about Eli Whitney would be that he improved performance by finding better uses for existing technologies. More recent proof of Say's point is everywhere around us today. Each of the entrepreneurs listed in Figure 2-1 found

	Entrepreneur	Industry	Application	Innovation
	Ray Kroc	Restaurant	Mass production	McDonald's
	John H. Johnson	Publishing	National magazine for ethnic/ racial groups	*Jet* and *Ebony* magazines
	Mary Kay Ash	Skin Care	Home sales/ distribution	Mary Kay Cosmetics
	Ted Turner	Television	Satellite telecommunications	TNT, CNN

Figure 2-1 Some Entrepreneurs and Their Innovations

a new application for a technology that was already being used for something else. How do you improve performance? J. B. Say and Eli Whitney's answer was to find better ways to use the resources we already have: new applications for existing technologies.

Robert Owen and the Soho Engineering Foundry

The kind of management experiments we see with Eli Whitney were also taking place in Europe. One of these efforts took place in New Lanaark, Scotland. The other involved the Soho Foundry in London.

Robert Owen was a cotton mill owner in New Lanaark, Scotland, who believed that improved working conditions for laborers would result in improvements in their performance. On the basis of this belief, he shortened the workday from thirteen to ten and one-half hours; built decent housing for his workers; and provided a company store where necessities could be purchased at reasonable prices, a school for the workers' children, and a recreation center where the members of the community could meet and entertain themselves.[5]

By all accounts, Owen's mills became highly profitable, and had a significant impact on child labor legislation. But the important point is that Owen was able to improve performance at his mills not by increasing the number of workers but by improving the way his workers were treated. The lesson from Robert

Owen is that the way people are managed can make a significant difference in performance.

At about the same time as Owen's experiment, the Soho Engineering Foundry in London was also trying out new ideas in an effort to improve performance. The experiment at Soho represents one of the earliest efforts to use forecasting and production planning, cost accounting systems, and training and incentive programs for its workers.[6] Most of these techniques are common practice today, but at that time they represented a unique willingness by the Soho Foundry to work with management tools and strategies that were all but untested at that time. As at New Lanaark, the results of the Soho approach were apparently very positive.

To the question of how to improve performance, Robert Owen's answer was to make the workplace a community and to treat your people well. The Soho answer was to plan production, develop effective systems of financial record keeping, and provide training and incentives for workers.

These early answers to the question of management are both interesting and important. They represent some of the first recorded efforts to improve performance. Not until the early twentieth century, however, were management and organization actually studied and analyzed in any systematic way in an effort to understand what worked and what didn't work to improve organizational performance.

Management writer John Case suggests an explanation for the increased interest in improving performance of organizations beginning around the turn of the century. "Back in 1870 the McCormick reaper plant's 500 employees made it one of the nation's largest. By 1900 some 70 factories counted more than 2,000 employees apiece, with a dozen or so in the 6,000–10,000 range."[7] With so many organizations suddenly reaching such unprecedented size and level of complexity, it became absolutely essential to develop an understanding of how management might make these massive business organizations more productive.

THE EARLY TWENTIETH CENTURY: THREE MILESTONES IN MANAGEMENT THINKING

During the first few decades of the twentieth century, three milestone responses emerged to the question of how to improve performance. They were the scientific management response of Frederick Taylor, the administrative theory response of Henri Fayol, and the human relations response of Elton Mayo. These three responses, more than any others, formed the basic foundation of the traditional, modern understanding of management. Each approached the central question of management from a different perspective. Each enriched our understanding of how to improve performance. And each has had a major impact on the way organizations are actually managed.

Organizations and Work at the Turn of the Century

As we mentioned earlier in this chapter, prior to the Industrial Revolution in the 1700s, products were produced mostly through craft, with one person performing all of the subtasks necessary to produce a finished product, whether it was an article of clothing, a weapon, or a piece of furniture. Crafters began with the raw materials, and through the application of a variety of skills completed the entire product themselves. With the dawn of the Industrial Revolution, however, the craft process was broken down into a set of fairly simple, specialized tasks, much as Adam Smith described in his pin-making example. As a result, while workers' output increased dramatically, the work itself became boring and repetitive, and—in the case of heavy manufacturing—exhausting as well.

Two other facts about the work environment of that period are also worth noting. First, while the work was broken down into specialized tasks, little or no attention was paid to how each task was done. Workers were often expected to provide their own tools, and would often develop their own "rules of thumb" about how to do the work and about what the quality of the work should be. There simply were no standards to speak of in terms of either procedures or quality.

The other fact worth noting is the role of managers in these turn-of-the-century factories. They might have been called overseers, or masters, or foremen, but their job was clear and simple: to keep workers working hard despite the boring, exhausting, and sometimes dangerous work. Given the nature of their responsibilities, it is probably safe to assume that the primary management tool at that time was intimidation.

As the twentieth century approached, these were the working conditions that prevailed: Work was repetitive and extremely tiring; it was performed according to "rules of thumb"; and management was mostly by intimidation. This was the kind of work environment that Frederick Taylor walked into when he went to work as a laborer at Midvale Steel.

The First Milestone: Scientific Management

Frederick Taylor was studying to be an engineer when he went to work at the Midvale Steel Company. Not surprisingly, he applied an engineer's problem-solving techniques to the work being done there. Taylor was convinced that by carefully observing and experimenting with all of the tasks being performed at the steel mill, he would be able to identify "principles" defining how the work should be done. According to Taylor, once these principles were defined, all the workers could be trained to do the work "the one best way," rather than relying on their own various rules of thumb.

For years, Taylor studied the work being done at Midvale, carefully noting where the workers stood to do certain tasks, how far they had to reach, the kinds of tools they used—everything having to do with how they did their jobs. Based on his extensive observations, he then experimented with ways to improve the worker's performance, changing everything from how they did their jobs to the tools they used to do them. Based on these experiments, Taylor then trained the workers to perform the tasks in the most efficient way. The results of Taylor's scientific approach were impressive. In one famous example, the "Taylor-trained workers" loaded nearly four times as much iron per day as the other workers, and the average earnings of these men went from $1.15 to $1.85 per day, a better than 50 percent increase.[8]

In 1911 Taylor published his conclusions from these and other experiments in a book titled *Principles of Scientific Management*. The principles Taylor suggested, outlined in Figure 2-2, were nothing short of revolutionary, especially given the rough-and-tumble work environment of that period.[9]

Taylor's concepts of task design and selection and training were radical enough at the time. Even more radical—and largely ignored—was his notion of cooperation between management and workers. Taylor took the position that by providing the workers with careful plans, the right tools, and training and incentives, management would get better performance from them than they would by using intimidation and threats. Taylor's other principles were widely adopted; his principle of cooperation was not.[10]

Of all of his "principles of management," however, none had a greater impact on the development of management thinking than Taylor's principle of "separating the planning from the doing."[11]

Separating the Planning from the Doing

In Taylor's scientific management, there is a clear difference between performing the tasks on the one hand and, on the other hand, designing and planning the tasks, selecting and training the workers, and developing incentive systems. Doing the work, suggested Taylor, is the worker's responsibility. The planning, the selection and training, and the incentive systems clearly are not. These are the responsibility of management.

In separating the planning from the doing, Taylor actually created the need for professional management. Scientific management obviously is very different from the management by intimidation and threat that was typical of Taylor's time. For Taylor, the management task is a professional task. It is the application of intelligence to work. In inventing the concept of the manager as professional, Taylor gave management a whole new face, a face that is still recognizable today, more than eighty years later.

- Develop a science of each element of a worker's task, which replaces the old rule of thumb.

- Scientifically select, and then train, teach, and develop the worker.

- Heartily cooperate with the worker so as to ensure all of the work is being done in accordance with the principles of the science which has been developed.

- Equally divide the work and the responsibility between the management and the workers.

Figure 2-2 Summary of Frederick Taylor's Principles of Scientific Management

To the central management question of how to improve performance, Taylor's response was both visionary and comprehensive: Separate the planning from the doing, design each task scientifically, provide training and incentives for the workers, cooperate with them, support them with effective planning; and give responsibility for all of this to the manager.

As we approach the twenty-first century, there are some questions about whether it still makes sense to separate the planning from the doing, especially with a much more highly educated workforce than there was in Taylor's time.[12] In fact, an increasing number of organizations have begun to experiment with self-managing work groups that are responsible for both planning and performing their tasks. Taylor would probably not object to this. After all, the heart of his contribution was that improvement in performance can only result from just such experimentation.

The Second Milestone: Administrative Theory

Frederick Taylor may have been the first to suggest that management is a professional set of tasks and responsibilities. As we noted in Chapter 1, however, it was another engineer, Frenchman Henri Fayol, who first defined in a comprehensive way just what those tasks and responsibilities might be. In 1916, he published *Administration industrielle et générale* (Industrial and general management) detailing the key elements and functions of management, which are listed in Figure 2-3.[13]

We have defined management as responsibility for organizational performance. Fayol defined that responsibility in the specific terms of planning, organizing, commanding, coordinating, and controlling. We pointed out earlier that Fayol's list no longer represents a complete description of the manager's responsibilities. So fundamentally sound, however, was his list of "elements" that it re-

- **Planning,** requiring the forecast of events impacting the organization, the development of an operating program taking those events into account, and the continuous updating of the organization's plans.

- **Organizing,** requiring the structuring of the organization's tasks and activities, and securing and coordinating the necessary human, financial, and material resources.

- **Commanding,** requiring setting the organization into motion, setting a good example, regularly visiting the shop floor, dealing with unproductive personnel, and maintaining the larger view rather than getting bogged down in day-to-day details.

- **Coordinating,** requiring regular meetings between managers and subordinates to ensure the harmony and unity of purpose necessary for effective organizational functioning.

- **Controlling,** requiring a constant monitoring of workers' activities, materials, and outputs to ensure that each is consistent with standards established in the plan.

Figure 2-3 Functions of Managers According to Henri Fayol

mains in essence a virtual job description for managers. Although more has been added to the foundation Fayol provided, the foundation is his.

Fayol's "Principles" of Management

Actually, Fayol's definition of the five elements or tasks of management, outlined in Figure 2-3, was only one of the two major contributions that he made to the development of management thinking. The other was the identification of a set of general principles of management, guidelines based on years of observation of what it takes for organizations to be successful. A few of the most frequently cited of Fayol's general principles are listed in Figure 2-4.

Fayol's principles may appear to be little more than common sense. However, like his basic elements or functions of management, most of Fayol's principles are as relevant and applicable today as they were more than seventy-five years ago. Thus, Fayol's response to the question of how to improve performance was really twofold: (1) Recognize the essential elements of the management process and train managers in each of them; and (2) identify and operate according to a set of general principles of management that will enhance the effectiveness of the organization.

Fayol's response to the question of how to improve performance might be summarized as "Improve the management": Train managers in planning, organizing, commanding, coordinating and controlling, and teach them to operate their organizations according to the principles of management.

The Third Milestone: The Hawthorne Studies

In the prosperity following World War I, there was a tremendous increase in demand for cars, home appliances, radios, telephones, and machinery. Naturally, with the huge increase in demand for these products, there came an increased in-

- **Division of labor** —Requiring people to specialize in their task will enable them to do their tasks well.

- **Unity of command** —Each person should have one and only one boss.

- **Unity of direction** —Each manager should provide direction consistent with an overall plan.

- **Remuneration** —Pay should be fair and at a level high enough to serve as an incentive, but not so high as to be unreasonable.

- **Equity** —Organizations run best when managers are fair with their people.

- **Stability of staff** —Turnover is unhealthy for organizations. Effective management encourages long-term commitment from employees.

- **Initiative** —People should be given the opportunity and freedom to conceive and implement a plan, even if it sometimes fails.

Figure 2-4 Henri Fayol's Principles of Management

terest in understanding how to make organizations better at producing them—in other words, how to improve performance.

In the early 1920s, General Electric began advertising that better lighting in the workplace would result in increased output by the workers. To support these claims, G.E. persuaded the Western Electric Company, manufacturer of telephones for the Bell System, to conduct illumination experiments at its huge Hawthorne Works outside Chicago in Cicero, Illinois. Consistent with Frederick Taylor's scientific management approach, an experiment was designed to determine whether better lighting in a work area would result in increased worker productivity. Worker output was measured as lighting was increased and then decreased.

The results of the experiment, shown in Figure 2-5, were totally unexpected. As the lighting was increased, productivity increased, just as G.E. had hoped. What was not expected was that even when the lighting was decreased, productivity continued to rise. In fact, productivity continued to rise until the lighting was as dim as moonlight; then productivity finally leveled off. These were clearly not the results G.E. was looking for, and it withdrew from the experiment at that point. But the search was on for an explanation for these totally unexpected findings.

The Hawthorne Effect

In an effort to get a clearer understanding of what had happened in the experiment at the Hawthorne Works, interviews were conducted with more than twenty thousand Western Electric workers. From the data from these interviews, Harvard professor Elton Mayo and his team of researchers began to piece together an explanation.[14]

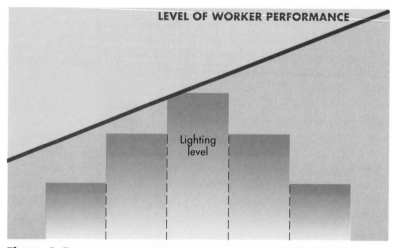

Figure 2-5 Hawthorne Experiment Results

According to Mayo, these interviews suggested that the workers viewed the experiments as evidence of increased management concern for conditions in the workplace. Mayo concluded that the workers increased their productivity in response to this increased attention from management. Whether the experimental conditions improved the workplace or not, the workers felt that at least management was trying to do something about working conditions. The workers apparently increased their output in response to what they viewed as management's concern for their well-being. The notion that increased attention by management results in increased productivity by the worker came to be known as the "Hawthorne effect."

One of the significant contributions of the Hawthorne studies, then, was the realization that the impact of management was not restricted to planning and task design, as Taylor had suggested, or to management by principles, as Fayol had suggested. Management—at least according to Elton Mayo and the Hawthorne effect—was every bit as powerful in its human impact as in its technical impact. The Hawthorne studies provided the first scientific evidence that management's attention to workers might have a major effect on their performance. There was, however, an even more significant finding from the Hawthorne studies.

The Interpersonal Factor

To further explore their conclusions, Mayo and the researchers at Hawthorne observed the activities and measured the performance of workers in the Bank Wiring Room. There, a group of fourteen operators accompanied by a single supervisor assembled terminal banks for telephone switchboards. The Bank Wiring Room phase of the study was, in a sense, a test of the Hawthorne effect, an experiment to see if increased management attention alone was enough to increase worker output. Once again, the results were unexpected. Unlike what occurred with the lighting experiments, in the Bank Wiring Room there was no increase in output. In fact, there were no observable changes at all in the group's performance. Despite the obvious presence and attention of management, the group turned out exactly the same amount of work as it had when no one was watching.[15]

Did this result mean that increased attention from management didn't necessarily result in increased productivity—that perhaps the Hawthorne effect doesn't always work? Mayo and his team's analysis of the results—or lack of results—from the Bank Wiring Room revealed that a strong group norm was operating there. This norm of a "fair day's work" was accepted throughout the group. No matter how much attention this group received from management, its members apparently shared the belief that a fair day's work was a fair day's work; they simply were not going to work any faster. For this group, it was not attention from management that most strongly impacted their productivity. In the Bank Wiring Room, performance was most strongly influenced by a different human factor: the group's own norms about how much work was considered reasonable.

Mayo and the Hawthorne studies provided a third (after Taylor and Fayol) critical response to the management question of how to improve organization performance: Improve interpersonal relations on the job. It is not enough to scientifically analyze and design each task, as Taylor suggested, nor to train managers to plan, organize, command, control, and coordinate effectively, as Fayol prescribed. (See Figure 2-6.) The Hawthorne studies pointed for the first time to the importance of positive interpersonal relations between management and workers, and among the workers themselves.

In recent years, there has been criticism of the way the Hawthorne studies were conducted.[16] Questions have been raised about whether the experiments there were sufficiently scientific to produce valid results. Nonetheless, there is no question that with the Hawthorne studies, management thinking expanded significantly to include consideration of people as a key factor in organizations' performance.

MORE RECENT CONTRIBUTIONS

During the second half of the twentieth century, new answers to the question of how to improve organizational performance have continued to emerge. As a result of the new management challenges, the changing environment, and the changing performance standards described in Chapter 1, the search for the most effective answers possible has become more urgent than ever before.

Partly in response to this urgency, there has been a steadily increasing flow of new theories and models of management. Many of these have faded after

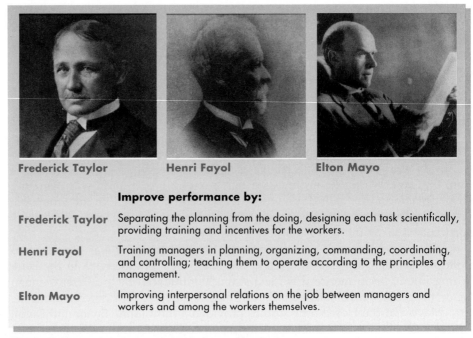

| | Frederick Taylor | Henri Fayol | Elton Mayo |

Improve performance by:

Frederick Taylor	Separating the planning from the doing, designing each task scientifically, providing training and incentives for the workers.
Henri Fayol	Training managers in planning, organizing, commanding, coordinating, and controlling; teaching them to operate according to the principles of management.
Elton Mayo	Improving interpersonal relations on the job between managers and workers and among the workers themselves.

Figure 2-6 Three Milestones in Management Thinking

promising beginnings. Still, a number of these more recent contributions to management thinking have endured and, taken together, they provide a sense of the range and diversity of the ideas now flowing within the management mainstream. We will consider five: (1) decision sciences, (2) systems theory, (3) contingency theory, (4) Japanese management, and (5) quality improvement.

Decision Sciences

During World War II, it became critical to utilize scarce military resources as effectively and as efficiently as possible. There were never enough personnel, aircraft, equipment, weapons, or supplies to meet the demands of all of the generals and naval commanders. To assist in making decisions about how all of these resources could be distributed to have the greatest impact, British military experts developed a technique called operations research (OR).

Decisions "by the Numbers"

Operations research (OR) uses mathematical equations to allow decision makers to evaluate which of all of the available options might represent the best use of resources. For example, World War II military planners would use mathematical formulas to try out all of the possible ways that various numbers and types of aircraft with various ranges between refuelings could carry various numbers and types of bombs. They would also factor in the probability of each type of plane's achieving the target and the probability of each type of plane's returning safely for additional bombing runs. Thus, using all of the quantitative or numerical information available to them, these planners were able to identify the option with the greatest likelihood of overall success. The United States military adopted operations research in the course of the war; and, not surprisingly, operations research was adapted to American industry following the war. Now it is called *decision sciences*.[17]

For Example

Perhaps the most commonly used decision sciences technique has been *linear programming*. The scheduling problems of the U.S. Air Force Military Aircraft Command (MAC) represent the kind of situation where linear programming is used to assist decision makers. For example:

> On a typical day thousands of planes ferry cargo and passengers among airfields scattered around the world. To keep those jets flying, MAC must juggle the schedules of pilots (whose flight times are severely limited) and other flight personnel. In addition, MAC must determine whether it would be more efficient to reduce cargo and top off fuel tanks at the start of each flight or to refuel at stops along the way and pay for the cost of shipping the fuel. To get the airplanes back into the air, cargo handlers need to be standing by, and ground crews must be ready to service the craft.[18]

All of the factors that MAC is attempting to take into consideration in this example can be expressed in numbers. This is the key factor for decision sciences.

Cargo weights, fuel weights and prices, aircraft and ground crew staffing requirements—even weather changes and emergency changes in priorities (which can be expressed in probability terms as percentages)—all are variables that can be quantified. This means that with the assistance of computers, every conceivable combination of variables can be systematically evaluated. Through the mathematical models of decision sciences, each alternative can be tried out before any decision is made.

The impact of decision sciences is seen everywhere. Banks, fast-food restaurants, and supermarkets, for example, now keep track of the number of customers at various times throughout the day, and how long it takes to service each one. The decision sciences approach is then used to calculate how many tellers, or ordering, or checkout stations will be needed; how many employees should be scheduled for each period; even how many spaces will be needed in the parking lot. Manufacturing organizations use decision sciences to decide how much production capacity they will need at various times, and how much warehouse space. The decision sciences approach is used by airlines to calculate how many flights they will need, and at which times, to service the greatest number of customers with the fewest possible planes.

Limitations of the Decision Sciences Approach

There is no question that decision sciences has had a tremendous impact in the kinds of areas described above, where the variables or factors involved can be counted and then included in mathematical calculations. In the area of a manager's job involving interpersonal relations, however, decision sciences obviously is less useful. How do you quantify the impact of layoffs, for example, on the performance of those workers who do not lose their jobs? Factors such as attitudes and norms and emotions can't easily be measured. Calculations involving the human factor are, by definition, simply less reliable.

Still, the decision sciences response to the question of improving performance continues to be valuable: Convert the factors in the situation into numbers, and calculate the effectiveness of the various combinations of those factors until the optimal combination is found.

Systems Theory

In 1928, biologist Ludwig von Bertalanffy introduced a theory of general systems suggesting that everything in nature is interrelated.[19] According to von Bertalanffy, every entity is part of a larger system. He pointed out that in nature nothing is totally independent and self-sufficient. Every living organism is part of a system and is affected by what happens both within and outside that system. Herbert Simon extended systems thinking to organizations by viewing them as systems that make decisions and process information.[20]

The Importance of What's Happening outside the Organization

Traditionally organizations were thought of as fairly closed systems. Organizations usually thought of themselves as fairly well insulated or protected from whatever was happening outside themselves. They tended to think the events most critical to their success were those that occurred inside the organization.

The major contribution of a systems perspective to the development of management thinking was the recognition that organizations are in fact open systems. That is, they receive input from the environment; they transform that input into output; and the output then reenters the environment, resulting in feedback which affects subsequent input, as shown in Figure 2-7.

The systems view forces us to recognize that what is happening outside the organization does matter. Events of the 1970s and 1980s, such as the 1973 Arab oil embargo, the rise of Japanese competition, and the deregulation of banking, airlines, and other industries, demonstrated conclusively that organizations are indeed open systems—they can indeed be seriously affected by social, economic, political, and technological changes in the environment. These changes include exactly the kinds discussed in Chapter 1: the changing environment, changes in the workforce, the new competition and advances in computer technology. These are factors that organizations usually can't eliminate by means of their own decisions. Organizations are open to the environment whether they want to be or not. This was Simon's point, and he made it almost a decade before the events of the mid-1970s made it clear that he was right.

Today organizations know that they are open systems. They are learning that their environments are a key factor affecting their performance. What they produce is driven more by customer tastes and preferences than by their own. Their success in meeting customer demands is determined by whether they can recruit a workforce capable of doing the work, and suppliers capable of providing affordable, high-quality materials. Their success in selling their output is strongly impacted by what the competition offers as an alternative, and by the state of the economy as well. Each of these environmental factors must be recognized and responded to in managing the organization.

Organizations can no longer be concerned simply with what's happening within their four walls. They must be equally concerned with customer relations, community relations, employee relations, supplier relations, and government relations. Von Bertalanffy and Simon were right: All organizations—from the very largest to the very smallest—are part of a system, and anything happening within that system is happening to the organization as well.

Figure 2-7 Open Systems Model

Systems theory also provides us with other valuable concepts, such as feedback and synergy, which we'll discuss in other chapters. But the principal value of the open systems perspective is that it forces managers to consider the full range of variables and factors—including those beyond the formal boundaries of the organization—that impact the organization and the performance of the people within it. Taylor, Fayol, and the Hawthorne studies all focused managers' attention on factors inside the organization. The systems theory answer to the question of how to improve organization performance was to recognize the importance of what is happening outside as well.

Contingency Theory

The search for universal or general principles of management did not end with Frederick Taylor and Henri Fayol. The emergence of systems theory, however, raised the question of whether, with so many environmental variables influencing the organization, it was still possible to develop a set of universal management principles that would apply in all situations. Was Frederick Taylor's concept of finding "the one best way" still valid, when there were so many factors to be considered?

The "Law of the Situation"

Social philosopher Mary Parker Follett developed the law of the situation in 1928.[21] Follett suggested that leaders would be more successful if they would adjust their style of leadership to the needs of the followers and to the requirements of the situation. For Follett there was no one best way. What was best would be determined by the situation. It was up to management to recognize what the situation required and to make the necessary adjustment.

Today, we call this the *contingency view,* and it is reflected in virtually every dimension of management. In terms of planning, we now have "contingency plans," options which ensure that an organization will have a plan in place for every likely situation or change in situations. In terms of organizing, we now recognize that an assembly line may be effective for long-term, high-speed production of an unchanging product, but that for flexibility in responding to specific customer demands, flexible work teams might be a more effective way to organize. In terms of quality control, in some cases every product needs to be fully tested and inspected, in other cases it makes more sense to inspect and test only a statistically selected sample of the total output. The evidence is everywhere: Effective organizations adjust to the situation.

For Example

For a clearer understanding of what the contingency views says, consider the case of a pizza shop which has steadily increasing sales, but no corresponding increase in profits. The question is: What can be done to improve performance in terms of profits? First, consider the alternatives to contingency theory. Frederick Taylor's scientific management approach would be to analyze the way the pizzas are made, determine how many movements were taken by the pizza maker, and try to reduce the number of movements or make them more efficient. Henri Fayol's administrative theory answer would be to train the pizza shop managers so that they could more effectively plan, organize, and control the activities of the shop, and coordinate and direct the workers. Elton Mayo's human relations theory would focus on the workers themselves, and on improving the relationships among the workers, and between workers and management.

In contrast, contingency theory would say that the solution to the problem depends on the situation, and that there is no single answer for how to improve performance. If the problem at the pizza shop is with the way the work itself is being done, the scientific management approach might be most effective. If the problem is with the management of the shop, providing management training for the managers might be the best solution. If the problem is workers' attitudes, human relations theory might hold the answer.

Mary Parker Follett's contribution was an important one, but it is often difficult to understand what is required in situations as complex and chaotic as those in which most organizations now find themselves. It can be even more difficult to implement the appropriate adjustment. Still, the challenge for management is clear: To improve performance, management must learn to adjust to the situation.

Japanese Management

For most of the period since World War II, the Japanese response to the question of how to improve performance has been very different from the American response. Given the Japanese success in the automobile industry, in consumer electronics, and in steel, Japanese management is a response worth studying. Characteristics of the Japanese management system are shown in Figure 2-8.[22]

So effective has the Japanese approach to management been that in the decades since World War II, it has transformed a resource-poor island nation into a first-rate economic power and the most successful trading nation in the world.

A Question of Culture and the Example of Saturn

For many years, critics questioned the usefulness of attempting to import Japanese management to American organizations. Some theorists, researchers, and

- The use of *group-based problem solving* or *quality circles* to improve organizational performance.
- *Management-labor cooperation* to avoid the problems associated with conflict and labor action.
- *Workers' pay tied* directly to the *performance of the organization.*
- Specific *manufacturing strategies*—for example, *flexible production systems,* and *JIT (just in time)* inventory systems.
- *Kaizen, a philosophy of continuous improvement* of the products and the processes of the organization.

Figure 2-8 Characteristics of the Japanese Management System

even practicing managers were convinced that Japanese management works well in Japan because it is Japanese. They felt that the Japanese approach to management couldn't be as effective in America, partially because the long history of bad feelings between management and workers in the United States would not permit the kind of labor-management cooperation that is at the heart of the Japanese system. They pointed to the even longer history in America of emphasis on individual rather than group achievement: the pioneer, the cowboy, and more recently the superstar. They argued that in a culture that focuses as much attention on the accomplishments of individuals as Americans do, the kind of teamwork required under the Japanese system would be all but impossible to achieve.

These are certainly legitimate concerns, but Japanese management actually reflects the influence of Peter Drucker, W. Edwards Deming, J. M. Juran, and other American management thinkers as much as it does Japanese thinking. Furthermore, many aspects of Japanese management are becoming commonplace in American organizations. One, in particular, is the concept of employee work teams.

As we noted in Chapter 1, workers in the United States are increasingly being organized into performance teams. In U.S. organizations, work teams are used not just for solving quality problems, as they are in Japan, but for the design, engineering, production, and marketing of new products.

It also appears that American organizations are capable of a level of labor-management cooperation that seemed doubtful only a decade ago. The Saturn project of General Motors, which yielded one of the most popular new American cars in a generation, was in many ways made possible by a productive labor-management partnership that some would have thought impossible given GM's long history of labor-management mistrust.[23]

Beyond teamwork at all levels, factories across the United States are also using Japanese-inspired *just-in-time* (JIT) systems to manage their inventories, or are committed to moving in that direction. JIT systems involve scheduling the delivery of materials and supplies as close as possible to the time when they will be used. And *kaizen*, the Japanese concept of continuously improving the product, the production process, and the people in the organization, is today an increasingly common practice being implemented in the offices and on the factory floors of the American workplace.

The Japanese response to the question of how to improve organizational performance—to create an atmosphere of cooperation among everyone in the organization, design more effective organizational systems, and constantly seek to improve the people, the process, and the product—has come to be viewed as so effective that elements of it are now in place within the mainstream of management systems throughout the world.

Quality Improvement

In Chapter 1, increased quality was emphasized as one of the new standards for management. Global competition, we said, requires that a product or service be of world-class quality if the organization producing it is to succeed. You will recall the comment by one executive that quality is the ticket into the stadium. The message was that quality alone is not enough to ensure success, but without quality there's no use even trying to compete.

Deming and the Concept of Variability

Over the past several decades, much has been written on the topic of quality by specialists from both the United States and Japan.[24] Perhaps no writer had a greater influence on business organizations in both countries than W. Edwards Deming, an American statistician and management consultant. Deming went to Japan after World War II to assist with rebuilding the Japanese economy. So successful were his methods, and so great is respect for him in that country, that the most prestigious award for Japanese business organizations is called the Deming Prize, which is awarded only to corporations achieving the highest standards of quality.

Central to Deming's view is the belief that problems with quality are the result of variability in the production or service process. For Deming, variability was the result of things that go wrong simply because no process is perfect. There can be a slight undetected change in the raw materials being used. A machine can be running too hot or too cold, too fast or too slow. Pieces can be damaged in handling, and there is always the possibility of human error. Deming suggested that through the use of statistics and other analytical tools, the source of the variability could be identified and eliminated. Deming defined this as management's responsibility: to ensure the analysis and problem solving necessary to eliminate or at least minimize variability.

Consider an example from education. For Deming, problems with quality in the form of poor grades would be viewed in part as a result of variability in the way different students prepared for the test: differences in how they read the material, the notes they took, how they studied, how much rest they got before the test, and so on. Deming would focus on the problems in each of these areas to reduce the variability and improve students' grades.

Deming's Program for Quality Improvement

To achieve an organization that is consistently producing high-quality goods and services, Deming recommended a fourteen-point program.[25] Figure 2-9 lists some of the key elements of his program.

Not surprisingly, Deming's response to the question of how to improve the organization's performance is similar to the Japanese management response: Focus on quality, continuously seek to reduce the variability that is the cause of a lack of quality, and engage the entire organization in seeking continuously to build quality into the process.

Rethinking Quality

Initially, American organizations were much slower than Japanese to listen to Deming's message, but that has changed as quality has become an increasingly

- A commitment by the entire organization to improve quality.
- Leadership by management to bring about changes toward improving quality.
- Eliminate the need for inspecting every product by building quality into the product from the beginning.
- Break down the barriers between departments. Solve problems through teamwork.
- Constantly seek to permanently improve the systems of production and service.

Figure 2-9 Key Elements of Deming's Fourteen-point Program

critical concern. In the early 1990s, *total quality management (TQM),* a concept rooted in the Deming approach, became one of the most widely practiced management responses in U.S. organizations trying to cope with pressures to compete. In fact, today it is rare to find a chief executive who does not claim to be a TQM advocate. However, too often organizations have pursued improvements in quality without considering customer needs or gauging whether the quality improvement would produce profits for the organization.

Most recently, the concept of *return on quality (ROQ)* has emphasized that quality improvements must have value to the customer, that investments in improved quality must ultimately result in increased sales and improved profits. While quality concepts such as improved product designs and increased speed in manufacturing are important, quality programs that result in no clear payoff can hardly be termed successful. In the ROQ approach, success in terms of quality can

- **Decision sciences:** Use mathematical and statistical models to decide on the best patterns and uses of an organization's resources.
- **Contingency theory:** Adjust the management approach to match the requirements of the situation.
- **Systems theory:** Recognize the importance of factors and events occurring outside the organization in the surrounding environment.
- **Japanese management:** Emphasize cooperation and continuously seek to improve the people, process, and the product or service.
- **Quality improvement:** Focus on quality. Engage the entire organization in identifying and eliminating the sources of problems with quality.

Figure 2-10 Recent Contributions to Management Thinking

only be measured in terms of larger market shares and increased customer satisfaction.[26]

There is no question that quality has become a focus of U.S. management, and one that, while possibly requiring continued refinements, such as ROQ, by all the evidence appears likely to endure.

These recent contributions to our understanding of management (shown in Figure 2-10) will certainly be followed by others. In the field of management it is clear that managers will continue to innovate and experiment with new approaches to make organizations more productive. The search will continue for ever more effective answers to the question of how to improve performance.

SUMMARY

Management is not a recent practice. Humankind has been engaged in activities requiring management since before the dawn of civilization. Certainly many of the achievements of ancient civilizations, from monuments to governments to religions, would have required the kind of coordination we today call management. At the time of the Industrial Revolution, management thinking began to emerge. From the late 1700s to the early 1900s, Adam Smith, J. B. Say, Eli Whitney, and Robert Owen all made contributions to our understanding of how to improve performance.

It was not until the twentieth century, however, that organizations were systematically studied in an effort to understand how performance might be improved. What emerged from these studies was remarkable. The scientific management approach of Frederick Taylor first recognized management as a separate and professional set of tasks within the organization. The elements and principles of management defined by Henri Fayol provided a description and agenda for Taylor's professional manager. And Elton Mayo and his research team at the Hawthorne Works concluded that in improving performance, the interpersonal relations within the organization are a factor that must be recognized.

From the contributions of Taylor, Fayol, and the Hawthorne studies, the stream of management thinking finally gained impetus and momentum. Although these were not the only contributions from that period, they were certainly among the most important.

There has been a steady flow of significant contributions to our understanding of management since World War II. Decision sciences, in fact, is a tool which was developed during that war. This approach converts factors of concern to the organization into numbers, allowing the organization to calculate the results of various options without actually trying each option out. Systems theory considers the organization as part of a larger system. To improve performance, organizations must improve their relations with every element of the system within which they operate—with their customers, their employees and suppliers, the government, and the public at large.

Contingency theory is similar to systems theory in that it provides a way of thinking about management rather than a specific management tool. Contingency theory recognizes that there is no "one best way" to manage. To improve performance, management must first understand what the situation requires, and then find a way to meet the needs of the situation, whether in the area of planning or organizing or leading. Management must adjust to what the situation requires.

Japanese management is a combination of specific management practices, some of which focus on the people of the organization, some on production and the product. In either case, in the constant effort to improve perfomance, the emphasis in Japanese management is always on cooperation, and on continuously improving both the people and the operational process.

Finally, there has been the expanding influence of the idea that improving performance goes hand in hand with improving quality. Deming suggested that most of our organizations are not set up to focus on the variability that is the real enemy of quality. In his approach, real improvement in organizational performance only becomes possible when management fully commits to the very difficult transformation necessary to make quality an organization's number-one priority.

This chapter provides a sense of the variety of answers to the question of how to improve the performance of organizations. Each of the responses discussed in this chapter represents an enduring contribution to the body of management thinking. In the chapters to come, we will consider in greater detail how these responses are shaping the practice of management as organizations approach the challenges of the twenty-first century.

QUESTIONS TO CHALLENGE YOUR UNDERSTANDING OF THE CHAPTER

1. Discuss why management is not considered a recent or modern invention.

2. Explain how Adam Smith's study of task specialization and J. B. Say's concept of the entrepreneur both represent contributions to the development of management thinking.

3. Contrast Frederick Taylor's response to the question of how to improve performance with the response of Henri Fayol. Are there any points upon which both agree?

4. Describe the Hawthorne effect and explain whether you agree or disagree with Mayo's findings about the importance of interpersonal relations between workers and managers.

5. Explain why decision sciences is less effective in decisions involving human factors. Provide an example of a human factor that may be difficult to quantify.

6. Provide an example of a factor or event that demonstrates that your college or university is part of an open system.

7. Use the "law of the situation" to explain why different styles of management might be used in managing a group of highly skilled workers versus workers who are new to a task.

8. Describe the similarities between Japanese management and the quality improvement approach.

9. Explain why some people think that Japanese management techniques cannot work in the United States.

10. Provide an example of "variability" in your own performance. Identify the sources or causes of this variability.

MANAGEMENT EXERCISE

Which Theories Apply?

The VideoLand Store

Maria Cartoni recently became manager of the Springfield VideoLand store, one of the largest stores in a nationwide chain that began renting videos over ten years ago. The store's volume of video rentals has increased steadily over the last three years; however, revenues from rentals have barely covered expenses. Last year, the store did not make a profit at all.

Maria spent her first week on the job studying the flow of customers, how employees handle their tasks and the transactions with outside suppliers. With regards to customers, at peak periods the store was so busy that there were always four or five customers in each line, which resulted in their waiting as long as ten minutes to be served. At other times, when business was slow, two clerks would descend upon the same customer. Customers noted the higher rental prices that VideoLand charged compared to the newer video store in the new supermarket several blocks away. One customer commented that the cost of renting movies at VideoLand's rates was getting close to the cost of the cable movie channels on televison.

The morning shift of employees was efficient and had a checklist of duties they performed daily. Several told Maria, however, that the layout of the store should be revised, but no one seemed interested in tackling the project. The evening shift, on the other hand, complained continuously about the pay level, the rudeness of customers, and each other's performance.

As Maria begins her second week, she is ready to make changes to improve performance at VideoLand. For each statement below, indicate the management perspective Maria appears to be utilizing or considering.

STATEMENT	DECISION SCIENCES	SYSTEMS THEORY	CONTINGENCY	JAPANESE MANAGEMENT	QUALITY
1. To determine the required number of clerks for a given period, Maria has recorded customer traffic in and out of the store for each one-hour period throughout the day.	_____	_____	_____	_____	_____
2. Maria is developing a brief training program for the employees on the evening shift. She will personally supervise their performance for the next month. She sees no need to provide training or special supervision for the morning shift because problems were minimal during that shift.	_____	_____	_____	_____	_____
3. Maria has discovered that the supplier of chips, soda, and other snacks sold at the store has a markup higher than any other local supplier's, and she is considering changing suppliers.	_____	_____	_____	_____	_____
4. Maria is assigning the morning shift workers to a work team to revise the store layout.	_____	_____	_____	_____	_____
5. Maria feels the best way to eliminate excess expenses is to consider the way customers are served and to revise the processes used through the operation.	_____	_____	_____	_____	_____
6. Maria has begun an in-depth review of the competition to compare the pricing policies, organization, and operation of other stores to VideoLand's.	_____	_____	_____	_____	_____

REFERENCES

1. C. S. George, *The History of Management Thought* (Englewood Cliffs, N.J.: Prentice-Hall, 1968), 4–5.

2. A. Smith, *The Wealth of Nations* (New York: Modern Library, 1937).

3. J. B. Say, *A Treatise on Political Economy* (New York: Sentry Press, 1964).

4. A. Cooke, *Alistair Cooke's America* (New York: Alfred A. Knopf, 1973), 197.

5. R. Owen, *A New View of Society*, 1st American edition, from the 3d London edition (New York: E. Bliss & F. White, 1825), 57.

6. George, *History of Management Thought*, 59–62.

7. J. Case, "A Company of Businesspeople," *INC*, April 1993, 80.

8. F. W. Taylor, *The Principles of Scientific Management* (New York: Harper & Brothers, 1947), 47.

9. Ibid., 36–37.

10. E. Locke, "The Ideas of Frederick W. Taylor: An Evaluation," *Academy of Management Review*, January 1982.

11. Taylor, *Principles of Scientific Management*, 122.

12. D. H. Freedman, "Is Management Still a Science?" *Harvard Business Review* 70 (6) (November–December 1992): 26–38.

13. H. Fayol, *General and Industrial Administration* (New York: Pitman, Publishing Corp., 1949).

14. E. Mayo, *The Human Problems of an Industrial Civilization* (New York: Macmillan, 1953).

15. F. J. Roethlisberger and W. J. Dickson, *Management and the Worker* (Cambridge, Mass: Harvard University Press, 1939).

16. B. Rice, "The Hawthorne Defect: Persistence of a Flawed Theory," *Psychology Today*, February 1982, 70–74.

17. For example, see E. Turban, *Decision Support and Expert Systems: Management Support Systems*, 2d ed. (New York: Macmillan, 1990), 16–19; and E. G. Mallach, *Understanding Decision Support Systems and Expert Systems* (Burr Ridge, Ill.: Irwin, 1994), 4–19.

18. W. G. Wild, Jr., and O. Port, "The Startling Discovery Bell Labs Kept in the Shadows," *Business Week*, September 21, 1987, 69.

19. L. von Bertalanffy, "General Systems Theory: A New Approach to the Unity of Science," *Human Biology*, December 1951, 302–61.

20. H. A. Simon, *The Shape of Automation for Men and Management* (NY: Harper & Row, 1965).

21. H. C. Metcaff and L. Urwick, eds., *Dynamic Administration: The Collected Papers of Mary Parker Follett* (New York: Pitman Publishing Corp., 1941).

22. W. Ouchi, *Theory Z: How American Business Can Meet the Japanese Challenge* (Reading, Mass.: Addison-Wesley, 1981); and A. Athos and R. Pascale, *The Art of Japanese Management: Applications for American Executives* (New York: Simon & Schuster, 1981).

23. J. B. Treece, "Here Comes GM's Saturn," *Business Week*, April 9, 1990, 56.

24. See W. E. Deming, *Quality, Productivity, and Competitive Position* (Cambridge, Mass.: MIT Center for Advanced Engineering Study, 1982); J. M. Juran and F. M. Gyrne, *Quality, Planning and Analysis* (New York: McGraw-Hill, 1980); and P. B. Crosby, *Quality is Free* (New York: McGraw-Hill, 1979).

25. Deming, *Quality, Productivity, and Competitive Position*.

26. D. Greising, "Quality: How to Make it Pay," *Business Week*, August 8, 1994, 54–59.

CHAPTER 3
Emerging Performance Issues

LEARNING OBJECTIVES

After studying this chapter, you should be able to:

- *Explain the concept of social responsibility and the difference between the classical economic and activist views of social responsibility.*

- *Distinguish among four levels of social contribution by organizations.*

- *Discuss the impact of information technology on the importance of education and training in organizations.*

- *Describe the value of information technology in making feedback on performance available throughout the organization, and the potential problems of using IT to monitor performance.*

- *Discuss the risks to the organization resulting from increased access to information.*

- *Distinguish among the various levels or stages of involvement in global markets.*

- *Discuss the guidelines for success in competing in global markets.*

The challenges facing management and organizations were identified and briefly discussed in Chapter 1. Many of these challenges, including ethical standards, speed and flexibility, quality, and workforce diversity, will be expanded upon in the chapters that follow. Three of them—social responsibility, information technology, and managing in global markets—are the special focus of this chapter.

SOCIAL RESPONSIBILITY

Social responsibility is the obligation of organizations not only to provide society with goods and services, but to contribute to the social well-being of the communities where they operate. When an organization is "socially responsible," its management has a broader view of its responsibility for performance than just realizing a profit. In addition to its responsibility to maximize profit, management views itself as having an obligation to society to set policies and make decisions that will enhance society's welfare.

Some organizations show an impressive sense of social responsibility. Consider the case of ice-cream maker Ben & Jerry's Homemade, Inc. Founders Ben Cohen and Jerry Greenfield have tried to ensure that every aspect of their business helps the world, not just the company's profits or bottom line. For example, in 1990 a new flavored ice cream was developed, Rain Forest Crunch. To supply the crunch, Ben & Jerry's ordered 100 tons of nuts, which are grown wild in the rain forest of the Amazon and processed in the small Brazilian town of Xapuri.[1] Their rationale was that if the rain forest nuts could provide a profitable venture for the Brazilians, the landowners might let the rain forests stand rather than destroy them to make cattle ranches.

As we noted in Chapter 1, an increasing number of organizations like Ben & Jerry's are involved in efforts of various types related to social responsibility. However, the expectation that business should commit to making a significant social contribution beyond providing jobs and support for the United Way is a relatively new concept in management.

The Concept of Social Responsibility

Through the 1950s, the relationship between business and the American public was always a good one. Consumers were eager to purchase products that had not been available during the Great Depression of the 1930s or during World War II, and businesses expanded rapidly to satisfy that demand. Business was viewed as the source of the jobs and the products that were at the heart of the American dream. A saying popular at the time was "What's good for General Motors is good for America." Large corporations made financial contributions for community projects, and most companies were strong supporters of the United Way and similar social service funds.

Beginning in the 1960s, however, the public began to view business differently. To meet the exploding consumer demand in the years following World War II, organizations had increased production at such rapid rates that the results unfortunately included pollution of the air and water, environmental decay from the dumping of industrial waste, and defective and sometimes unsafe products and services. Frustration with the Vietnam War added to the public's discontent, as many people blamed big businesses with defense contracts, such as McDonnell Douglas and DuPont for profiting from the prolongation of the war. An even stronger sense of resentment was directed toward Dow Chemical Company, maker of napalm, a chemical used by U.S. forces with tragic consequences for the landscape of Vietnam and its people. Additionally, there was the growing sense that business organizations were not offering equal employment opportunity to the minority members of society. "Suddenly consumerism, stockholderism, racial equalitarianism, antimilitarism, environmentalism, and feminism became forces to be reckoned with by corporate management."[2]

The result of all of these factors was a significant increase in the public's demand that organizations of all types act in a more socially responsible way. As we noted in Chapter 1, as a result of this public pressure, some areas of social responsibility, including protection of the environment, equal employment opportunity, and safe working conditions, are now regulated by law and monitored by federal agencies. In the areas not covered by laws and regulations, however, the question of how much social responsibility business organizations should take on has generated a wide range of responses.

Two Views of Social Responsibility

The most common approaches to social responsibility reflect either of two very different philosophies. As summarized in Figure 3-1, these two views vary in their

Arguments for Classical Economic Approach

- Management's responsibility is to earn profits for owners (stockholders).
- Potential conflict of interest when managers must meet profit goals and simultaneously enhance social welfare.
- Businesses lack expertise to manage social problems.

Arguments for Activist Approach

- Business is a member of society and has responsibilities to other "shareholders," such as employees, customers, suppliers, distributors, creditors, government, unions, special interest groups, and the general public.
- Business has technical, financial, and managerial resources to help solve social problems.
- Government intervention is less likely when business takes the initiative in addressing social problems.

Figure 3-1 Two Views of Social Responsibility

conception of the level and type of involvement management should undertake in terms of activities to benefit society.

The Classical Economic Approach

The classical economic approach to social responsibility suggests that a business organization should limit its involvement to activities that improve its own economic performance. This approach maintains that the first and foremost responsibility of management is to earn profits for owners (stockholders). According to economist Milton Friedman, a strong proponent of this view, there is a potential conflict of interest when society holds managers responsible to owners for meeting profit goals and at the same time holds them responsible to society to enhance the social welfare.[3] From this perspective, every dollar spent on social problems or donated to a charity is one less dollar distributed to the owners in the form of dividends and one less dollar available for the kind of investment that creates jobs.

For example, William Norris, the former chairman of Control Data, spent large sums of money involving the company in socially responsible activities such as urban renewal, vocational training for prisoners, and farm experiments in Alaska. When Control Data lost millions of dollars in the 1980s, critics suggested that Norris's priority should have been to maximize profits for the stockholders, and they blamed Norris's "do-gooder" mentality for Control Data's poor financial performance.[4]

The classical economic approach further argues that requiring management to pursue socially responsible activities could be unethical, since the money managers are spending belongs to other people:

> Insofar as the actions of [an employee of the owners of the business] . . . reduce returns to stockholders, he is spending their money. Insofar as his actions raise the price to customers, he is spending the customers' money.[5]

A final argument against managers' being involved in social responsibility programs is that businesses lack the expertise to determine which programs have the greatest needs. For example, should an organization donate to the local YMCA, or is there a program with greater needs?

In sum, the classical economic approach to social responsibility insists that business organizations have the social responsibility not to do harm to customers, employees, or the environment. But managers do not have the right to invest stockholders' profits in activities focusing on social problems. According to this view, management's only social responsibility is to follow the legal and ethical rules of society while making business organizations profitable.

The Activist Approach

The activist model of social responsibility argues that business does in fact have a responsibility to deal with social problems, since business is both part of the cause of these problems and part of society.[6] And social responsibility activists argue that organizations *do* have the technical, financial, and managerial resources to help solve society's difficult problems.

There is growing evidence that to some extent businesses agree with this view. For example, large and small companies all over the United States have entered partnerships with local schools. These business partners not only encourage their employees to volunteer at the schools; they provide training for teachers and administrators in key skill areas and donate surplus computers, furniture, and other equipment that the school might not otherwise be able to afford.

Another part of the activist argument is that business has a responsibility not just to owners and shareholders, but to everyone who has a stake in the company's operations. As we noted in Chapter 1, stakeholders include employees, customers, suppliers, distributors, creditors, government, unions, special interest groups, and the general public. In the activist view, business—as a corporate citizen—has an obligation to respond to the needs of all these stakeholders while pursuing a profit.[7] In other words, business has an obligation to be responsible to all of the elements of the communities from which it profits. This argument gains strength considerably the more closely the success of the business is presented as linked to the health of the community that supplies it with workers and customers.

Lastly, the activist argument holds that when business itself takes the initiative in addressing social problems, costly government intervention is less likely. In recent years, for example, both the cable TV industry and the video game producers have taken the initiative to create commissions to monitor the level of violence in their products. Their actions came in response to consumer concerns as well as concern on the part of management that the government would impose potentially more costly standards if this industry did not take the initiative and act on its own.

A Difficult Choice

In the classical economic approach, business is viewed exclusively as an economic entity whose nearly exclusive purpose is profit. The activist approach, on the other hand, views business as a member of society, with broader social responsibilities. When an action is required by law, or when investment in a socially responsible activity is profitable, there is no conflict between the two views, and both approaches would support the activity.

It is when the socially responsible activity neither is required by law *nor* is it in itself profitable that the two approaches differ. The classical approach would argue against business's becoming involved, while the activist view would support involvement if the costs were not prohibitively high.

Many business organizations find themselves caught squarely in the middle. For example, at Stride Rite, maker of shoes for young children, Keds sneakers, and Sperry Top-sider shoes, a long-standing commitment to social responsibility has begun to clash with the competitive pressures to lower costs. Over the years, the company has received numerous awards for setting aside 5 percent of pretax profits to help fund such programs as providing scholarships to inner-city youths, paying employees to tutor disadvantaged children on company time, and funding Harvard graduate students to work in a Cambodian refugee camp.

However, in recent years, to save on labor costs, the company has closed three plants, including its children's shoe factory in Roxbury, Massachusetts, and moved the jobs to the Far East. According to a company spokesperson, it was a difficult decision, since this meant five hundred lost jobs for workers who were mostly low-skilled immigrants.[8] Famous for its commitment to its workers and the community, Stride Rite found itself unable to both compete successfully and maintain the high standards of social responsibility it had set for itself.

The degree to which a business advances societal versus economic objectives depends to a great extent on factors such as the organization's size, the nature of competition in the industry, the type of problems involved, and the costs of pursuing an activity—as with Stride Rite—versus the consequences of not doing so.

Thus, the forms and extent of corporate social responsibility vary across a broad spectrum, from traditional philanthropy at one end to organizations for whom social responsibility is the primary mission of the company at the other.

Levels of Social Contribution

One model of the various options for social responsibility suggests four levels of contribution. As shown in Figure 3-2, as business becomes increasingly active in terms of social responsibility, the level of social contribution increases.[9]

The point of this model is not to label organizations according to these categories, or to imply that one category is superior to another. In fact, frequently organizations do not fall squarely into one level. For example, a company might donate money to a charity with no strings attached (Level 1) and might also have a policy where employees can take paid leaves to work on community projects (Level 2). The model simply shows the range of possibilities.

Level 1: Traditional Philanthropy

Philanthropy, or the charitable donation of a company's resources, was the most common form of social responsibility practiced by large organizations in the nine-

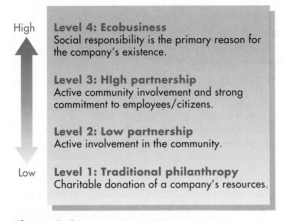

High

Level 4: Ecobusiness
Social responsibility is the primary reason for the company's existence.

Level 3: High partnership
Active community involvement and strong commitment to employees/citizens.

Level 2: Low partnership
Active involvement in the community.

Low   **Level 1: Traditional philanthropy**
Charitable donation of a company's resources.

Figure 3-2 Levels of Social Contribution

teenth century and is a form still practiced today. Typically, the amount of resources donated and the charities or programs that will benefit are determined by the company's CEO or a group of senior executives. Employees do not participate in deciding where the money goes, and there is no mechanism for guaranteeing contributions once the CEO leaves.

Often, there is no real sense of connection between the company and the larger community, which is viewed as something "out there" to which contributions are made. Although not in all cases, this failure to make the connection to the community can lead to a contradiction between a company's practices and its philanthropic activities. For example, critics question the motives of tobacco companies that sponsor athletic and artistic events with profits from products that cause health problems. In such cases, there appears to be no genuine concern for the welfare of society. The concern of many organizations at this level of the model is for goodwill or public relations.

Level 2: Low Partnership

At the next level of social contribution, called *low partnership,* a company recognizes the connection between itself and the larger community. The social contribution of organizations at this level extends beyond traditional philanthropy to active involvement in the community. The schools/business partnership mentioned earlier is an example of this low-partnership level. Employees are encouraged to volunteer for community activities, such as donating blood, serving on nonprofit boards, or taking on large-scale community projects. At Aetna Life & Casualty, for example, employees support a volunteer lawyers' project that gives free legal advice to elderly low-income people.

Concern for employees' welfare is also part of this strategy. The company might invest in child care facilities, for example, or provide free counseling services for employees and their families.

In contrast to traditional philanthropy, when these low-partnership companies donate money to a cause, they select organizations that they know will have an impact, and they track the results of the programs funded.

Level 3: High Partnership

The difference between the low and high partnership levels is that the high-partnership approach has a greater impact on the day-to-day internal workings of the company. High-partnership companies change their structures and the way they function in response to the interests of their employees in the community. They tend to foster employee participation, focus on teamwork, and often value diversity in their workforce. Ben & Jerry's Homemade, Inc., tries to set an example within its own structure by sharing profits with workers, and for years had a rule that the highest-paid employee could make no more than seven times as much as the lowest-paid worker.

In addition, companies at this level of social contribution strive for partnership externally with their customers, suppliers, and other stakeholders. One such external partnership involved Levi Strauss & Co. and its Bangladesh supplier. In

1992, the company discovered that the supplier was employing children as full-time seamstresses. Levi decided to follow its ethics code and enforce International Labor Organization standards that bar children under the age of fourteen from working. The supplier agreed to fire the underage children but argued that most of them provided sole economic support for their families. Rather than ignore its ethics code or just insist that the children be let go, Levi developed an agreement with the supplier: Levi would send the children to school and pay for uniforms, books, and tuition if the supplier would agree to pay the children their wages and hire them back when they turned fourteen.[10]

Level 4: Ecobusiness

Like the companies at the high-partnership level, businesses at the ecobusiness level of social contribution promote social equality within their organizations by viewing employees as fully participating partners. They provide high-quality products and processes that show concern for customers as much as for profits. They go to great lengths to reduce harmful effects on the environment by recycling materials, developing pollution-free production processes, and supporting environmental causes. In this model, what distinguishes this highest level of social contribution is that these companies consider their social responsibility as the *primary* reason for their existence. The organization's mission is social responsibility; its profits help to fulfill that mission.

The Body Shop, a company selling body lotions and shampoo, is an example of an organization at the highest level of social contribution. Anita Roddick, the founder of the company, sees education as one of the company's major goals. The Body Shop outlets offer cards, pamphlets, and videos about products and ingredients. No money is spent on advertising and there is no marketing department. Whether the cause is saving the whales or working for the preservation of Brazil's rain forests, Roddick devotes her organization to educating the public with messages on company trucks and sometimes by leading employees in public demonstrations. Roddick, who sees no conflict between operating a business for profit and supporting environmental concerns, feels business should lead the way in solving the world's problems.[11]

Another ecobusiness is Newman's Own, a company started by actor and director Paul Newman. Newman's Own makes salad dressings, pasta sauces, salsa, and lemonade, and all profits from the company go to charities and social causes. Examples of companies at the ecobusiness level are still rare. Only time will tell whether a primary focus on social responsibility represents a viable business strategy.

The issue as organizations move through the 1990s is not whether managers and their firms should behave in socially responsible ways, but rather how to define the appropriate scope of social responsibility. As society demands more from its organizations, the message to management is that responsibility for performance must also include a social responsibility dimension. The management challenge is to define that dimension in a way that meets both the organization's goals and society's.

INFORMATION TECHNOLOGY

The impact of computers and of *information technology (IT)* is being felt in every kind of organization in every industry. Information technology has transformed the way work is done in small businesses and large corporations. Consider the examples in Figure 3-3.

In the 1990s, it has clearly become management's task to recognize and integrate IT both as a tool for improving performance and as a force actually shaping the organization itself.

Part of the IT challenge for management is to determine how best to use computers to speed up or improve the way goods are produced and services are provided, as shown in the examples in Figure 3-3. But IT also creates challenges for management in at least two other areas. First, there is the challenge to provide employees with the education and training necessary to operate and take advantage of IT. The second challenge is to use IT effectively to support and improve human performance. Finally, there is the challenge to effectively manage the access to information made necessary and possible by IT.

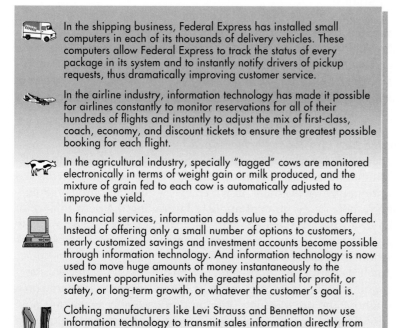

In the shipping business, Federal Express has installed small computers in each of its thousands of delivery vehicles. These computers allow Federal Express to track the status of every package in its system and to instantly notify drivers of pickup requests, thus dramatically improving customer service.

In the airline industry, information technology has made it possible for airlines constantly to monitor reservations for all of their hundreds of flights and instantly to adjust the mix of first-class, coach, economy, and discount tickets to ensure the greatest possible booking for each flight.

In the agricultural industry, specially "tagged" cows are monitored electronically in terms of weight gain or milk produced, and the mixture of grain fed to each cow is automatically adjusted to improve the yield.

In financial services, information adds value to the products offered. Instead of offering only a small number of options to customers, nearly customized savings and investment accounts become possible through information technology. And information technology is now used to move huge amounts of money instantaneously to the investment opportunities with the greatest potential for profit, or safety, or long-term growth, or whatever the customer's goal is.

Clothing manufacturers like Levi Strauss and Bennetton now use information technology to transmit sales information directly from their stores to their factories to make sure that the factories are producing items that the customers are buying, almost eliminating the need for costly warehouses in the process.

Figure 3-3 Innovations through Information Technology

The Importance of Education and Training

As information technology has changed the way business is being done by organizations, it has changed the very nature of jobs within the organization as well. Employees in every kind of position are now required to use IT to do their work. Even manufacturing jobs, jobs that had little if any information processing requirements in the past, increasingly require workers to use computerized machinery and equipment to perform their tasks. The same is true for clerical staff and for maintenance and transportation workers. Virtually every kind of job now requires that workers know how to operate at least some elements of information technology to gain access to information, process it, modify and reconfigure it, and pass it along to others.

As a consequence, the need for training in IT has increased dramatically. No matter what business or service an organization is in, it also is in the training business. Managers are now responsible for ensuring that everyone in the organization possesses and continually updates the skills and understanding necessary to take advantage of the performance potential available through IT. Training has always been a responsibility of management, but with the IT revolution, the training challenge is more demanding than it has ever been. And with the continuous development of new hardware and software, the training task will continue to be of paramount importance.

IT and Performance Improvement

Information technology not only makes performance demands on people to learn new skills and to develop new competencies. It also represents a tool for improving and enhancing their performance in other ways. One of the most powerful uses of IT is to provide performance feedback, the kind of timely information that can dramatically enhance performance.

Feedback on Individual and Team Performance

There are several levels or kinds of performance feedback made possible by IT. One is feedback on individual or team performance. In Chapter 12 we will discuss the process of continuous improvement, in which every member of the organization shares in the responsibility for continuously improving the performance of the organization. It is no longer enough for the manager alone to know how things are going; for continuous improvement to work, everyone needs to have access to information on performance.

The move toward continuous improvement coincides with the development of the computers and software necessary to make timely feedback available on a broad scale throughout the organization. Workers on assembly teams are now provided continuously updated information on the rate of production, quality, level of inventory, costs, and other variables that represent important feedback about performance. Bank tellers have available on their terminal screens a steady flow of feedback on the number of transactions they have completed during a time period, the types of transactions, the average waiting time in line for each customer, etc. Insurance claims processors receive similar feedback in terms of number of claims processed, error rates, average and total dollar values, processing time per claim, and more.

Organizations in every industry are beginning to see the improvements in performance that are the result, at least in part, of this kind of IT-based feedback. According to Harvard Business School professor Gary W. Loveman, "Gains [in performance] come not because the technology is whiz-bang, but because [IT] supports breakthrough ideas in business processes."[12] In other words, the kind of feedback made possible through IT allows individual and team performers to see what kind of progress they are making toward performance goals, and to identify and solve performance problems.

Feedback on Organizational Performance

In addition to feedback on individual and team performance, IT also makes feedback on overall organizational performance available to employees throughout the organization. For example, an increasing number of companies are sharing the financial performance data found on income statements and balance sheets with their employees. Formerly, information about financial performance was available only to the highest level managers in the organization. Managers now realize that this kind of information allows employees to better understand how their own performance impacts the overall performance of the organization, and to engage in activities and problem solving for improving performance at the organization level.

Traditionally, information of this type has been available only to top-level managers. As an executive from Chesapeake Packaging noted, however, "I've never seen a parade yet that was very impressive where only the drum major had the sheet music."[13] With IT, it is possible for an organization to make its "sheet music" available to virtually everyone in the organization and to keep it updated continuously.

Feedback on Ideas

A third category of IT-based feedback is feedback on ideas. With the demands of the changing environment and changing performance standards, increasing the speed of transmission of ideas and feedback on them as they work their way through the organization has great strategic value.

Before the availability of IT, the process of having an idea considered by others in an organization was slow and time-consuming. An individual had to either wait for an appropriate time to have the idea placed on the agenda of some future meeting, or prepare a typed memo, have it circulated through the organization's mail system, and wait for a typed reply to be prepared and forwarded. Obviously this process could take days. Today organizations use electronic mail (E-mail) to dramatically reduce the lag between idea and feedback. *E-mail* uses electronic circuits to send written messages from one person's computer to another computer. An idea can now be prepared on anyone's desktop terminal, and instantaneously mailed electronically to anyone hooked up to the system, who in turn can immediately electronically mail back a response or feedback on the idea. In fact, E-mail is increasingly being used to hold spur-of-the-moment electronic meetings among several participants to resolve issues or determine a course of action—all with the participants never leaving their offices.

Cellular telephones, video conferencing, fax machines, and PCs are all part of the IT revolution. The dramatically improved flow of information and feedback made possible by these technologies have become a requirement for improving the performance of both the organization and its members. As we will see in the coming sections of this discussion, however, effectively utilizing IT is not without its own special challenges.

The Computer Terminal: Coach or Cop?

In terms of managing performance, IT provides not only the means for giving performance feedback to individuals and groups, but the means to carefully monitor individual and group performance as well.

The number of organizations with people working in front of computer screens or at video display terminals (VDT's) has increased dramatically over the past decade. Literally millions of people now sit at computer terminals to provide services over the telephone for catalog companies such as L. L. Bean and J. Crew, for TWA, American, and other airlines, for the home shopping networks, the telephone companies, telemarketing services, and a whole variety of 1-800 and mail-order customer services. As we have already noted, through the use of IT these workers can receive a steady flow of feedback about the number of calls they handle, the average length of a call, and other factors about their performance. At the same time, this information is being used to evaluate and grade the performance of the operator.

Consider the regimen at TWA's Chicago reservation office. The computers keep track of when their operators sign on in the morning and sign off for breaks and at the end of the day. Beyond this, supervisors regularly listen in on calls to rate operators on how effective they are in delivering TWA's eight-point sales pitch. The operators each receive a weekly evaluation based on the computer data, and a monthly evaluation that includes both their performance data from the computer and the ratings from when their supervisors listened in on their telephone conversations with customers.[14]

Supporters of this system of electronic performance monitoring suggest that it is an effective way to provide strong performers with the feedback they desire while at the same time ensuring that weaker performers stay on their toes. Opponents of the system insist that it not only is an invasion of the workers' privacy, but also pressures them constantly to complete their calls more and more quickly. Some critics charge that the companies program high performance goals into the computers, automatically pushing employees to work faster to meet them, much as manufacturers might speed up assembly lines.

Perhaps more to the point, some workers say that the impact of IT in this case may actually be to discourage improved performance. In attempting to meet their electronically imposed goals, workers may become more concerned with completing calls in the shortest possible time rather than taking the time necessary to satisfy the needs of the customer.

The case of the killer software. Information technology for monitoring and managing individual performance is being used to "manage" managers as well. A graphic example of this is the case of the "killer software" used by CEO T. J. Rodgers at Cypress Semiconductor Corp.[15] In one example, Rodgers developed a computer program to scan purchase orders from customers. When the program discovers missed delivery dates, it automatically shuts down the computers of whichever department is responsible. This effectively cripples the department until the appropriate steps are taken to eliminate the late deliveries.

In another example, Rodgers started electronically tracking how long parts were sitting on the shelf in inventory before they were used in production. If any parts were found to sit for more than two hundred days, again, the tracking software automatically shut down that department's computer system. In fact, Cypress tracks the performance of all its managers electronically. Each manager at Cypress is required to establish performance goals, to provide performance updates regularly, and to provide explanations where goals are not being met.

Cypress managers say that the goal system improves morale, since people always get credit for what they have done. Still, there is concern among some observers that, because the performance monitoring is so detailed and so constant, IT could become as much an instrument of intimidation and punishment as a means for improving performance.

At its best, IT can be the means for improving the way work is done, a source of valuable feedback on performance, and the media of speeding feedback and ideas through the organization. As we have just seen, however, if used inappropriately, IT risks becoming a source of the kind of intimidation and pressure that might actually hurt performance in the long run. Obviously, the key for management is to find the right balance to ensure the most appropriate uses of IT possible to enhance and support the performance of the organization and its people.

Risks from Increased Access to Information

While the potential for improved performance through IT is significant, even when used effectively it is not without risks. An additional area of challenge for managers is to effectively manage the access to information made possible by IT and required in the workplace.

IT: The Need for Access and the Threat of Leaks

As employees' participation in the responsibility for speeding up and improving the firm's performance increases, what also increases, as we have pointed out, is their need for access to information on such factors as inventory levels, delivery schedules, costs, and levels of staffing, as well as the performance of various units within the organization. Futurist Alvin Toffler explains, "Today, workers are demanding more and more access to information because they can't do their job effectively without it."[16]

Obviously, this greater access to information throughout the organization results in an increased possibility that important information might leak outside the organization to competitors, the media, and elsewhere. This is a reality, and organizations must learn to manage this reality and the risk it represents.

Yet on closer examination, it appears that the fear of leaks may be greater than the actual threat. Companies like Tandem Computer, GM, and Herman-Miller have been sharing "secret" information with front-line employees for a number of years, with no evidence of any damaging leaks. Tom Peters also makes the point that since information is everywhere anyway, competitors can get the kind of information they are seeking without the help of leaks. Finally, the potential performance advantages of sharing information with employees far outweigh the value of keeping this information "secure."[17]

The Possibility of Sabotage

Perhaps more serious than the potential for damaging leaks is another risk arising from the presence of IT in the workplace: the risk of employee sabotage of the company's information system. Toffler points out that a single angry employee armed only with a computer virus is now capable of doing irreparable harm to a company's databases and information systems. Toffler also raises the possibility of the one-person "strike," where a single anonymous, dissatisfied employee could interrupt the information system to call attention to a particular issue or to attempt to gain concessions from management. As Toffler points out, "No laws, clever programs, and security arrangements can totally protect against this. The best defense is likely to be social pressure from one's peers. Or the simple feeling that one is treated with dignity and justice."[18]

To guard against viruses, employees can be trained not to use software and disks from unknown sources. In addition, security software has been developed to protect against viruses.[19] However, as with leaks of crucial information, organizations must now learn to manage their employees in ways that minimize the likelihood that they will want to do damage to the information and the IT to which they have now gained access. Fortunately, surprisingly little evidence to date exists of this kind of sabotage.

Minimizing these risks, Toffler suggests, is primarily a process of treating employees fairly and justly. But as we saw with the TWA and Cypress Semiconductor examples, there can often be differences of opinion about what is fair and what is just. In all probability, it will have to be the employees' sense of fair treatment that management will have to satisfy, if the threat of information leaks and IT sabotage is effectively to be minimized.

MANAGING GLOBALLY

In 1992, the Walt Disney Company opened its $4 billion Euro Disneyland eighteen miles outside of Paris, France. By the end of 1993, Euro Disney had drawn more than 17 million visitors, making it the largest tourist attraction in Europe. Unfortunately, the park also lost more than $900 million in its first full year. In fact, Disney was able to ensure the continued operation of Euro Disney only with the financial involvement of an investor from Saudi Arabia.[20]

In this situation one of America's top companies, doing business in Europe, is saved from major embarrassment by a financier from the Middle East. The Euro Disney example provides vivid evidence of two key trends in managing: first, that managing is increasingly a global activity; and second, that even for the very best managed companies, managing globally is not easy.

As we pointed out in Chapter 1, some 95 percent of the world's population, and almost all of the market growth, reside beyond the boundaries of the United States. In addition, companies from all over the world are competing in the United States for American customers. These two facts make it clear that to genuinely prosper, business organizations have to learn to move beyond the familiar American markets and prepare themselves for competition in markets around the globe.

It's not just the Walt Disneys, the Ford Motor Companies, and the McDonald's who must learn to manage globally; it's the "little guys" as well. The example of Ohio-based Vita-Mix is becoming more and more typical. In 1991, Vita-Mix hired an international sales manager to export its high-powered blenders to twenty countries. Managing through a global sales force resulted in 20 percent of sales coming from exports in the following year.[21]

In the final section of this chapter, we will review the options that organizations have in terms of the various stages or levels of involvement in global business. We will also discuss some of the key strategies for ensuring that a company's global involvement is well managed, regardless of the level of that involvement. It is one thing to recognize the need to compete globally. As Disney has discovered, it is quite another to succeed.

Stages of Global Involvement

Companies can participate in global markets in many ways. It is not an all-or-nothing proposition. Each form of global participation has advantages and disadvantages. Effectiveness in managing the global challenge begins with understanding what these options are.

Global Sourcing

One of the most basic forms of global involvement is when a business turns to a foreign company to manufacture one or more of its products. This practice is called *global sourcing,* since the company will turn to whatever manufacturer or "source" around the world will most efficiently produce its product. This approach is common in the clothing and footwear industries, for example, where companies in countries like Mexico, China, and Malaysia have much lower production costs because workers are paid at much lower wage rates than American workers. The foreign producer, or "source," manufactures the product to a particular company's specifications and attaches that company's label or logo to the product.

Nike, Reebok, Bennetton, and Banana Republic are examples of companies that do a great deal of global sourcing. Companies that engage in global sourcing take advantage of manufacturing expertise or lower wage rates in foreign countries, and then sell their products either just in their home market or in markets around the world.

Licensing/Franchising

In a second of the more basic stages of global participation, the company authorizes both the production and the marketing of its products by a company in a foreign country. Athletic clothing companies like Starter and Champion engage in *licensing*, which consists of allowing their labels and logo to be attached to clothing that will be both produced and marketed in a foreign market by a company from that market. While the licensing company, say, Champion, receives only a negotiated fee, this arrangement allows them to enter foreign markets with no direct investment in either production or marketing.

Franchising is the equivalent of licensing where the business involves a service rather than a product. A franchising agreement allows the use of a company's logo and business systems in a foreign country, usually in return for a fee and a percentage of the revenues from those services. Holiday Inn, KFC, and Coca-Cola, with its licensed bottlers around the world, are examples of companies that benefit from foreign markets while minimizing their investment to enter those markets.

Exporting

One of the most common forms of participation in global markets is *exporting:* the practice of selling goods or services produced in one country directly to customers in foreign markets. While most major corporations use exporting as part of their overall mix of global strategies, for small businesses, exporting frequently is the only global strategy, because it represents the most direct form of involvement in global markets. Exporting allows a small business to participate in global markets by finding a means or channel through which it can distribute its product in the foreign market.

The advantage of exporting over other kinds of global involvement is greater control over the quality of the product, as well as receiving the full share of profits. The complicated aspect of exporting is that it often requires the assistance of local agents or local representatives with expertise in how best to gain entry and acceptance in their country's markets. For example, U.S. slot-machine manufacturer IGT tried without success for several years just to get a copy of the regulations that would allow it to sell its machines in Japan. When, finally, IGT hired a Japanese agent to assist in this process, it received a copy of the regulations within weeks.[22]

Local Assembly and Packaging

Sometimes trade restrictions in a foreign country prohibit the direct import of some large products, such as automobiles or large pieces of machinery or equipment. To enter markets with these kinds of restrictions, a company ships major components of the finished product to a company-owned facility in the foreign country for final assembly. This is the approach taken by Honda, Toyota, BMW, and other foreign car manufacturers doing business in the United States. Major components, such as the engine and transmission, are manufactured in Japan or Europe and shipped to Honda's American facilities for assembly of the finished automobile. Although this approach can be more expensive than simply exporting a final product to a foreign market, trade restrictions in that market may leave no other alternative for gaining access to that market.

Joint Venture/Strategic Alliance

One of the more complex levels of participation in global markets involves a company from one country pooling its resources with those of one or more foreign companies. Sometimes the joint venture is necessary as a result of laws in foreign countries prohibiting a company from another country from owning more than 49 percent of a business in the host country. Other times, these agreements simply provide faster entry into a marketplace. AT&T, for example, has utilized the joint venture strategy extensively, as shown in Figure 3-4.[23]

In other cases, called *strategic alliances,* the purpose of the partnership is to take advantage of particular expertise or other resources in the foreign companies. For example, Ford has formed an alliance with Mazda to take advantage of Mazda's manufacturing expertise in building subcompact cars. GM has a similar

AT&T's Foreign Affairs

Venture	Date signed
A 20% stake in Canadian long-distance provider Unitel Communications Inc.	January 1993
An 80% stake in Poland's Telfa, which makes phone switching gear and other equipment	November 1992
A 60% investment in Chinese fiber-optic-cable venture	October 1992
A 50–50 venture with Tata Telecom Ltd. to make phone transmission equipment in India	June 1992
A 68% stake in a joint venture with Dalnya Sviaz of St. Petersburg to sell phone equipment	February 1992
A 19.5% stake in a joint venture to design, build, and operate Ukraine's long-distance network	January 1992

Figure 3-4 Joint Ventures Established by AT&T (*Source: Reprinted from March 8, 1993 issue of* Business Week *by special permission, copyright © 1993 by McGraw-Hill, Inc.*)

arrangement with Toyota, and Apple notebook computers were initially manufactured by Sony.

Both joint ventures and strategic alliances represent highly complex approaches to participating in the global marketplace. Achieving effective overall management of a venture when the ownership is shared by companies from different countries is challenging, to say the least. But research suggests that a majority of these arrangements do work well, especially when both parties have a strong need for the venture or strategic alliance.[24]

Direct Foreign Investment

Perhaps the most fully developed form of participation in the global marketplace is when a corporation produces and markets goods or services in a foreign country through a wholly owned company or subsidiary in that country. A wholly owned local company is an existing company that has been purchased by the corporation to allow it to take advantage of the market position, management, workforce, and other resources already in place at that company. For example, Whirlpool bought the European appliance business of Philips Electronics NV several years ago in order to capitalize on Philips's strong brand name in Europe.[25]

Forming a wholly owned subsidiary in a foreign market (versus buying an existing company) has the advantage of allowing the corporation to do business entirely its own way. The disadvantage of this approach is that it requires the corporation to develop its own market position and its own workforce, its own facilities and suppliers, all in a foreign market. For companies like Disney, building a European theme-park subsidiary meant creating a replica in France of the company's successful parks in the United States. Besides the cost associated with constructing the park, mistakes were made in designing the infrastructure. For example, six large hotels with fifty-seven hundred rooms were built on the mistaken assumption that visitors would stay at the park instead of making day trips from Paris. Disney also built an American-style parking lot with eleven thousand spaces, only to discover that people primarily use public transportation such as trains and buses.[26] The point here is that even a company as well-managed as Disney stumbled over the difficulties of establishing a venture in a foreign market.

As shown in Figure 3-5, the various levels or forms of participation in the global marketplace can be thought of as stages or degrees of involvement, from the simpler levels of global sourcing and licensing to the more complicated stages of strategic alliances and wholly owned foreign business units. Management's task is to recognize the advantages and disadvantages of each, and to select and pursue the option that presents the greatest opportunity for successful involvement in the global marketplace.

Guidelines for Global Success

Given the range of possible options for participating in the global marketplace, there is no simple recipe, no single set of guidelines for managing success in foreign markets. Still, observers who have followed the efforts of companies at every phase of "going global" suggest that the success stories in foreign markets do have several ingredients in common.[27]

Figure 3-5 Stages of Global Involvement

Learn the Culture

Both organizations and individuals reflect the cultures of their homeland. For example, Japanese companies make decisions only after what by American standards seems to be endless series of meetings to arrive at consensus. In conversing, many Americans and Northern Europeans prefer to be at a distance of arm's length or more, while many Asians and Arabs prefer to stand much closer. Attitudes regarding the roles of men and women in the workplace vary dramatically around the world. And there is always the problem of language. Even nonverbal gestures like eye contact and hand movements have different meanings in different cultures.

To learn a foreign culture, there is probably no substitute for spending time in that culture. But an increasing number of companies, such as Motorola and British Petroleum, are trying to speed up the learning process by developing courses in which trainers strive to change employee's attitudes by identifying and challenging the biases that can result in confusion or conflict when dealing with an unfamiliar culture.[28] The bottom line is that managing successfully in a foreign market requires understanding the culture of the local marketplace. Or, as it is often put, learning to think global and act local.

Customize Your Product or Service

Successful businesses are willing to modify and adapt their products or services to meet the preferences of customers in foreign markets. Pen maker A. T. Cross discovered that German men prefer very thick, black pens and that Europeans prefer fountain pens to ballpoints overall. Companies have had to reduce the amount of packaging around their products to satisfy customers from markets where the "throwaway" mentality of American packaging is considered to be unacceptably wasteful. McDonald's serves black currant shakes in Poland and veggie burgers in Holland. Even Coca-Cola modifies its syrup and packaging to reflect the preferences of its various foreign markets.

People are not the same everywhere. Companies that are successful in foreign markets do the market research and make the adjustments necessary for their products and services to reflect these important differences.

Recognize the Risks

There are risks associated with entering the global marketplace that go well beyond lack of familiarity with a foreign culture or with foreign customer preferences. Three of the most important sources of risk are shown in Figure 3-6.

A number of American businesses that moved to Mexico, for example, to take advantage of low labor wage rates there have returned to the United States because the factors listed in Figure 3-6 represent less of a risk here. In another example, McDonald's risks none of its own money in politically unpredictable countries. Instead, it licenses the use of the McDonald's logo for a fee, secures agreement from the purchaser to adhere to strict standards, and takes an option to buy in later.[29] Successful global competitors carefully assess the risks involved in entering foreign markets and develop strategies for minimizing those risks.

Exercise Patience and Persistence

It takes time to succeed in the global marketplace and to learn another country's culture and consumer preferences. It takes time to identify the individuals and companies that represent the right match in terms of who a company should work with in a foreign market, as well as to overcome being perceived as an outsider. It takes time to project the kind of longer-term presence that allows a foreign customer to develop a sense of familiarity with and trust in an international company.

- The political stability and efficiency of the government.
- The infrastructure, including distribution systems, transportation and communication systems, and the availability of professional support in terms of computer and information systems.
- Managerial considerations, including the availability of a skilled and productive workforce, the ability to enforce contracts, and the availability of reliable suppliers.

Figure 3-6 Risks Associated with Global Involvement

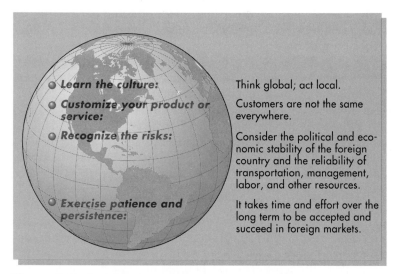

Learn the culture:	Think global; act local.
Customize your product or service:	Customers are not the same everywhere.
Recognize the risks:	Consider the political and economic stability of the foreign country and the reliability of transportation, management, labor, and other resources.
Exercise patience and persistence:	It takes time and effort over the long term to be accepted and succeed in foreign markets.

Figure 3-7 Guidelines for Participating in Global Markets

Persistence is the key. In the case of IGT, the slot-machine maker mentioned earlier, to actually do business in the Japanese market they were asked by the Japanese government to rework their application and paperwork not once or twice, but more than twenty times.[30] Experience suggests that successful companies enter global markets with a very long-term view. Ten years is not an unusual length of time before the global efforts of a company begin to yield significant results. It took even Apple computer that long to succeed in the Japanese marketplace.

Participation in global markets is both a competitive necessity and an important strategic opportunity. Regardless of the approach taken, from global sourcing to exporting to strategic alliances, the four guidelines discussed here and shown in Figure 3-7 represent essential ingredients for success.

SUMMARY

This chapter deals with three of the issues that have gained priority as organizations approach the twenty-first century: social responsibility, information technology, and managing globally. Each represents an important challenge to management.

Social responsibility is the concept that organizations, especially business organizations, have a responsibility for more than just economic performance; they have a responsibility to contribute to the social well-being of the communities where they operate. The classical economic view rejects this concept, saying that business organizations exist exclusively to generate profits for owners and stockholders. The activist perspective holds that all organizations have the obligation to involve themselves in solving problems in the communities from which they profit.

Even within the activist view, however, there is the question of how fully an organization should become involved in social issues. One model suggests four possible levels of social contribution, ranging from traditional philanthropy at the lower end to ecobusiness at the upper level of involvement. Management's task is to define the scope of social responsibility the organization should seek to sustain.

Also demanding attention from management and organizations as a whole is the permeation of information technology (IT) into virtually every process and job in organizations of every type. One consequence of this explosion of IT in the workplace is that to take advantage of the performance gains available through IT, every organization must become a training organization, providing its workforce with the skills and information necessary to use and keep pace with the never-ending developments in technology.

A second consequence of IT in the workplace is the ready availability of information throughout the organization. The feedback provided through information technologies enables the entire organization to become fully involved in continuously improving performance at every level.

The presence of IT in the workplace is not without risks. The widespread availability of IT in an organization increases the threat of potentially damaging leaks of information, as well as of sabotage to the organization's information system. Evidence to date suggests that the threat is not great, but the security of information remains a very real management concern.

Finally, there is competitive pressure for organizations to become involved in global markets. With intense competition in U.S. markets and with most of the growth coming from outside the United States, business organizations must learn to succeed in markets around the world. There are a variety of options or degrees of global involvement, but regardless of the approach, success in global markets requires that management learn the culture, customize the product or service, recognize the risks involved in global environments, and be patient and persist.

QUESTIONS TO CHALLENGE YOUR UNDERSTANDING OF THE CHAPTER

1. Why does Milton Friedman argue that the only responsibility of a business is to make a profit? What is the counterargument?

2. What level of social contribution does your college/university appear to be at? Explain your answer.

3. What is the impact of information technology on education and training in organizations?

4. How does the move toward continuous improvement coincide with the development of computers?

5. Discuss how the computer terminal can be both a coach and a cop.

6. What is the best strategy for an organization to minimize information leaks and potential sabotage of the company's information system?

7. Briefly describe the stages of involvement in global markets. Which stage is associated with the greatest risk?

8. If your school was starting a satellite campus in Japan, what would you recommend that it do to implement the four guidelines for global success?

MANAGEMENT EXERCISE

Trouble at Global Chemical Company

You are plant manager for the Ashton, West Virginia, processing facility of Global Chemical. Nearly two years ago a citizen environmental group from Kentucky began complaining about the health hazards they claim are being carried downstream from your plant across the state border and into several small towns along the river in their state. They have brought in health specialists to support their claims that pollutants from the river are causing serious health problems in these towns. An independent study conducted by the state of West Virginia concluded that while the residents of these towns do experience higher-than-normal levels of a number of types of cancer, there is no proven link between these diseases and the chemicals from Global.

Despite this lack of proof, it appears that Global Chemical's board of directors will be considering the charges against your facility at its next meeting. As part of the materials to be sent to board members, the CEO would like to include your recommendations about what action to take on this problem. You know that your filtering system is too old to be upgraded. To put in a new system would cost millions and would close the plant for months. You're also concerned that some board members think it would make more sense to build a new plant somewhere else (maybe overseas, where environmental laws are not as strict) rather than put an entirely new filtering system in such an old facility.

Further complicating the situation is the fact that almost half of the workers in this community work at Global. Closing the plant for even a few months not only would cause extreme financial hardship but also would threaten the existence of many local businesses. Understandably, the unions at the company are totally opposed to any actions that might hurt their members, especially since none of the pollution charges have been proven.

The citizens' environmental group from Kentucky is threatening to do a *60 Minutes*-type program on the situation. If it gets to that point, it might not matter that there is no proof that the chemicals from Global cause the diseases found in the Kentucky towns.

1. Identify Global's stakeholders in this situation.

2. What response would the classical economic view of social responsibility

suggest in this situation? What would the activist social responsibility view be?

3. What do you see as the company's alternatives?

4. Which alternative would you select? Which stakeholders are being satisfied by your decision?

5. What specific steps would you suggest to deal with the other company stakeholder claims?

REFERENCES

1. "Brazil's Tropical-Forest Murder Trial," *Newsweek,* December 17, 1990, 38; "Ben & Jerry Save the World," *Fortune,* June 3, 1991, 247–248. Business Brief, *Wall Street Journal,* September 7, 1989, A-1.

2. Neil H. Jacoby, *Corporate Power and Social Responsibility* (New York: Macmillan, 1973), 6.

3. Milton Friedman, "The Social Responsibility of Business Is to Increase Its Profits," *New York Times Magazine,* September 13, 1970.

4. Eric J. Savitz, "The Vision Thing: Control Data Abandons It for the Botton Line," *Barron's,* May 7, 1990, 10–11, 22.

5. Milton Friedman, "Does Business Have Social Responsibility?" *Bank Administration,* April 1971, 13–14.

6. Frederick D. Sturdivant and Heidi Vernon-Wortzel, *Business and Society: A Managerial Approach,* 4th ed. (Homewood, Ill.: Irwin, 1990), 3–24; Keith Davis, "Five Propositions for Social Responsibility," *Business Horizons,* June 1975, 19–24.

7. An example of a stakeholder audit is given in Nancy C. Roberts and Paula J. King, "The Stakeholder Audit Goes Public," *Organizational Dynamics* 17 (Winter 1989): 63–79.

8. Joseph Pereira, "Social Responsibility and Need for Low Cost Clash at Stride Rite," *Wall Street Journal,* May 28, 1993, A1, A6.

9. The social contribution continuum is based on the models of social contribution described in Charles Garfield, *Second to None: How Our Smartest Companies Put People First* (Homewood, Ill.: Business One Irwin, 1992), 333–39.

10. "Managing by Values," *Business Week,* August 1, 1994, 51.

11. Bo Burlingham, "This Woman Has Changed Business Forever," *INC.,* June 1990, 34–46; Mark Maremont, "A Cosmetics Company with a Conscience," *Business Week,* May 23, 1988, 136.

12. "The Technology Payoff," *Business Week,* June 14, 1993, 57.

13. John Case, "A Company of Businesspeople," *INC.,* April 1993, 90.

14. Peter T. Kilborn, "Workers Rise Up against Use of VDT as Monitor," *Springfield Sunday Republican,* January 6, 1991, G-1, G-2.

15. Richard Brandt, "The Bad Boy of Silicon Valley: Meet T. J. Rodgers, CEO of Cypress Semiconductor," *Business Week,* December 9, 1991, 70.

16. Alvin Toffler, *Power Shift* (New York: Bantom Books, 1990).

17. Tom Peters, *Thriving on Chaos* (New York: Harper & Row, 1987), 611.

18. Toffler, *Power Shift,* 212.

19. "Is Your Computer Secure?" *Business Week,* August 1988, 64–72.

20. William Echikson, "Disney's Faux Pas," *Boston Sunday Globe,* December 26, 1993, 81–82.

21. William J. Holstein and Kevin Kelley, "Little Companies, Big Exports," *Business Week,* April 13, 1992, 70.

22. Jacob M. Schlesinger, "A Slot-Machine Maker Trying to Sell in Japan Hits Countless Barriers," *Wall Street Journal,* May 11, 1993, A1, A8.

23. Bart Ziegler, "AT&T Reaches Way Out for This One," *Business Week,* March 8, 1993, 83.

24. J. Bleeke and D. Ernst, "The Way to Win in Cross-Border Alliances, *Harvard Business Review,* November–December, 1991, 127–35.

25. Robert L. Rose, "Whirlpool Is Expanding in Europe

despite the Slump," *Wall Street Journal,* January 27, 1994, B4.

26. Echikson, "Disney's Faux Pas," 82.

27. Tom Peters, *Liberation Management: Necessary Disorganization for the Nanosecond Nineties* (New York: Alfred A. Knopf, 1992), 673–74; Ira Magaziner and Mark Patinkin, *The Silent War: Inside the Global Business Battles Shaping America's Future* (New York: Random House, 1989), 171–98.

28. Bob Hagerty, "Trainers Help Expatriate Employees Build Bridges to Different Cultures," *Wall Street Journal,* June 14, 1993, B1, B6.

29. Andrew E. Serwer, "McDonald's Conquers the World," *Fortune,* October 17, 1994, 112.

30. Schlesinger, "A Slot-Machine Maker in Japan," A1, A8.

FROM THE MANAGER'S E-MAIL
Improving Performance at Windansea Surfboard Company

You came to California almost ten years ago, after completing your degree in engineering. Your first job was with an aerospace company; but despite your workload, within two years you had become a dedicated surfer.

You basically just surfed on weekends, but the more you surfed, the more you began to think about ways to improve the design of your surfboards. At first you built boards for yourself. Before long, however, your friends were asking you to build boards for them. Soon word got around about the quality of your designs and surfboards, and in less than a year you had more orders than you could handle building only in the evenings and on weekends. When you found yourself with almost no time left for surfing, you left your engineering job and set up your own custom surfboard design and production company, called Windansea Surfboard Company.

Within eight years, Windansea consisted of more than thirty craftspeople, each of whom performed all of the tasks necessary to construct the surfboard from start to finish. In a sense, everyone was their own boss. And while sales continued to increase for both the custom designs and Windansea's standard models, the company's overall profit leveled off.

Because your background was in engineering, you brought in a team of management consultants to provide some recommendations about how to improve the performance of Windansea. The main points of their recommendations are included in the following E-mail:

Date:	August 30, 1995 10:00 am
From:	LOCALSYS (The CalWest Consulting Group)
Subject:	Recommendations on Windansea

Summary of recommendations:

1. Convert the production system from a craft-based approach to a mass-production approach in which each board moves from one end of the factory floor to the other, with each person trained to perform only one or two of the tasks necessary for producing each board.

2. Create a management team responsible for planning and scheduling production, inspecting the finished boards, and supervising the workers building the boards. . .

There was more to the E-mail, explaining the reasons for the consultants' recommendations. You are concerned, however, because even though you have a constantly changing workforce, a number of the people who have been with you for a long time might have trouble adjusting to such a drastic change. In response to this concern, the consultants recommended the following:

Date:	September 15, 1995 1:00 pm
From:	LOCALSYS (The CalWest Consulting Group)
Subject:	Recommendations on Windansea—Part 2

. . . We know you are concerned about the possible negative reaction of some of your longtime employees to the plan we are proposing. We suggest promoting four of your most senior and valued workers to the newly created management positions. For those who are not promoted immediately, there is the possibility of creating additional management positions as the company grows and expands. . .

1. How would (a) Frederick Taylor, (b) Henri Fayol and (c) Elton Mayo react to the consultants' recommendations? Would they agree or disagree? What additional suggestions might each make?

2. Will you follow the consultants' recommendations? Why or why not?

SECTION

II

The Critical
Management Tasks

In the changing environment of the 1990s, the organizations that survive and prosper will be those that are able continuously to improve their performance. As this section title suggests, there are certain basic management tasks associated with improved performance. We consider goal setting and decision making two of the most critical.

Chapter 4 describes goal setting. Clearly stated goals can provide people and organizations with the focus, direction, and understanding they need to perform well. The chapter defines the task of developing effective goals in terms of several key criteria, reviews the numerous benefits from developing goals in this manner, and examines the challenges and difficulties that are part of the goal-setting process.

Once goals have been defined, whether they are achieved depends in large part on the effectiveness of management's decisions. **Chapter 5** outlines a six-step process designed to ensure that decisions will actually move the organization closer to its goals. Included are techniques for enhancing the decision process, and discussions of the importance of personality, group-based decisions, and other issues impacting decision making, and of the ethics challenge in the decision-making process.

CHAPTER 4
Developing Goals

LEARNING OBJECTIVES

After studying this chapter, you should be able to:

- *Discuss the concept of vision and its importance to the organization.*

- *Explain the criteria for effective goal statements.*

- *Identify the benefits of developing effective goals that result in improved performance.*

- *Specify the problems associated with developing effective goal statements.*

- *Discuss the guidelines for developing a goal-based system of managing organizations.*

Nearly twenty-five years ago, Peter Drucker suggested that it is the "first responsibility of the manager . . . to give others vision and the ability to perform."[1] For Drucker, vision is the clear shared sense of direction that allows people to achieve a common purpose. Drucker insists that vision is the essential contribution of management because without this shared sense of direction, it becomes all but impossible to achieve the cooperation and commitment necessary for organizations to succeed.

Drucker suggests that the most effective means for communicating the organization's vision is through goals. More specifically, he suggests that it is management's first responsibility to develop a system of goals that provides a sense of direction so clear that it guides the organization on its course much as the stars guided navigators at sea for thousands of years.

Consider the case of Chrysler Corporation. In the summer of 1990, Chrysler set out to do what no American automobile manufacturer had ever accomplished: to build a subcompact automobile that didn't feel like a small car and was reliable, fun to drive, and safe.[2] The recent history of American car companies was littered with failed attempts at achieving this goal, including such efforts as the Dodge Omni, the AMC Gremlin, the Chevy Vega and Chevette, and the Ford Pinto and Escort.

Chrysler was more than aware of the odds against its efforts' succeeding, so it was careful from the outset not to simply adopt the goal of "doing better" in terms of developing and manufacturing an American subcompact. Instead, it pushed itself to define its goals in the most specific terms possible. Chrysler knew it must minimize both the time and the cost of planning and developing its new small car, so the goal included a budget of $1.3 billion and a deadline of forty-two months. It knew the car must be competitive in terms of price, so it set as its goal a selling price in the $8,000 range for the base model, and a goal of manufacturing the car at a lower cost than any of its competitors. In terms of quality, the goal was to not exceed 76 problems per 100 cars produced, the standard set by the Toyota Corolla, the most problem-free car in its class. Similar goals were set for safety, driving pleasure, and every key area of performance in the development and production of a subcompact automobile.

In January of 1994, three months ahead of schedule, the first Chrysler Neons began rolling off the assembly lines. Car experts and potential buyers alike raved about the newest entry into the small-car competition. Due largely to its highly disciplined focus on carefully defined goals, Chrysler appeared to be well on its way to doing what many experts in the automobile industry had begun to think was impossible: developing an American small car that could compete with the best from anywhere around the world.

The lesson from Neon—and from successes like Neon in virtually every industry—is clear: Achieving high-level performance requires the development of a comprehensive network of highly effective goals.

Later in the chapter we will consider how such a network of goals might be constructed or developed. First we need to understand what a goal is and why goals are so essential to performance.

WHAT IS A GOAL?

A *goal* is a statement of a specific, desired performance result or outcome with a time frame.[3] A well-written goal should state what is to be accomplished and by when. John Naisbitt illustrated this point in his book *Megatrends*.[4] He compared the following statements:

1. To become the world leader in space exploration.

2. To place an American on the moon by the end of this decade.

Naisbitt noted that although the first statement sounds like a goal, it is not a goal. It is not specific. What exactly do "world leader" and "space exploration" mean? And there is no time frame. The second statement, made by President Kennedy in the 1960s, is a goal statement. It is very clear in its direction and desired result. The desired performance result is landing on the moon, and we are seeking to place an American there before 1970. History shows that this goal was so effective that it provided the basis for all of the important decisions of NASA during the 1960s that resulted in Americans landing on the moon in July 1969.

Or consider the following goal statement of a company concerned about customer satisfaction: "To improve customer service." Although this statement seems to describe a goal, like Naisbitt's first statement, it is too vague to be useful. It does not pinpoint how much improvement is desired, or by when, or even what is meant by "customer service." A more effective goal statement would be: "To respond to every customer inquiry or problem courteously and completely within four hours." The reworded goal is very clear about the performance result it seeks. It defines what the focus is (effective response to customer inquiries) as well as the time frame (within four hours).

Only goals defined as clearly as these provide the members of the organization with the vision essential to the organization's success. Only clearly defined goals provide people with the focus, direction, and understanding they need to perform effectively and contribute to the organization achieving its purpose.

Developing Effective Goals

A number of key criteria need to be met in developing effective goals—that is, goals that define and support organizational performance. Paul Hersey and Ken Blanchard developed the acronym "S.M.A.R.T." to help emphasize the critical elements of an effective goal.[5] We have adapted their device but changed it slightly to suggest that for goals to be effective they must be **s**pecific, **m**easurable, **ac**cepted, **r**ealistic yet challenging, and **t**ime-framed, as shown in Figure 4-1.

Specific Enough to Provide Focus

We have already made the point that goals must be specific to be effective. A goal can be effective only to the degree that it provides focus. The customer service goal "To respond to every customer inquiry or problem courteously and completely within four hours" is effective because it focuses clearly on three things:

Specific enough for focus and feedback

Meaningful enough to engage participants

Accepted by the participants

Realistic yet challenging

Time-framed

Figure 4-1 Critical Elements of an Effective Goal

courtesy, completeness, and timeliness of service. The emphasis is not one or two of these things to the exclusion of the other; the goal distinctly states that the focus is on all three areas.

Similarly, "To place an American on the moon by the end of this decade" allowed NASA to focus on that single priority. The goal made it clear that neither unmanned nor interplanetary programs should be considered unless they contributed to the goal of landing an American on the moon. Only then should either be a priority in terms of funding or other resources.

In sum, goals that are specific provide the kind of clarity that can enhance the focus of organizations and improve performance. It's not enough to tell someone to "do better." Instead, the desired outcome should be spelled out so that those working toward it know specifically what they are attempting to achieve.

Meaningful Enough to Motivate

In the early 1980s Ford Motor Company set the goal "Quality is Job 1." This meant that in every activity and in every decision, quality was to take priority over cost or schedule or any other consideration. Ford has standards that define quality, so this goal was specific enough to be effective. But it was likely to be successful only if the employees at Ford also found it meaningful—that is, if it mattered to them.

By "meaningful," we mean that organizational goals must relate to employee needs. When people see in a goal the possibility of satisfying one or more of their needs, they become engaged by the goal, and their performance is likely to be enhanced. At Ford, the meaningfulness of the goal came from the fact that over the previous several years the company had lost hundreds of millions of dollars in sales, primarily to foreign automakers who produced cars rated much higher in quality. These losses forced Ford to close a number of its plants and to lay off thousands of its workers. Ford's goal of "Quality is Job 1" was—and continues to be—meaningful to the workers at Ford because their own need for continued employment was met through achieving that goal.

The question arises, Shouldn't the "M" in "S.M.A.R.T." stand for money rather than meaningful? Isn't money the primary factor in determining how meaningful goals are? In organizations, aren't people more likely to improve their performance when there's a financial payoff in terms of a raise or a bonus? Isn't the possibility of making more money what finally makes goals meaningful? The answer is yes and no. Edwin Locke and Gary Latham, two of the foremost theorists and researchers on goal setting, reviewed sixty studies on the effect of various motivation strategies on performance.[6] The results, in part, of their review are shown in Figure 4-2.

Money clearly does increase the impact of goal setting, especially where the incentive is based on individual rather than group performance. Still, it is important to realize that significant performance improvements can be achieved even without bonuses or monetary rewards. One interesting example of the effectiveness of goals even without financial incentives is provided by Emery Air Freight. One key part of the operations at Emery involved handlers and sorters placing small packages in large cargo containers that were then loaded on the appropriate aircraft. Because no emphasis was being placed on filling these containers to their full capacity, package handlers were only filling them approximately two-thirds full. This meant that many more cargo containers were being used than was necessary, significantly increasing the cost that Emery was being charged to ship them.

To improve performance in this area, Emery set a goal of filling the cargo containers to 95 percent of capacity. (Because of the irregular shape of some packages, 100 percent would not have been a realistic goal.) The package handlers were offered no bonus for achieving this goal. They were merely asked to keep a record of how full the containers were before they were closed for shipping. Within days, the handlers achieved the 95 percent goal and they have maintained it ever since, at a savings to Emery of millions of dollars annually.[7] The lesson from Emery is that money is not the only thing that makes goals meaningful. At Emery, for example, apparently the challenge of attaining higher levels of performance was sufficient to make the new goals meaningful.

Clearly, individuals have needs for more than just money. Management has come to realize what psychologists have been saying for a long time: People have needs for recognition, for responsibility, for challenge, and for a sense of accomplishment, among other things, that are every bit as strong and real as their need for money. To the extent that goals represent the possibility of satisfying these

Motivation Strategy	Median Improvement in Performance
Money, individual incentives (goals)	30%
Money, group incentives (goals)	20%
Goal setting (no money)	16%

Figure 4-2 Money, Goals, and Performance Improvements

other needs, goals will have the kind of meaning to employees that results in increased motivation. This is an important realization for management. In this era of controlling costs to increase competitiveness, by setting goals that are meaningful to the members of the organization, management can improve performance without simply "throwing more money" at performance problems.

Accepted by the Participants

For a long time it was assumed that for goals to improve performance, an organization had to allow its employees to participate in goal setting. This kind of participative goal-setting was viewed as a problem by managers who felt there wasn't enough time available to involve employees in goal setting, and that they would somehow give up some control in the process.

Research, however, has revealed that goal setting does not have to be participative to be effective. Having a goal *accepted* by the members of the organization is more important than whether or not they participate in setting it.[8] The acceptance of the goal, not the level of participation, is the key element in whether or not that goal will result in improved performance. Apparently, people are willing to pursue goals set for them by others as long as they find those goals acceptable.

The question then becomes, When are goals likely to be accepted? The answer appears to be, in part, the same as the answer to the question of when are goals meaningful: An organization's goals are likely to be accepted when achieving them also allows individuals or teams to achieve their own goals. A team that is assigned the goal of completing an extremely difficult task—creating a new advertising campaign in record time, for example—is likely to fully accept that goal if it also represents an opportunity to meet the needs of its members. These might include the need to meet a challenge, for example, or the need to be involved in important work, or the need to be creative.

There is another consideration, however, that affects the extent to which a goal will be accepted by organizational members. That consideration is whether or not they view the goal as realistic.

Realistic yet Challenging

People are more likely to accept a goal when there is a realistic chance of their achieving it, when the necessary resources are available in terms of skills, time, equipment, funding, cooperation, etc. Someone who has been working hard to complete forty units of a product a day is unlikely to accept a goal of eighty units a day. The goal will be viewed as unrealistic unless some additional resources are also made available in terms of training in improved techniques, faster equipment, or overtime.

In fact, a goal that is perceived to be unrealistic might actually result in a *decrease* in effort and performance rather than an increase. An individual might conclude that there's no sense in wasting effort even trying to achieve a goal that appears to be unattainable.

But goals also can't be viewed as too easily attained. To be effective, goals must also be challenging. Research shows that difficult goals result in greater improvements in performance than goals that are perceived as easy to attain.[9] Whether in terms of an increase in sales, in units produced per day, or in the number of insurance claims processed, challenging goals result in better performance. Why? Because people work harder to achieve them. There appears to be something in most of us that causes us to rise to a challenge, as long as the challenge is not perceived as unattainable. As Edwin H. Land, the founder of Polaroid, noted, "The first thing you naturally do is teach the person to feel that the [goal] is manifestly important and nearly impossible. That brings out the kind of drive that makes people strong."[10]

To be effective, then, goals must be perceived as realistic or attainable, but also difficult enough to be challenging. This relation between performance and goal difficulty is shown graphically in Figure 4-3. If goals are too easy, people are less likely to be motivated by them. If goals are too difficult, people actually decrease their efforts because they become convinced that they can't succeed. Although this necessitates a difficult balancing act for the manager, the task is clear: to develop goals that are both realistic and challenging.

Time-framed

The final criterion of an effective goal is that it must have a time component—more specifically, a deadline. Deadlines are one of the most powerful and effective means available to managers for ensuring performance. Even goals that are specific, meaningful, accepted, realistic, and challenging, if they are without a time frame, run the risk of never quite getting done. For several years in the 1980s, Kentucky Fried Chicken attempted to develop a new design for its restaurants, and for several years the new design remained uncompleted. Under new management, a specific deadline was added to the goal of the design team, and the new design was successfully completed in just six months.[11]

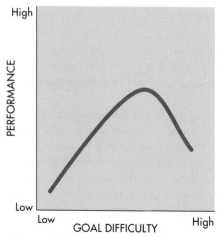

Figure 4-3 Relationship between Goal Difficulty and Performance

In sum, not every statement of desired or intended results is a goal. "To be the world leader in space exploration," "To do well in school," "To improve customer service," "To increase utilization of our cargo containers" are all statements of desired or intended performance results, but none of them represents an effective goal. They are not sufficiently S.M.A.R.T. and challenging. Only through goals that are S.M.A.R.T. and challenging can managers fulfill Drucker's charge to give others vision and the ability to perform.

Why Goals Improve Performance

We've already discussed some of the most powerful consequences of effective goals. They provide the kind of focus that channels an organization's energies and efforts, and they make possible the kind of feedback needed for motivation and performance adjustments. There are other significant contributions that goals make as well.

Goals Provide a Blueprint for Performance

At every level of the organization, goals provide the critical means for ensuring that performance stays on course. Rather than just reacting to problems that occur or to events in the environment, organizations with clearly defined goals can respond in ways that are consistent with a game plan. Without goals, when things go wrong, the tendency is to "put out fires" and to lose sight of what the direction is. A blueprint ensures that everything a builder does is consistent with the design or plan. Goals serve the same purpose in an organization.

Goals Provide a Basis for Feedback

Goals that are specific also make it possible to track progress toward achieving them. This information about progress toward a goal is called *feedback* and is critical for improving performance.

Feedback comes from a comparison of where you are at any given point in time with where you want to be. Feedback in a performance situation is essential for at least two reasons. First, feedback can be an important source of motivation. It can either reinforce performance where the progress is positive or spur greater effort where it is not. Feedback motivates by either confirming that we are on the right track or warning us that we are not.

Second, knowing how much progress we've made allows us to make the adjustments and corrections that are necessary to move us closer to the goal. Feedback not only tells us where we stand relative to a goal, in the process of doing so it can help clarify what adjustments or corrections are necessary to achieve that goal. For a student whose goal is to make the dean's list, for example, midterm grades become a source of valuable feedback, reinforcing or warning the student and indicating in which courses he or she must adjust or correct performance.

A goal that is not specific makes feedback on progress all but impossible. And if you don't know where you presently stand, how can you determine what adjustments and corrections are necessary to move you closer to that goal?

Goals Focus Attention on the Right Agenda

Individuals bring many different needs to their activities within the organization. For some the strongest need is for money; for some it's power; for others, the strongest needs are social, or related to security or achievement. The existence of a strongly shared set of clearly defined organizational goals helps to ensure that everyone's primary focus is on achieving those goals, rather than on satisfying their own individual needs. It is human nature to pursue goals. Clear organizational goals focus everyone's attention on the right agenda, and ensure that individual goals do not interfere with the effectiveness of the organization.

Goals Provide a Basis for Cooperation and Teamwork

Just as individuals have their own priorities, so too do the different departments or units within the organization. A well-defined set of overall goals helps ensure that activities and efforts throughout the organization do not conflict with each other or with the plan. Goals ensure that, as in an orchestra, everyone in the organization is "playing from the same sheet of music."

Specific performance goals can also have the effect of "leveling" the members of an organization, of eliminating some of the problems that can occur when members of a team are from different levels or from different departments. For example, if the team's goal is to cut costs by 40 percent by the end of the year, everyone—despite their rank in the organization—focuses on how to achieve that goal. Successful teams concentrate on how each individual can best contribute to reaching the goal, not on distinctions in terms of titles or positions within the organization.[12]

Goals Provide Criteria for Decisions

You will see in the next chapter that the first step in the decision-making process is to define the goal or goals of the decision. One of the greatest benefits of clear goals is that they then become the standards for evaluating decision options. Without clearly defined goals, decisions become arbitrary and potentially inconsistent. Without a strongly shared sense of exactly what the organization is attempting to accomplish, decision makers are more likely to base their decisions on the demands of the particular situation rather than on the goals of the organization.

At Burger King, the decision whether to offer pizza as a menu item was dictated in part by Burger King's goal of having customers served within three minutes of entering the restaurant. Clearly Burger King recognizes the importance, especially in the fast-food industry, of competing on the basis of speed. Since pizza takes fifteen minutes to produce, and the typical customer eats and exits in twenty minutes, the company decided to eliminate pizza from its menu entirely.[13] The existence of well-defined goals will ensure that decisions like this reflect the longer-term direction of the organization, rather than the more immediate needs of the decision maker or of the situation.

Effective goals provide all of the benefits and advantages to the organization shown in Figure 4-4. However, goal-based management does present problems.

- A blueprint for perfomance
- A basis for feedback
- Focus attention on the right agenda
- A basis for cooperation and teamwork
- Criteria for decisions

Figure 4-4 Benefits of Goals

Problems with Goals

Three major hurdles must be cleared in order to fully achieve the potential for improving performance that goals can bring. The first is the challenge of setting goals for outcomes that are difficult to measure. The second is the longer-term problem of setting challenging goals without also creating unwanted stress. The third is the problem of avoiding too narrow a focus in defining goals. If unsuccessfully dealt with, each of the problems can hinder the development of an effective goal-based management system.

The Measurability Problem

One barrier to developing a goal-based system of management is that it is difficult to define specific goals in some performance areas. For example, consider a claims processor in an insurance company. This person's job is to review insurance claims submitted by customers, determine whether the customer's policy covers the claim, evaluate whether the claim is legitimate, calculate how much of the claim should be covered, and so on. Unlike manufacturing a product, the amount of work required to fully process a claim can vary widely. The claim itself can be simple or complex, telephone conversations may or may not be required, memos or meetings with supervisors or colleagues may or may not be necessary. It is very difficult to set a specific goal for this kind of work. What is the standard for good performance? Because of the variation in types of claims, the goal can't be the number of claims a person processes in a day. Nor can it be the dollar value of the claims processed, or how quickly the claim is processed.

The problem of *measurability* is the problem of setting specific goals when it is difficult to define exactly what the performance result should be. It is a problem that has become more important as we have become a service economy with fewer manufacturing organizations and more organizations in health care, education, government, social services, travel and entertainment, and so on. The challenge is to find a way to define in highly specific terms the teacher's goal in education, or the nurse's goal in health care, or the manager's goal in areas like problem solving and communication. Because of the complexity of the work these people do, and since there is no easily measured unit of output, it is difficult to define specific goals to focus and challenge their performance.

However, it is not impossible. Consider the case of the customer service representative or the nurse. Both provide services that are not easily quantified. How do you measure the personableness of a nurse, for example, or the effectiveness of a service representative's communication? Still, it is possible to set goals for at least some aspects of these positions. For example, goals can be set in terms of customers or patient waiting time, or specific courtesies such as using the customer's/patient's name, or how quickly and effectively customer/patient problems are resolved, and so on.

The problem of measurability actually represents a healthy challenge for management. Knowing the power of goals forces managers to be as specific as they can, even in areas of performance that are difficult to define. It forces them to go beyond simply telling people just to "do a good job."

The Stress Problem

While our emphasis in this chapter has been on the potential of goals for improving performance, there is a point at which goals may become a part of the problem rather than a part of the solution.

When goals are extremely demanding and performance is closely monitored, there may be a point at which the effect on the employee is chronic fatigue or performance-sapping stress that leads to burnout. In the mid-1980s, the New United Motor Manufacturing, Inc. (NUMMI), a joint effort by General Motors and Toyota, produced Chevy Novas at the rate of sixty cars an hour. Although this was the average for American automobile assembly plants, NUMMI was doing it with one-third fewer workers. "To produce the same number of cars per hour as the industry average, but to do it with one-third fewer workers" was a goal that was both specific and challenging, and workers at NUMMI initially felt energized by it.

However, as time went on, the grueling pace required to meet this goal began to take its toll. Workers claimed that the excitement of the early days at NUMMI was gone. Fewer team members arrived early at the plant to maintain their equipment as they had in the early days. They reported being tired when they arrived and tired when they went home.[14]

Workers at airline reservation centers, mail-order houses, and 1-800 customer service centers, as we mentioned in Chapter 3, report the same pattern: exhaustion and stress from long periods of working too hard to meet goals that are too demanding. And as organizations in every industry try to increase productivity by trying to do the same work with fewer workers, the potential for this problem is rising.

That goals have the potential to reduce stress for workers by making clear what is expected of them is not at issue. Rather, the question for managers is: At what point do goals move from the productive effect of providing a challenge to the counterproductive effect of causing performance-threatening stress? There is perhaps no more difficult hurdle confronting management than to identify goals that remain a prescription for effective and satisfying performance rather than a prescription for burnout.

The Problem of Too Narrow a Focus

We said earlier that an effective goal statement provides direction and focus in terms of what should be emphasized in the organization. But when this focus is too limited, it could cause unwanted results. For example, suppose the goals of customer service representatives are focused entirely on a time frame. Their statement of purpose is to resolve all customer inquiries within four hours. The end result could be a lack of courtesy to customers, or a lack of completeness in answering inquiries. Meeting the time limit of four hours might force representatives to cut communication short or to cut corners in researching problems. As a result of a too narrowly defined goal, customer satisfaction declines rather than increases.

A goal with too narrow a focus was exactly the problem facing Domino's Pizza not long ago. For years, Domino's promised to deliver pizzas within thirty minutes. This goal not only served as a challenge and target for its drivers and pizza makers, it positioned the company against the competition in terms of speed of home delivery. For the most part, Domino's was successful in achieving its goal of delivery within thirty minutes. In fact, the company became known as much for its speed as for its pizza. However, in 1993, after a St. Louis woman was hit and injured by a Domino's delivery driver hurrying to meet the thirty-minute goal, the company stopped promising to deliver pizza within a half an hour.[15] This was a classic example of a goal with too narrow a focus. The emphasis on performance in one area, speed, resulted in performance problems in another area, safety. This kind of incident and the negative publicity that resulted from it were the unwanted results of a too narrowly focused goal.

This same problem can occur with individuals. A student who focuses too much on athletic performance, for example, might find that too narrow a focus on that one area results in unwanted consequences in other areas, such as low academic performance.

While we have emphasized in this chapter that goals must be specific enough to provide focus, the challenge for management is to develop goal statements that do not limit the focus to the point where unwanted outcomes result. The potential problems with defining organizational goals are summarized in Figure 4-5.

These problems of measurability, employee stress, and too narrow a focus are significant challenges for managers working to set goals with the greatest per-

---

- *Measurability:* In some areas performance results are difficult to quantify or measure.

- *Stress:* Goals that are too demanding can result in stress and performance problems over the long term.

- *Too narrow a focus:* Some goals are so concentrated in their focus that they result in negative performance results in other areas.

Figure 4-5 Potential Problems with Goal Statements

formance-enhancing potential. As significant as these challenges may seem, however, they have not diminished the commitment of organizations in every industry to the development of effective goal-based systems of management.

Guidelines for Creating a Goal-Based Organization

The potential of goals to improve performance is clear, as are the challenges that must be met in setting organizational goals. Effective goals in and of themselves, however, are only part of the solution. To maximize the overall impact of goals on organizational performance, to create a truly goal-based organization, at the very least requires following four guidelines shown in Figure 4-6.

Create a Network or System of Goals

The concept of a network or total system of goals suggests that specific end results should be identified for every department, team, and individual in the organization, and that these desired results should contribute to meeting the organization's larger goals. In other words, the individual, department, team, and overall company goals should build upon one another, with the attainment of each goal moving the organization closer to achieving its purpose. Figure 4-7 provides an example of such a network, with specific goals for individuals at different levels in an organization.

Consider the case of General Motors. At one time each division of GM, in fact each car model, was assigned a profit goal. The problem with this approach was that it resulted in competition rather than cooperation for resources and rewards within the organization. Every unit of the organization had goals, but all of the goals weren't pointing in the same direction. Then, in 1994, GM created a goal system focusing on a single financial goal for the North American division. According to CEO Jack Smith, "The leaders of each area of the vehicle business are working toward the common goal of positive financial results for all of North America rather than just the individual units."[16] The new goal is actually a system; that is, the goals of each performance unit contribute to the overall attainment of the financial goal.

Another way to state this guideline is that goals must be consistent and

- Create a network or system of goals
- Prioritize among multiple goals
- Benchmark: Set goals from the outside in
- Build in flexibility

Figure 4-6 Guidelines for Creating a Goal-Based Organization

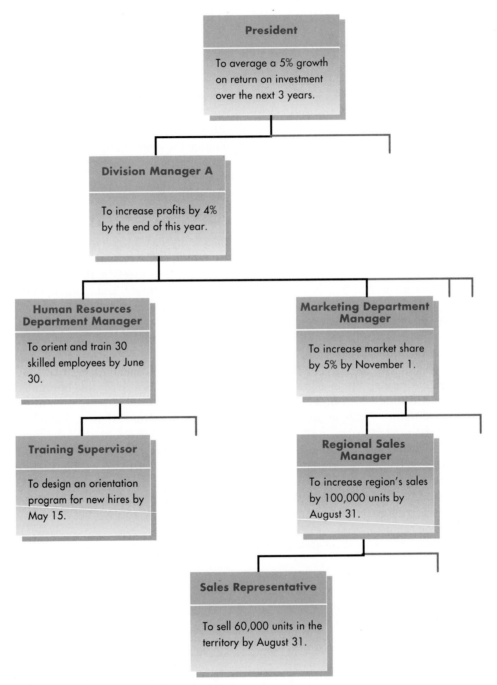

Figure 4-7 A Portion of a Network of Goals

coordinated throughout the organization, both top-to-bottom and across every department.[17] That is, goals must be consistent from one level to another (*vertical*), as well as among departments (*horizontal*). Figure 4-7 illustrates vertical consistency. The salesperson's goal is in line with the sales manager's goal, which is in line with the division manager's goal, and so on. The consistency that is achieved through a network of goals is an important criterion for an organization's success.

The first requirement of a network of goals, then, is that the network be comprehensive, that there be specific goals for every unit and every position in the organization, and that all the goals in the network point in the same direction.

Prioritize among Multiple Goals

A network or total system of goals would be easier to carry out if only one goal were identified for the entire company, and if individuals and departments each pursued only that goal. However, in today's complex and dynamic environment most organizations pursue multiple goals. A firm may have a goal of increased profits as well as goals involving social responsibility and employee development, both of which might increase expenses that potentially reduce profits. For example, a company's social responsibility goal of decreasing pollution could compete with a goal of lowering production costs. To deal with multiple goals, organizations must learn to prioritize them—they must determine which goal is first in terms of importance, which is second, and so on.

It is not unusual for organizations to have customer-related, employee-related, community-related, and stockholder-related goals. At Lincoln Electric Co., a manufacturer of arc-welding products and electric motors, customer goals are given first priority. According to the company's legendary founder, the late James Lincoln, customer interests, not stockholders' interests, should come first. In his opinion, the first priority should be how to make a product better, cheaper, and more useful to the customer. Stockholder gains would follow if this first goal was achieved.[18]

At Johnson & Johnson, the organization's responsibilities are prioritized in a statement of values and beliefs which the company calls its "Credo." The first responsibility is to customers, ". . . to the doctors, nurses and patients, to mothers and fathers and all others who use our products and services." Next are company employees, the communities in which they live and work, and lastly, stockholders.

Multiple goals make the job of managing much more complicated. But they are often unavoidable, even in small organizations, and management needs to prioritize them if the organization is to succeed.

Benchmark: Set Goals from the Outside In

Benchmarking is defined as the process of researching other companies' goals and setting goals that match those of the best companies.[19] For years, American managers refused to believe that anyone else could do things better. Managers tended to believe that because they were doing their best, it was the best that could be done. As long as competition was weak, this mind-set was not a problem. However, the changing competition forced American firms to recognize that the Japanese, for example, had set more ambitious goals and were outperforming U.S. firms, at least partially because they were more effective in meeting those goals. With this realization began the practice of benchmarking: adopting the goals and standards of other highly effective organizations.

Ford Motor Company provides an example of this outside-in goal-setting. Ford set a goal of reducing its accounts payable staff by five hundred people, or 20 percent. When Ford viewed the same operation at Mazda Motor Corp., it found that Mazda had 80 percent fewer people handling the accounts payable function, adjusting for its smaller size. Ford raised its target to 75 percent from the original 20 percent, and reached that larger goal.[20]

With benchmarking, the search is on for role models. Remember, Neon used the Toyota Corolla as the standard in defining its own goals for quality. Similarly, both Xerox and Chrysler have copied the goals and warehousing practices of L. L. Bean, Inc. And even small businesses are benefiting from researching larger firms. Manco, Inc., a small producer of duct tape, imitates the practices of Wal-Mart, Rubbermaid, and Pepsico. As Terri L. Rock, chief operating officer of Convex Computer, noted, ". . . benchmarking is critical to our strategy. Without the resources to hire in-house experts, borrowing from larger companies is the only way for us to win."[21]

Build in Flexibility

Some critics charge that commitments to specific goals result in organizations that are too rigid to be responsive to changes in the environment. A focus on specific goals, according to this view, restricts the ability of organizations to be flexible enough to take advantge of unexpected opportunities or unanticipated changes in their environment.[22]

It is difficult to argue against the importance of flexibility in terms of the direction of an organization. Speed and flexibility, you will remember, are among the key new performance standards. But it is also difficult to argue against the effectiveness of goals in improving organizational performance. The solution to this dilemma is not to eliminate specific goals, but to ensure that the goal system includes the ability to review and revise goals in response to significant changes as they occur.

This kind of flexibility was an important element in GM's success with the Saturn automobile project. At the beginning, GM committed to a goal of assembling the Saturn automobile almost entirely by robots. During the several years that it took to develop Saturn, however, GM learned from its other automobile divisions that robot assembly did not ensure the high level of quality that was part of GM's overall goal for the car. Reflecting this experience, GM redefined its goal in this area, committing to a goal of assembly by self-directed work teams rather than by robots.[23] This shift in goals in response to changing conditions was a key element in the success that Saturn has experienced since its introduction several years ago.

As we noted in Chapter 1, flexibility is an essential performance standard for organizations competing in the changing environment. The key to flexibility is not to eliminate goals, but to develop a system in which goals are continually reviewed to ensure they make sense in terms of the changing environment.

The practices of creating goal networks, prioritizing among multiple goals, setting goals from the outside in, and building flexibility into the system are all essential elements of an effective goal-based management system. If well implemented, such a system makes possible the kind of performance improvements seen with Neon and other similar achievements in goal-based organizations.

Vision Again

In the intense competition of the changing environment, organizational vision that consists of a clearly defined, fully developed network of goals is no longer optional. The need to compete and survive in every industry and sector of our economy now requires the levels of organizational and human performance achievable only through the development of effective, comprehensive, goal-based management systems.

Much progress has been made in our understanding and implementation of goal-based systems, but as we have seen, significant challenges remain. It is in finding effective responses to these remaining challenges that managers will fulfill what Drucker defines as management's "first responsibility": to give others vision and the ability to perform.

SUMMARY

The first responsibility of management is to give others vision and the ability to perform. In this chapter, we've shown how such vision can be established by means of a total system or network of goals. Goals must satisfy several criteria in order to ensure that they provide individuals with the kind of focus, direction, and understanding they need to perform well. The acronym "S.M.A.R.T." identifies the key criteria for effective goals. Each should be specific enough for focus and feedback, meaningful enough to motivate individuals, accepted by the participants, realistic yet challenging, and time-framed.

The benefits are numerous. Goals that are S.M.A.R.T. and challenging provide consistency throughout the organization, a blueprint for effectiveness. They ensure that individuals focus on achieving the organization's goals rather than on satisfying their own needs. Effective goals provide a basis for cooperation and teamwork. They ensure that the efforts of the different units in the organization are coordinated. Lastly, they are an integral part of the decision-making process in that they provide decision makers with the criteria for generating and evaluating options.

Despite the advantages that a total system of goals provides, there are still challenges for management. In areas where output or performance is not easily measured, such as service or management, defining specific goals is more difficult. In addition, goals that are too challenging can cause stress and burnout for the participants. Finally, goals that are too narrow in focus can be counterproductive, as the Domino Pizza case illustrates.

As significant as these challenges are, they have not diminished the commitment of organizations to develop effective goal-based systems. To achieve the full impact of these systems, certain conditions must be met. First, separate goals must be woven into a system or network. Goals are most effective when they are defined for every task and area of the organization and where they all work in synergy to move the organization toward achieving its purpose.

Second, goals must be prioritized. Organizations have complex, sometimes competing goals. Care must be taken to establish priorities, identifying which goals are more important.

Third, benchmarking, or setting goals from the outside in, has become an important management task in the 1990s. Comparing goals of other companies and copying what they do to achieve them is a process that improves the effectiveness of individuals and organizations alike. Rather than reject methods that were "not invented here," managers are looking to openly benchmark their activities against the best-performing companies to ensure that their goals are the right ones.

Finally, building flexibility into the system is essential. Goals must be reviewed and revised to ensure they are the right ones for the changing environment.

In the next chapter, we build on the foundation that goals provide and examine the process of decision making, the process that strongly influences whether the organization's goals are actually achieved.

QUESTIONS TO CHALLENGE YOUR UNDERSTANDING OF THE CHAPTER

1. Explain Peter Drucker's concept of vision and why he describes vision as management's first responsibility.

2. Develop a goal statement regarding your professor's classroom performance so that it satisfies the S.M.A.R.T. criteria.

3. Describe the relationship between performance and goal difficulty. How might a manager tell if a goal is too easy or too hard?

4. Explain two of the reasons why well-defined goals tend to result in improved performance.

5. Explain the difference between the measurement problem in goal setting and the problem of too narrow a focus.

6. Explain why an organization must have a network of goals to be effective. How might the concept of a network of goals apply to a student's personal goals?

7. What are some goals that a student could have that might conflict? How could the conflict be resolved?

8. If you were a manager, would you share your goals and performance standards with another organization doing research to establish benchmarks? Explain your answer.

9. What is the potential drawback of goals that are very specific? How can management counteract this drawback?

MANAGEMENT EXERCISE

Goals for Healthco

Christine Johnston is the manager of a regional office of Healthco, an insurance company specializing in health insurance programs for corporations and small businesses. The office serves as a source of clerical and computer support for Healthco field representatives, and as a customer service center for processing claims and questions from individuals insured by Healthco.

Johnston is responsible for an office staff of seven individuals who type up proposals, help prepare presentations for the sales representatives, and answer questions about policies, billings, and claims from customers either by telephone or in person in the office. She has been office manager at Healthco for less than a year, but is already determined to take action to improve the performance of the office staff.

Johnston would like to target several areas for immediate improvement. First, she believes that the staff can do better in terms of the quality of information they give to clients. Too often it turns out that a staff member provides inaccurate or incomplete answers to client inquiries. This almost always results in a second telephone call from an understandably upset client once he or she has discovered the error. Johnston is not sure exactly what the reason might be for the mistakes, but she is certain the staff can do better.

The second area Johnston would like to focus on is the interpersonal relations of the staff. At least once a week there is a disagreement or argument between two or more staff members that requires her to intervene. Those arguments are rarely over personal matters; almost always they involve some task that needs to be done when everyone feels they already don't have time to do their own work. All too often these conflicts take place in full view of clients who are being serviced. When Johnston was new to her position, she felt these episodes would resolve themselves. Now she knows that it's up to her to take action.

Finally, Johnston is concerned that two of the more senior staff members are not able to work with the rest of the staff in customer service. Customer service requires extensive use of the computer terminals. These two staff members spend all of their time working with the sales representatives on the work they need done. The other five staff members alternate between customer service and working with the sales representatives, and most of them view customer service as more stressful. There has been steadily increasing resentment over the unfairness of this situation, and Johnston feels that it's time to do something to resolve the problem.

1. Write a goal statement that defines better performance in each of the three areas Christine Johnston has targeted for improvement. Review what you have written to see if they are S.M.A.R.T. and challenging.

2. Under each of the goal statements you have written, list the activity or activities that might be undertaken to ensure that the goal will be achieved.

REFERENCES

1. Peter Drucker, *Management: Tasks, Responsibilities, Practices* (New York: Harper & Row, 1973), 3, 9–10.

2. David Woodruff and Karen Lowry Miller, "Chrysler's Neon," *Business Week* (May 3, 1993), 116–26.

3. The terms "goal" and "objective" are used interchangeably in this book, although some authors suggest that objectives are more specific and encompass a shorter time frame than goals.

4. John Naisbitt, *Megatrends* (New York: Warner Books, 1982), 94.

5. Paul Hersey and Kenneth Blanchard, *Management of Organizational Behavior* (Englewood Cliffs, N.J.: Prentice Hall, 1988), 108, 382.

6. Edwin Locke and Gary Latham, *Goal Setting: A Motivational Technique That Works* (Englewood Cliffs, N.J.: Prentice Hall, 1984), 117.

7. "Productivity Gains from a Pat on the Back," *Business Week* (January 23, 1978), 56–62.

8. Hubert H. Meyer, E. Kay, and J. R. P. French, "Split Role in Performance Appraisal," *Harvard Business Review* (January–February 1965), 123–129; J. R. P. French, E. Kay, and H. H. Meyer, "Participation and Appraisal System," *Human Relations* 1966 (19): 3–19.

9. Andrew C. Stedry and Emmanuel Kay, "The Effects of Goal Difficulty on Performance" (New York: General Electric: Behavioral Research Service, 1964).

10. Warren Bennis and Burt Nanus, *Leaders* (New York: Harper & Row, 1985).

11. From a presentation by Mr. Hicks B. Waldon, president and CEO of Heublein, Inc., at the Eastern Academy of Management, Baltimore, Maryland, 1982.

12. Jon R. Katzenback and Douglas K. Smith, "The Discipline of Teams," *Harvard Business Review* 71(2) (March–April, 1993): 111–20.

13. Marcia Berss, "A Tale of Two Strategies," *Forbes* 152(11) (November 8, 1993): 198–200.

14. D. Forbes, "The Lesson of NUMMI," *Business Month*, June 1987, 34–37.

15. Krystal Miller and Richard Gibson, "Domino's Stops Promising Pizza in 30 Minutes," *Wall Street Journal* (December 22, 1993), B1, B3.

16. Alex Taylor III, "GM's $11,000,000,000 Turnaround," *Fortune* (October 17, 1994), 70.

17. William Ouchi, "Markets, Bureaucrats, and Clans," *Administrative Science Quarterly* (March 1980), 129–41.

18. James F. Lincoln, *A New Approach to Industrial Economics* (New York: The Devin-Adair Company, 1961).

19. David A. Garvin, "Building a Learning Organization," *Harvard Business Review* 71(4) (July–August,

1993): 86; "Beg, Borrow and Benchmark," *Business Week* (November 30, 1992), 74–75.

20. "Beg, Borrow and Benchmark," 74–75.

21. Ibid., 75.

22. James B. Quinn, "Strategic Goals: Process and Politics," *Sloan Management Review* (Fall 1977), 21–37.

23. James B. Treece, "Here Comes GM's Saturn," *Business Week* (April 9, 1990), 56–62.

CHAPTER 5
Decision Making

LEARNING OBJECTIVES

After studying this chapter, you should be able to:

- *Define and explain the term "decision making."*

- *List and briefly discuss the steps in the decision-making process, as well as some of the ideas and practices for improving decision making.*

- *Discuss intuition and experience as factors in decision making.*

- *Describe the impact of the decision maker's personality, values, and power on the decision-making process.*

- *Identify the advantages and disadvantages of involving others in the decision process, and the various degrees of involvement that are possible.*

- *Explain the problem of "groupthink," and some steps for avoiding this problem.*

- *Discuss ethics in the context of decision making, and describe the conditions that encourage ethical decisions.*

The second critical management task is decision making. Once the organization has defined the goals that determine its direction, it is essential that the decisions made by management are consistent with those goals. We've defined management as responsibility for an organization's achieving its goals. Success in exercising this responsibility is determined to a large degree by the effectiveness of the manager's decisions. Just as Frederick Taylor tried to understand how a task could be organized to make it as productive as possible, we will consider here how decisions can be made to make them as effective as possible.

Three decisions made by organizations in the recent past have become classics in the study of management decision-making. Each provides dramatic evidence of just how important the decision-making process is.

- In 1982, seven deaths in the Chicago area were attributed to Tylenol capsules that were said to be laced with cyanide. Johnson & Johnson, the maker of Tylenol, could have decided to try to disprove the charge, or to say these were isolated incidents, or to remove the product from Chicago-area stores only. Instead, Johnson & Johnson decided to remove every bottle of Tylenol from every store where it was sold across the entire United States, a decision that ultimately turned a potentially disastrous situation into an incident that actually enhanced the image of Johnson & Johnson.[1]

- In 1985, in response to Pepsi's taking an increased share of the soft drink market, Coca-Cola developed a new formula that was sweeter than the original formula, more like Pepsi. In blind taste tests all over the United States, people consistently preferred the new-formula Coke over both Pepsi and regular Coke. Based on these results, Coca-Cola decided to replace original Coke with "New Coke." This decision resulted in such an outcry from loyal Coke drinkers everywhere that within weeks Coca-Cola was forced to withdraw New Coke and reinstate "Coke Classic," a move that cost the company millions of dollars and caused it significant embarrassment.[2]

- In 1986, NASA was confronted with the decision of whether to launch the space shuttle Challenger with temperatures at the launch site falling below the levels usually required for a safe launch. Despite concerns voiced by lower-level engineers, top-level NASA officials decided to proceed with the launch, a decision that resulted in the deaths of all the astronauts on board.[3]

We will return to these three examples over the course of this chapter for the lessons each offers about the decision-making process. First, we will consider the decision-making process itself.

DECISION MAKING: DEFINITION AND PROCESS

Decision making is the process of selecting and implementing alternatives consistent with a goal. It is a series of activities that begins with defining the purpose or goal of the decision and then involves developing and evaluating alternatives, selecting and implementing the optimal alternative, and monitoring the results to ensure that the decision goals are achieved. We call this entire process, from setting the decision goal to making sure the goal has been achieved, "decision making."

There are a variety of ways to describe the activities in the decision-making process. They can be reduced in number to three or four, or increased to eight or more. Virtually every decision model, however, includes in one form or another the phases or steps shown in Figure 5-1.[4] Each of these phases of the decision process is worth considering in greater detail.

Decision Step 1: Define the Decision Goals

The purpose of any management decision is to move the organization closer to the attainment of its goals. When we speak of the "goal of a decision," we mean that there needs to be established, in very specific terms, just what the decision is intended to accomplish.

As we discussed in Chapter 4, goals that are specific provide a target to aim for and make feedback possible. In that sense, decision making is like any other activity: Performance is enhanced when the decision process itself is in pursuit of specific goals. When a goal is defined, decision making has the critical focus necessary to ensure that the decision will actually move the organization closer to attaining the goal(s). Also, specific goals enable feedback to be provided in progress reports.

In addition to focus and feedback, there are benefits in defining specific goals that are unique to the decision process. Specific decision goals, for example, provide criteria for focusing the information search, for determining which alternatives might be most relevant, and for evaluating the relative strengths and

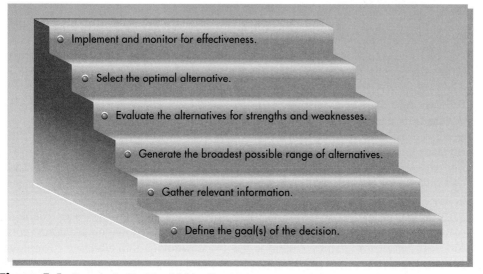

Figure 5-1 Steps in the Decision-Making Process

weaknesses of each alternative. When Burger King set the goal of serving customers within 3 minutes, this eliminated the alternative of offering the menu item pizza, which required 15 minutes to prepare and serve. Specific decision goals also provide the standards for evaluating the effectiveness of the decision itself once the selected alternative is actually implemented. Only with specific decision goals can the organization evaluate whether the decision is actually moving it closer to those goals.

Decision Step 2: Gather Information

Once the decision goals are clear, the next step is to gather as much information as possible relevant to them. Clearly defined decision goals help focus the information search by defining which information is relevant. In the example from Chapter 4, for example, NASA needed only to focus on information relevant to placing an American on the moon. This is an important advantage to goal-based decisions. In an age when the amount of information available to management is expanding rapidly, clearly defined decision goals allow managers to set boundaries on their information search to target the most relevant information.

While efficiency in gathering information is essential, we cannot emphasize enough the importance of gathering as much information as possible before moving too quickly through the rest of the decision process. Quality decisions require quality information. Coke's switch from the original Coke to "New Coke" is a graphic example of what can happen when decisions are based on incomplete information. It has been suggested that Coke made the very crucial decision to change its already successful formula on the basis of incomplete information. While people did prefer New Coke in blind taste tests, Coke discovered the hard way that people don't buy their soft drinks blind. The managers at Coca-Cola learned that they should have tested not only whether people preferred the taste of New Coke, but whether they would give up their long association with the original Coke and switch to the new formula.

Once the storm of protests had provided an obvious answer to this question, Coke was forced to reverse itself and reintroduce the original Coke as Coke Classic. The message from this episode: Having the right information on which to base a decision is absolutely critical to the effectiveness of the decision.

Barriers and One Solution

A variety of barriers can prevent management from having the information they need to make effective decisions. Managers often feel they lack the time to fully research important information. Some managers consciously try to avoid becoming overwhelmed by information, especially during the crunch time of decision making. And managers sometimes tend not to ask others for information for fear of appearing uninformed.

One approach to overcoming these information barriers is called "management by walking (or wandering) around," or "MBWA." Management commentators Tom Peters and Nancy Austin suggest that managers in effective companies get the information they need simply by walking around, by getting out of their offices and talking with people—employees, suppliers, other managers, and customers.[5] MBWA enables managers to avoid both appearing uninformed and having to frantically search out essential information when an unexpected decision suddenly needs to be made. Through MBWA, managers maintain a constant flow of information, and they keep that information continuously updated.

Managers admit that for all of the reasons we've just discussed—but time and pride chief among them—MBWA isn't easy at first. But they've also found that MBWA is a powerful tool for making sure that they are hearing what they need to hear, so that their decisions reflect the broadest possible range of information.

Decision Step 3: Generate Alternatives

In the third phase of decision making the challenge is to *not* move too quickly to a consideration only of the obvious alternatives. In this era of accelerating change and global competition, the obvious alternatives, the traditional solutions to organizational problems, have become increasingly ineffective. Innovative alternatives need to be generated, and as this need intensifies, creativity becomes an ever more critical ingredient in the decision-making process.

The Importance of Creativity

Creativity in the sense we are using here might be described as the ability to discover relations between things that were formerly considered unrelated.[6] The main barrier to creativity, according to researchers, is our lack of flexibility in the way we view things. We tend to place the elements of our experience in fixed categories. The longer we operate using these categories, and the longer they work for us, the more difficult it is for us to see beyond them. If we place two elements in unrelated categories, over time it becomes more and more difficult for us to relate them.

Take, for instance, rubbish and garbage. People tend to view them only as a problem, but inventor Buckminster Fuller suggested they be thought of as potential sources of energy. Today communities across the country are experimenting with electrical and steam generating facilities fueled by rubbish and garbage.

Another example of generating creative alternatives occurred with the development of Post-it notes by 3M Corporation. When one chemist at 3M had a problem with an adhesive that was not sticky enough, another chemist took the same adhesive and turned it into a creative solution for the problem he was working on. This chemist used this not-too-sticky adhesive to temporarily attach notes to paper without tearing or marking the page when they were removed. The results were Post-it notes, one of 3M's most successful products.

A technique for enhancing creativity.   Over the years, a number of techniques have emerged to help us loosen up our categories, to enhance our creative capacities. The most familiar of these is brainstorming. *Brainstorming* is a group technique for generating the broadest possible range of alternatives. The rules for brainstorming are summarized in Figure 5-2.

These rules reflect two basic realizations about the creative process. The first is that creativity is very often a synergistic process; that one person's ideas can

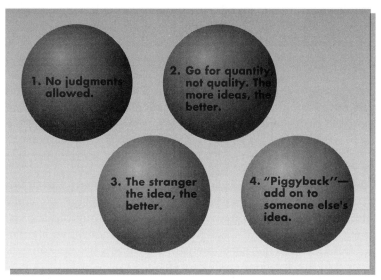

Figure 5-2 Rules for Brainstorming

spark ideas in someone else's mind. The rules emphasizing quantity, strangeness, and piggybacking ideas are intended to encourage the synergistic potential of the group.

These rules also reflect the fact that judgment or criticism tends to restrict the flow of ideas. It takes courage to suggest an off-the-wall idea, especially in a group setting. The knowledge that our ideas might be judged or criticized is usually enough to convince us not to risk sharing them. The no-judgments-allowed rule helps create a climate that enhances the willingness of group members to risk sharing their ideas, again increasing their potential for developing innovative alternatives.

Decision Step 4: Evaluate Alternatives

When the broadest possible range of realistic alternatives has been identified, the focus of the decision process shifts to evaluating those alternatives, to identifying the strengths and weaknesses of each option. Perhaps no dimension of the decision process has been as well developed as the evaluation phase.

Quantitative Approaches for Evaluating Alternatives

One set of methods that is used to evaluate decision alternatives has been found extremely useful in situations where all of the variables relative to the decision goals and alternatives can be expressed in numbers. These are called *quantitative approaches* because they use mathematical and statistical techniques to analyze the decision alternatives.

Linear programming. In Chapter 2 we mentioned linear programming as a decision sciences technique that allows the decision maker to use mathematical formulas to analyze and evaluate the full range of decision options before committing to one option.[7] The Military Air Command (MAC) uses linear programming to decide how many of what kind of aircraft will be needed on a particular day, given the number of passengers and the amount of cargo that must be transported, as well as their destinations.

Break-even analysis. Another common quantitative evaluation technique is called break-even analysis. This technique is used to determine how many units of a product (or service) must be sold, and at what price, for the producer or service provider to at least break even, given the cost of producing or providing that item or service. The *break-even* point occurs when revenues from the sale of a product or service exactly equal the cost of producing and selling it. For example, a pharmacist can decide whether a full-time assistant or a part-time assistant would be a better option by considering the additional cost of both options and the additional revenues each option would likely generate. Break-even analysis allows the decision maker to clearly understand the financial impact of various alternatives before deciding which one to pursue. The example of whether to hire a full-time or part-time assistant pharmacist is detailed in Appendix 5A.

Decision tree analysis. There is another technique for evaluating decision options, called the decision tree. There are some decisions where there is certain important information that can't be known ahead of time. The Military Air Command, for example, can't know what the weather will be during the period for which it is planning. So it makes probability estimates about the weather based on forecasts and weather data from previous years. *Decision tree analysis* uses probability estimates to help compare various alternatives.

Consider the case of a family restaurant owner trying to choose between a location that seats 150 customers and one that seats only 100. Obviously the smaller location would be less expensive to lease, but it would also be too small on nights when more than 100 seats are needed. On the other hand, why lease a larger location if there are not a sufficient number of nights when 100 seats are needed? By estimating what percentage of the time this location is likely to require more than 100 seats, management can evaluate which location provides the better payoff. A complete decision tree analysis of this example is given in Appendix 5B.

Of course, this kind of analysis is only as accurate as your probability estimates, which depend either on the quality of your research or the amount of experience you have with the business about which you are estimating, or both. Nevertheless, quantifying your expectations enables you to evaluate your alternatives in a way that is extremely objective and that would not otherwise be possible.

The T-chart: A Qualitative Technique for Evaluating Alternatives

Not all decisions involve factors that can be easily quantified or measured. For example, suppose a decision has to be made about which individual to appoint as a team leader. Imagine that there are two prime candidates for this appointment, and management needs to assess the strengths and weaknesses of both. One tool used to compare alternatives in this kind of situation is the T-chart, which gets its name from the T-shaped format used to list and compare the alternatives. A T-chart for the decision described above is shown in Figure 5-3.

The characteristics being compared in T-charts aren't like the costs or the number of items in quantitative-type decisions. They are more qualitative or subjective in nature. They might include communication and organizational skills, for example, which are not easily expressed in numbers. The value of the T-chart is that it puts on paper the qualitative considerations that otherwise would have to be juggled in the decision maker's brain. The T-chart registers all the factors the manager is attempting to consider in a decision, and freezes the action so that each factor can be considered carefully. In the example in Figure 5-3, the T-chart allows the decision maker to compare the two job candidates on each factor that is relevant to the decision. For a more detailed discussion of a T-chart analysis, see Appendix 5C.

As with the earlier phases of the decision process, the emphasis in the assessment phase is on *not* moving too quickly to selecting an alternative. Like the other phases, the evaluation phase is an attempt to impose a discipline on the decision maker to ensure that each alternative is considered carefully enough.

Decision Step 5: Select the Optimal Alternative

The fifth phase of the decision process is to select the alternative that comes closest to satisfying the decision goal. Nobel laureate Herbert Simon was among the first to recognize that there is no such thing as a perfect decision. Simon uses the term *bounded rationality* to describe the fact that no matter how systematic the manager has been, in most cases it is impossible to have *all* of the relevant information, to generate *every* possible alternative, or to fully comprehend the advantages and disadvantages of *each* option. Furthermore, since most decisions are attempting to achieve a variety of goals, a single alternative will rarely satisfy all of them. These limitations of the decision process "bound" or reduce the rationality of the decision.

Recognizing these realities about decision making, Simon coined the term

	PERSON A	PERSON B
Time with Company	5 years	3 years
Education	Associate's degree	Bachelor's degree
Interpersonal skills	Very strong	Fair to good
Management skills	Weak organizer Strong motivator	Strong planner Strong organizer
Knowledge of other departments	Extensive	Extensive

Figure 5-3 T-Chart for Team Leader Division

satisfice to describe the way alternatives really are selected.[8] According to Simon, about the best we can do in making a decision is to select the best available alternative, recognizing our lack of time, the lack of complete information, and the variety of goals most decisions are attempting to satisfy.

Students often satisfice when it comes to making decisions regarding how to allocate their time at college. Exams, social events, and work obligations may occur simultaneously, each involving separate goals (i.e., get an A on the Biology exam Monday morning; attend the evening wedding and reception of a close friend, and still work the weekend shift at the pharmacy). Since it would be virtually impossible to achieve all of the desired outcomes, students might satisfice by selecting an alternative that is not ideal, but is the best one available. This decision might be to forgo the wedding, or to study fewer hours than might be needed to get an A on the exam.

Satisficing, says Simon, is the way most selections of alternatives are actually made. The challenge for management is not to compromise too easily, but to ensure that the alternative selected is truly "the best available," given the bounded rationality of the decision-making situation.

Decision Step 6: Implement the Decision and Monitor for Effectiveness

All too often, especially with difficult decisions, we tend to consider the decision process complete once we have selected the optimal alternative. There is often a definite sense of relief once the decision has been made. However, all the effort invested in the decision process will have been wasted unless the alternative selected is effectively put into action. A decision is just a choice until it is acted upon. Johnson & Johnson's decision in the Tylenol incident is a graphic example of the importance of the action phase of decision making. Having ensured that Tylenol was fully removed from the marketplace, Johnson & Johnson followed up with letters to doctors and pharmacists, a 1-800 number for worried consumers, and a major media campaign that reported on the development of a tamper-proof version of the product, and announced the return of all-new bottles of Tylenol to the shelves several months later. As a result of implementing its decision so effectively, Tylenol returned to 95 percent of its previous market share almost immediately.

An interesting contrast is provided by Perrier & Co., whose bottled water was found to be tainted in a few instances in the early 1990s. Like Johnson & Johnson, Perrier immediately removed all its bottled water from stores and restaurants all around the world. Unlike Johnson & Johnson, however, Perrier did not implement a comprehensive strategy to protect its market share from competitors. Consequently, when Perrier was ready to return to the market, it discovered that many of the bars and restaurants where the water had been sold had switched to other brands of bottled water. Here were two companies, confronted with similar decisions, who selected essentially the same alternative. Johnson & Johnson's decision succeeded; Perrier's did not. The difference was primarily in how well each implemented the chosen alternative.

Even effective implementation does not complete the action phase of the decision-making process, however. Once it is implemented, the decision must be monitored to ensure that the alternative put into action is in fact moving the organization closer to its goals. As we said at the beginning of the chapter, moving the organization closer to its goals is the ultimate purpose of every decision, and this cannot be assumed to be happening just because the decision has been implemented. An organization that attempts to improve performance by implementing a particular management approach, for example, needs to evaluate how well that approach is actually meeting the goals of that decision. Only when the monitoring phase confirms that the decision goals have been achieved is the decision-making process finally complete.

THE DECISION MAKER

As important as the decision process is, there is another key variable that determines the effectiveness of decisions: the decision maker. The decision maker is not a neutral factor. Decisions reflect the person making them as much as the process by which they are made. A number of dimensions of the decision maker are worth considering.

Intuition and the Impact of Experience on Decisions

As part of his research on decision making, Simon studied chess masters to try to understand how they are able to consistently make high-quality decisions when there are so many variables and so little time. What Simon discovered is that chess masters do not use a purely logical or rational decision process of the type we have been discussing. It would be virtually impossible for them to systematically evaluate the consequences of each of the available alternatives at every point in a match, especially in the very brief period of time allowed between moves in a chess match. Based on his observations, Simon concluded that it must be "intuition" that allows chess masters to select such effective alternatives in so little time.[9]

For Simon, however, intuition is not merely a "hunch" or a "gut instinct"; it is ability based on extensive experience. Intuition based on years of experience allows the chess master or the veteran manager to select and implement the most appropriate course of action without exhaustively evaluating each alternative.[10]

It took Ray Kroc less than thirty-six hours to decide to buy a restaurant company from the McDonald brothers. His decision was based not on a logical and systematic evaluation of all of the facts and figures; that would have taken weeks, even months. Instead, Kroc's decision was based on intuition reflecting his own years of experience selling milk-shake mixers to drive-in restaurants. It was his extensive experience with this type of business that allowed Kroc to decide so quickly and so successfully. His decision effectively created the entire fast-food industry.

As this example shows, it is experience that makes intuition much more than just instinct. If decisions must be made more quickly and with less information than logic allows, then extensive experience with the situation becomes the key input, and the experience level of the decision maker becomes a key factor. In management, as in sports, the experienced player tends to make the better decisions.

Personality, Values, and Power

Like any behavior, a person's decision making reflects his or her personality, values, and power. By *personality*, we mean an individual's consistent pattern of behavior. An *aggressive* personality, for example, is revealed in a consistent pattern of risk taking and confrontation. Similarly, the *perfectionist* personality emerges from a pattern of constantly pursuing the one best way, the only right answer. The *impulsive* personality, on the other hand, shows a pattern of leaping to conclusions and preferring action to analysis.[11]

We can reasonably expect that when confronted with all of the same goals and information, and even sharing all of the same experiences, each different personality might actually decide very differently. The aggressive personality might be expected to make decisions in ways that some might find argumentative or confrontational. The perfectionist might postpone taking action, preferring to seek the ideal alternative. The impulsive personality might hurry through the decision process, just to have it over. For this reason it is critical that managers recognize the powerful influence of personality in decision making and minimize any negative effects a decision maker's personality might have on the effectiveness of the decision process.

Beyond personality, decisions tend also to reflect the *values* of the decision maker, those things which are personally most important to him or her in the decision context. Steven Jobs, when he was leading Apple Computers, strongly valued innovation and creativity—so strongly that even when the future success of the company required greater emphasis on efficiency and control, his decisions continued to more strongly reflect his own personal values rather than the company's needs. Apple's board of directors became convinced that Jobs's decisions could never reflect the values the company needed, and forced him to leave the company he had started.

In 1993, Robert Stemple stepped down as CEO of General Motors reportedly because he was unwilling to make the difficult decision to eliminate thousands of jobs, a decision that apparently ran counter to his own personal value system. For Stemple, as for Jobs and every decision maker, personal values strongly color and influence both the goals and the outcomes of the decision process.

Finally, there is the issue of power. Some alternatives, including sometimes the best alternatives, are beyond the power of the decision maker to implement. Managers, especially team leaders and middle managers, often do not have the power to select what they feel would be the optimal alternative. The Challenger launch decision is a tragic example of how the lack of power of a group of decision makers resulted in a decision with fatal consequences. The evidence that has emerged since that tragedy suggests that the engineers and project managers with the best understanding of the situation knew that the optimal alternative would be not to launch the shuttle at such low temperatures. Unfortunately, this group did not have sufficient power to ensure that the no-launch alternative would be selected.

Like experience, personality, and values, the power of the decision maker strongly influences the effectiveness of the decision-making process.

GROUPS AND DECISION MAKING

Organizations, as we have said, are built on the necessity for people to engage in cooperative efforts to get things done. Frequently, the effectiveness of decisions hinges not on the decision maker's ability to take direct action, but on how successfully he or she involves other people in making and implementing the decision. Typically, this includes both those whose input would improve the decision and those whose commitment is needed for the decision to be effectively implemented.

The Advantages and Disadvantages of Involving Others

Although group involvement can improve the decision-making process, there are both advantages and disadvantages to group-based decisions.[12] A summary of these is shown in Figure 5-4.

There is no question that the involvement of others, no matter how great the potential benefits, complicates the decision-making process. Anyone who has ever been involved in a group project or committee has experienced firsthand the difficulty of actually making a group decision. On the other hand, the price of not involving others in decisions can also be high, particularly in terms of lack of valuable input, understanding, and commitment to the decision from them.

Levels of Involvement in the Decision Process

Management theorist and consultant Victor Vroom and his associates have described five levels of involving others in decision making.[13] These levels are shown in Figure 5-5.

In Vroom's model, a decision about what to include in a report summarizing a work group's activities for the year would require very little participation, if

ADVANTAGES	DISADVANTAGES
● A better understanding of the reasons for the decision	● Increased time spent in discussion at each stage of the process
● A greater commitment to making the decision work	● Difficulty in reaching a consensus
● Greater creative potential	● "Winners" and "losers" in terms of suggestions
● More careful evaluation of alternatives	● Compromise rather than selection of the optimal alternative

Figure 5-4 Participative Decision Making

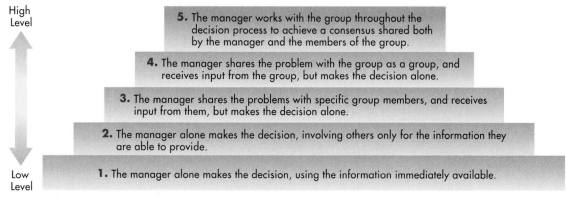

High
Level

5. The manager works with the group throughout the decision process to achieve a consensus shared both by the manager and the members of the group.

4. The manager shares the problem with the group as a group, and receives input from the group, but makes the decision alone.

3. The manager shares the problems with specific group members, and receives input from them, but makes the decision alone.

2. The manager alone makes the decision, involving others only for the information they are able to provide.

Low
Level

1. The manager alone makes the decision, using the information immediately available.

Figure 5-5 Levels of Group Involvement in Decision Making

any. Participation is probably not essential for identifying the group's accomplishments, and there is little necessity of the group's commitment to the report. A decision on how to redesign the group's work area, on the other hand, would almost certainly benefit from a higher level of group participation. Both the group's input and its commitment would be essential to the success of the new design.

Vroom's point is that the same level of participation is not necessary in every decision. But the more important the group's acceptance of the decision is, or the more the decision might benefit from group input and ideas, the higher the level should be of individual and group participation, at least to the extent that time permits.

Interestingly, the amount of group-based decision making has increased significantly in recent years. In Chapter 1 we pointed to teamwork as one of the key elements of the changing workplace. One of the defining characteristics of this trend has been the steadily increasing responsibility of teams for making many of their own decisions. Organizations now recognize that for them to compete in the changing environment, decisions must reflect the commitment, the expertise, and the creativity that can only come with highly participative decision making. For this reason, the challenge for managers is to improve not only their own skills as decision makers, but the decision-making skills of their teams as well.

Groupthink: A Potential Problem with Group Decisions

While group-based decision making unquestionably offers the potential for more effective decisions, it also has potential drawbacks, even beyond those mentioned earlier. One of the most serious is groupthink.

Psychologist Irving Janis coined the term *groupthink* to describe the tendency of close-knit groups to lose their ability to function effectively in the decision-making process.[14] In reviewing group decisions around famous events in recent history, Janis found that the more cohesive or unified a group was, the less willing the members were to present their own opinions, especially when they differed from the opinions of other group members. Instead of benefiting from the differing points of view of various group members, the decision process in groups suffering from groupthink unconsciously focused on not rocking the boat.

This unspoken desire to avoid creating conflict within the group appears to have been another piece of the puzzle in explaining the Challenger disaster. We now know that individual members of the decision-making team did have serious doubts about launching the shuttle. But they never forcefully stated their concerns to the group, apparently for fear of being viewed as disloyal to the decision team.

While the Challenger tragedy is an extreme example, the consequences of groupthink are always serious. Groupthink decisions are lacking both in terms of challenging the status quo and in critically evaluating the alternatives that are presented. For example, if the group seems satisfied with one member's view of what a particular problem is and how it should be solved, not only are alternative points of view not raised, but even the single alternative that is suggested tends not to be very critically or carefully evaluated.

Janis describes a number of symptoms of groupthink, including self-censorship by members and the appearance of total agreement among them, even when consensus does not exist. Perhaps more importantly, he suggests strategies for avoiding groupthink. Some of these strategies are summarized in Figure 5-6.

With the trend toward more group- and team-based decisions, the tendency toward groupthink becomes an increasingly serious problem. By implementing Janis's strategies, groups can take much greater advantage of their potential for making higher-quality decisions.

ETHICS AND DECISION MAKING

In Chapter 1 we introduced ethical behavior as a key challenge to management in the changing environment. We defined ethical behavior as behavior that recognizes the difference between right and wrong, behavior that conforms to society's standards. Two easily justifiable moral standards might be honesty and fairness. We expect our organizations to conduct themselves in a way that the average person might consider to be honest in terms of telling the truth, and fair in terms of

- Assign the role of critical evaluator to every member of the group.
- The group leader should avoid stating preferences or positions early in the process.
- Encourage input from individuals and experts from outside the group.
- Assign one member to play devil's advocate at each group meeting.
- Hold a "second chance" meeting to review the decision once a consensus has been arrived at.

Figure 5-6 Strategies for Avoiding Groupthink

how they treat their customers, their employees, and society in general. In no area of organizational performance is ethical behavior more important than in decision making.

In Chapter 1 we pointed to Sears, Ernst & Young, and Dow Corning as three companies who have had problems meeting the ethics challenge during recent years. Unfortunately, these are only three examples of what began in the 1980s and has continued as a steady drumbeat of charges of unethical behavior in virtually every kind of organization in our society. During the past ten years we have heard stories of defense contractors being fined hundreds of millions of dollars for overcharging the government for the work they performed, rental car agencies overcharging customers for repair work they never performed, food producers intentionally mislabeling their products, scientific researchers tampering with experimental results to maintain their funding from foundations and the government, Wall Street investment firms rocked by "insider trading" scandals in which brokers used information unavailable to the public to make millions of dollars in personal gains—and on, and on.

Ethics matter. At the most basic level we are still a free-market society based on honesty and fair play. In that sense, unfair and dishonest behavior threatens the very existence of our society. Every unethical act by organizations threatens the trust which is the foundation of a free society.

At another level there is very real concern that a growing lack of trust in our business organizations may result in demands for additional legislation and regulations to control their behavior. The fear is that such restriction's would further limit the ability of our organizations to compete globally against businesses from other societies that operate without such regulations.

Finally, unethical behavior, when discovered, invariably results in a loss of confidence in the organization by customers, investors, and employees. For example, the price of Sears stock fell 15 percent in the weeks following the charges that its Tire and Auto Centers in California were performing unnecessary repairs on customer cars.

Nor is this continued pattern of ethical abuse the result of a lack of effort to correct it. As the abuses of the 1980s came to light, they triggered a major effort on the part of corporate America to become more ethical in its practices. To achieve this, managers in as many as 40 percent of medium- and large-sized companies received some form of ethics training, and 75 percent of the surveyed companies developed codes of ethics to clarify their expectations in terms of right and wrong.[15] Many set up councils and committees to review company practices and procedures to ensure ethical conformity. But despite these efforts in the 1980s, ethical misconduct continued into the 1990s. Consider the case of Dow Corning.

Dow Corning was the producer, among other things, of the most popular version of the silicon breast implant. When some of these implants began to fail, leaking silicon into the bodies of the women in whom they were implanted, the Food and Drug Administration (FDA) began an investigation. One of its findings was that Dow Corning had not shared all of its own research on the implant device during the period when the FDA was originally reviewing the product for approval. More specifically, Dow Corning had not shared its own findings that suggested there was some danger the breast implant might leak in a small number of cases.[16]

The irony is that Dow Corning is reported to have one of the most fully developed ethics policies and procedures of any company in any industry. Its ethics code is under constant review, and its ethics committees are staffed with high-level managers. Observers point out that even the most effective ethics committee structure won't work, however, if no one raises questions about the fairness or honesty of a particular practice or decision. It has been suggested that Dow Corning's very fine system for dealing with ethical questions never had a chance to work because no one at Dow ever raised questions about the silicon implants.

What this and other similar examples suggest is that as important as ethics training, an ethics code, and ethics committees may be, the key to ethical decisions in organizations is probably the example of top management. For unethical behavior to be avoided, top management not only must support a system for dealing with ethical questions once they are raised, they must actively encourage people to raise ethical questions whenever they exist. Without that kind of management support, even the best ethics committees and procedures are likely to sit idle.

In other words, ethical decision-making in an organization may have much more to do with the climate management creates than with the decision process itself. This means that if organizations are to achieve the goal of ethical decision-making, they must commit themselves to creating an environment in which questions about ethics are a required part of the evaluation phase of every decision, an environment in which ethics is a key priority in every decision process. Management must insist that the question "Is this decision fair and honest?" be answered for all of the organization's decisions.

SUMMARY

Making effective decisions is one of the critical tasks of management. Only decisions that actually move the organization closer to its goals can be considered effective. For this reason, decision making must be viewed as a series of activities. These activities begin with an understanding of the decision goals; move through the phases of information gathering, generating and evaluating alternatives, and selecting and implementing the optimal alternative; and conclude only when the decision has actually achieved its goals. Management's responsibility is to ensure a decision process equal to this challenge. MBWA, creativity, and satisficing are all essential elements of effective decisions.

Besides recognizing the importance of an effective decision-making process, managers also need to recognize the importance of the person making the decision. The decision maker's intuition, if based on extensive experience, represents a significant potential asset in the decision process. The personality, values, and power of the decision maker can also strongly influence the decision process, and the decision itself.

Increasingly, there is an emphasis on involving others in the decision process. There are advantages and disadvantages to involving others, and there are various degrees of group involvement. But clearly, the greater the value of group input to the decision, or the more important the group's commitment to the decision, the greater the need for group involvement in the decision-making process.

However, with group decisions there is also the risk of groupthink, a decision process that reflects the group members' desire not to rock the boat more than a desire to achieve the actual decision goals. The challenge for management is to maximize the advantages of involving others in decisions, while managing that process to minimize the potential disadvantages.

Finally, the decisions reached in the decision-making process must be ethical. Meeting this requirement begins with developing a code of ethics, establishing committees to review questions of ethics in the organization, and offering employees and management training in ethical decision-making. Ultimately, however, ethical decisions require a belief that pervades the organization from top to bottom that decisions and the decision process must be both fair and honest.

QUESTIONS TO CHALLENGE YOUR UNDERSTANDING OF THE CHAPTER

1. Discuss whether you had specific goals in your decision about which college or university to attend. If you had goals, what were they? Describe what effect, if any, having or not having goals may have had on the quality of your decision.

2. Describe an unsuccessful decision you are familiar with. Use the decision-making process described in this chapter to explain why the decision was not successful.

3. Define creativity, and explain how it can improve the decision-making process.

4. Define satisficing, and describe a situation from your own experience when the "good enough" or best available alternative was selected.

5. Explain how intuition is related to experience in decision-making.

6. Discuss which kinds of personalities or values might actually facilitate or support an effective decision process.

7. Consider a college professor who begins the semester by asking students for input on how the class material might be delivered. What are the advantages and disadvantages of this process?

8. Describe the problem of groupthink and two of the steps for avoiding this problem.

9. Explain the concept of ethical decision-making and discuss two of the pressures against and two reasons for insisting on ethical decisions.

MANAGEMENT EXERCISE

The Chicago Decision

John Riordan is CEO of Wentech, an environmental engineering company headquartered in Fairfield, Connecticut. Wentech's growth during its first ten years has been slow but steady, with most of its customers consisting of large companies, cities, and towns located in the northeastern part of the United States. Lately, however, Wentech has successfully bid on projects in the Midwest, and Riordan has decided to open up a Chicago office to serve as a base of operations in that region.

Now Riordan must decide who to send to manage the Chicago office. He's clear on his goal: he needs the best decision maker available, someone who's very independent since he or she will be on their own most of the time. After a careful review of the possibilities and a lot of conversations with people he respects, Riordan has narrowed the field down to three candidates: Jason Carpenter, Maureen Lyons, and Michael Jones. All three have been with Wentech for at least fifteen years, all three have had extensive experience with major management responsibilities, and all three would be willing to move to another part of the country. These are some of John Riordan's thoughts as he considers the options.

Jason Carpenter is an intense and hard-working individual who, in his own words, "has never missed a deadline yet." Actually, this can sometimes be a problem. From time to time, Jason appears to be more concerned with finishing a project on time than with getting it 100% right. For example, a major computer report Jason was recently working on had to be redone and months of work involving several departments were wasted. Jason hadn't wanted to take the time required to speak with everyone he needed to in order to make sure the report was on target, thus the report was done quickly, but it did not contain the information needed by various departments. Jason actually works well with others. He has a reputation of being "firm but fair." But there's no question he would be even more effective if he would just take the time it takes to make sure he's heading in the right direction.

Maureen Lyons is one of the most thorough and respected managers in the company. She has extremely high standards, works very well with others at all levels of the organization, and prides herself on making high-quality decisions. Maureen's weakness is with deadlines. She is so thorough in gathering information and evaluating options that she is extremely slow in her decision making. For example, Maureen's lack of timeliness on a recent decision resulted in the company spending additional money to lease equipment until Maureen was finally able to decide which machine to purchase. Once the decision was made, everyone agreed that the machine was a good choice. Maureen calls herself a perfectionist. You wonder if she might also be something of a procrastinator. She disagrees and says that what's important isn't time; it's whether or not the decisions are good ones.

You are convinced that good decisions are also timely, and you wonder how well Maureen's approach would work at the new Chicago office.

Michael Jones is one of the most decisive managers at Wentech. He has a reputation for balancing thoroughness with the ability to get right to the heart of the question. Once he has completed his analysis, he wastes no time in taking action, and his decisions almost always are on target. On the other hand, Michael is not easy to work with. He tends to consult only a few trusted associates—some say he plays favorites. This frustrates the people outside of Michael's "circle" who feel they have something worthwhile to offer. Michael is aware of this, but feels his job is to make good decisions, not to make people "feel good." There is no question that Michael can be counted upon to make the "safe" decision, but you're also convinced that his decisions could be even better if he took greater advantage of the skills and knowledge of the people around him.

1. Write John Riordan's goal as a goal statement.

2. What are the strengths and weaknesses of each of the three candidates in terms of this goal?

3. If you were John Riordan, which one of the three would you send to head the Chicago office. Why?

4. What would you do to implement the decision to increase the likelihood of its success?

APPENDIX 5A — Break-Even Analysis

The break-even point (BEP) for a product or service can be calculated whenever you know three things:

1. What the fixed costs are for the operation—items like rent, the cost of equipment, legal costs to set up the operation—costs that will be there whether you provide or produce 1 unit of the service or product or 1,000 units.

2. What variable costs per unit are, such as labor and material costs that will vary depending on how many units you produce or provide.

3. The selling price per unit.

The *break-even point* (BEP) for a product or service—how much of the product or service must be sold in order not to lose money on it—equals the total fixed costs divided by the selling price per unit minus the variable cost per unit.

$$\frac{Total\ fixed\ cost}{Selling\ price - Variable\ cost\ per\ unit} \quad = \quad BEP\ (units)$$

This formula allows you to evaluate various alternatives by determining how many units of the product or service you must sell before you start to make any money. For example, say you are the owner-operator of a professional pharmacy, and you are trying to decide whether or not to hire a full-time assistant. Hiring an assistant means increasing your fixed costs by approximately $25,000 for salary and benefits. These are considered fixed costs because you will have to pay salary and benefits regardless of how many—or few—additional prescriptions the new person fills. From your records you know that the average variable cost of each prescription—the wholesale price of the drug—is $5.00, and the average selling price of each prescription is $9.00. Substituting these values into the formula as follows:

$$BEP \quad = \quad \frac{\$25,000}{\$9 - \$5} \quad = \quad 6,250\ units\ (prescriptions)$$

you determine that you will need to fill 6,250 additional prescriptions per year—an average of about 20 prescriptions each business day—to break even on hiring this full-time assistant. Or you could increase the average charge for each prescription to $10.00 and reduce the BEP to 5,000 prescriptions per year. Or you could hire the assistant on a half-time basis for $15,000 and reduce your BEP to 3,750 additional prescriptions. Again, where each of the key variables in the decision can be quantified, it becomes possible to play out each decision alternative for detailed evaluation.

APPENDIX 5B — Decision Tree Analysis

Suppose you are operating a restaurant, and you are trying to decide which of two properties to lease. Property A allows seating of 100 customers per meal and costs $1,800 per month to lease. Property B seats 150 and leases at $2,700 per month. Obviously your break-even point will be lower if you lease Property A. But whether Property A is the better choice actually depends upon how much seating you anticipate needing on a night-to-night basis. You can't know exactly how many seats you'll need until you've been open for a while, so for the purposes of your decision, you'll have to estimate. This is where the decision tree comes in. Using the decision tree format, rather than estimating an average number of seats you'll need, you estimate the relative probabilities for three levels of seating: low, moderate, and high. Assuming that each seat will generate revenues of $10 per night above all other costs, the decision tree evaluation of the two leasing alternatives is as follows:

	ESTIMATE	PROBABILITY	$ PER SEAT	DAYS PER MONTH	EXPECTED VALUE
Property A					
High =	150	0*	$ 0	—	—
Moderate =	100	.7	$10	30	$21,000
Low =	75	.3	$10	30	6,750
Total					$27,750
				Less Lease	1,800
				Net expected value	$25,950

*Property seats 100 maximum.

	ESTIMATE	PROBABILITY	$ PER SEAT	DAYS PER MONTH	EXPECTED VALUE
Property B					
High =	150	.2	$10	30	$ 9,000
Moderate =	100	.5	$10	30	15,000
Low =	75	.3	$10	30	6,750
Total					$30,750
				Less Lease	2,700
				Net expected value	$28,050

By multiplying, for each "branch" of the decision tree, (1) the estimate of the number of seats needed per day by (2) the probability of needing that many seats by (3) the average revenue above other costs per seat by (4) the days in the month, you obtain an expected value, or the revenue you would expect under each of the three conditions (high, moderate, and low) under both leasing alternatives. In this case, you have estimated that you expect your capacity needs to be high 20 percent of the time, moderate 50 percent of the time, and low 30 percent of the time. Using the decision tree, it becomes obvious that even though you estimate that Property A would provide sufficient seating 80 percent of the time, by not allowing for the larger crowds that you expect 20 percent of the time, you would be sacrificing $2,100 per month in additional revenues.

APPENDIX 5C — T-Chart Example

Suppose you are attempting to evaluate two employment alternatives: one an entry-level position with a large regional organization offering a lower initial salary, but with opportunities for advancement requiring relocation; the other a position with a local firm offering a higher initial salary and more responsibility immediately, but with much less opportunity for advancement. Other than in terms of salary, the possibility of evaluating these two alternatives on any kind of quantitative basis is clearly limited. In cases like this, the focus is on the qualities of the alternatives. If the goals of the decision have been well defined, the qualities that are important will be clear.

If, as we said in an earlier chapter, your goal for the decision has been stated in such general terms as "a good job with satisfying work," the two alternatives are difficult to compare and evaluate. What exactly does "a good job with satisfying work" mean? If, on the other hand, your goals for this decision include (a) significant immediate responsibility, (b) opportunity for continued advancement and professional development, (c) not a large corporation, (d) no requirement to relocate, and (e) starting salary of $25,000 a year, the potential for effectively evaluating the two alternatives is greatly enhanced. Now it becomes possible to compare the two opportunities on the basis of five fairly specific dimensions. This is where the T-chart comes in.

T-charts get their name from the T-shaped format they use to list and evaluate alternatives. In the example being considered here, the T-chart would be set up as follows:

	LOCAL FIRM	*REGIONAL CORPORATION*
Significant responsibility	*Now*	*Later*
Opportunity for advancement	*No*	*Yes*
Not a large corporation	*Isn't*	*?*
No relocation required	*None*	*Maybe*
$22,000+	*Yes*	*No, but . . .*

Given the mixed results from this evaluation, it becomes clear why the relative importance or the priority of each decision goal should be understood, as discussed in Chapter 4.

It is important to note, as with the other evaluation techniques, the purpose of the T-chart is not to make the decision. Rather, the purpose of the T-chart is to assist the evaluation process, in this case (a) by getting down on paper what otherwise would have to be juggled in your brain, and (b) by raising additional issues to be considered in evaluating the two alternatives. For example, is the regional corporation a large corporation by your definition? Or, might it be worth taking a lower starting salary where the potential is greater for a higher salary later on? The answers to these kinds of questions are themselves a critical part of the evaluation phase.

REFERENCES

1. "Johnson & Johnson's Class Act," *Business Week,* March 3, 1986, 134.

2. T. Oliver, *The Real Coke, The Real Story* (New York: Random House, 1986).

3. A. J. Large and L. McGinley, "NASA Is Asked to Explain Why Shuttle Was Launched despite Warning on Cold," *Wall Street Journal,* February 12, 1986, 62.

4. See P. Rivett, *Model Building for Decision Analysis* (New York: John Wiley & Sons, 1980), 4–11; and M. Zeleny, *Multiple Criteria Decision Making* (New York: McGraw-Hill Book Co., 1982), 85–94.

5. T. Peters and N. Austin, *A Passion for Excellence* (New York: Random House, 1985), 6.

6. For example, see R. J. Sternberg, "Implicit Theories of Intelligence, Creativity and Wisdom," *Journal of Personality and Social Psychology* 49 (1985): 607–27; M. D. Mumford and S. B. Gustafson, "Creativity Syndrome: Integration, Application and Innovation," *Psychology Bulletin* 103 (1988): 27–43; and E. T. Smith, S. Yanchinski, M. Sabin, and P. E. Simmons, "Are You Creative?" *Business Week,* September 30, 1985, 84.

7. B. Kolman and R. E. Beck, *Elementary Linear Programming with Applications* (New York: Academic Press, 1980).

8. H. A. Simon, *Administrative Behavior* (New York: Free Press, 1957).

9. H. A. Simon, "Information Processing Models of Cognition," *Annual Review of Psychology* 30 (1979): 363.

10. For example, see W. Agor, "How Top Executives Use Their Intuition to Make Decisions," *Business Horizons,* January–February 1986, 49–53.

11. A. Etzioni, "Humble Decision Making," *Harvard Business Review* (July / August 1989), 122–26.

12. P. F. Drucker, *Management: Tasks, Responsibilities and Practices* (Harper & Row, 1974), 468–69.

13. Adapted from Victor H. Vroom and Phillip W. Yetton, *Leadership and Decision Making* (Pittsburgh: University of Pittsburgh Press, 1973); Victor H. Vroom, "A New Look at Managerial Decision Making," *Organizational Dynamics* 1 (Spring 1973):66–80.

14. Irving L. Janis, *Groupthink* (Boston: Houghton Mifflin, 1982).

15. R. Eric Reidenbach and Donald P. Robin, "A Conceptual Model of Corporate Moral Development," *Journal of Business Ethics,* April 1991, 273–84.

16. "Chronology of Dow Corning's Breast Implant Saga in 1992," *Chemical and Engineering News* 71 (2) (January 11, 1993):16.

FROM THE MANAGER'S E-MAIL

Teams at Young Rehab Hospital

You are a member of the management team at Young Rehabilitation Hospital. The hospital is named after its founder and CEO, Dr. Sydney Young, and specializes in the rehabilitation of spinal-cord-injury patients. Because of its excellent reputation, the hospital receives patients from all over the United States.

During the past year, the hospital has been experimenting with a team-based approach to patient care. The experiment created a team of twenty employees (one doctor, two social workers, two occupational therapists, two physical therapists, six nurses, and seven nurses' aides). This team cares for only one ward of ten patients. The rest of the staff works on patients throughout the hospital, as they traditionally did.

The team has been in operation for a full year, and as a member of the hospital's management team you are part of the group that will evaluate the success of the treatment team's approach. The evaluation group will be meeting to prepare its recommendation later in the week, and you have begun to prepare for that meeting by reviewing your E-mail messages.

Date: April 4, 1995 11:30 am

From: LOCALSYS (Sydney Young, M.D.)

Subject: Treatment Team Experiment

As you know, I am requesting a recommendation from your group based on our experience with the treatment team. I am asking that your group review the information about patients and staff members who have participated in the team experiment, and suggest whether we should expand the team concept, discontinue the experimental team, or pursue some other course of action.

Please identify at least three alternatives, assess the strengths and weaknesses of each, and provide me with your recommendation of which alternative we should pursue and why. I ask you to keep in mind that our reason for trying the treatment team approach was to improve the performance and job satisfaction of the staff, and the process of rehabilitation for the patients.

I look forward to receiving your report by the end of this month.

Date: April 4, 1995 8:30 am

From: LOCALSYS (Angela Duclos, Director of Staff Services)

Subject: Data from survey of treatment team members

The following is a summary of the results of our survey of staff members who have been serving on the treatment team. As you can see, their reaction to the experiment is mixed.

1. Team members reported greater satisfaction with their teammates.

2. There was concern about a lack of a "true supervisor" to provide overall direction for the team.

3. There is significantly lower satisfaction among team members because of fewer opportunities for promotions.

4. Overtime hours were 48 percent lower for team members.

5. Frequent conflicts were reported about who had primary responsibility for patient care.

6. Significant satisfaction was reported with having the opportunity to focus on a limited number of patients for their entire treatment process.

7. Absenteeism was 42 percent lower for team members.

8. Ten of twenty team members have requested to return to their departments.

Date: April 5, 1995 10:15 am

From: LOCALSYS (Victor Sanchez, Coordinator of Patient Services)

Subject: Data from survey of patients treated by treatment team

Dr. Young asked that I share with you the information we have gathered about patients who participated in the team treatment experiment. I would be happy to provide clarification of any of these points.

1. Patients recovered significantly faster with team-based treatment.

2. Patients put forth more effort during exercise periods.

3. Patients appeared less accepting of staff who were not team members.

4. Patients were discharged 10 percent earlier than the average sixty days.

5. Closer relationships were established between patients and team members.

6. Patient treatment costs were 12 percent higher for the team approach.

1. Define the goal(s) of the decision Dr. Young must make.

2. Identify three options as alternatives.

3. Create T-charts to assist you in assessing the strengths and weaknesses of each of these options.

4. Based on your analysis, indicate which option you'd recommend to Dr. Young and why.

SECTION
III

Planning for Performance

W e have said that vision is the network of goals that gives an organization a sense of purpose and direction. Developing this network of goals is the first responsibility of management; it is the planning responsibility. Through planning, managers develop the organization's goals and identify the resources and actions required for achieving them. In recent years this organizational planning process has come to be called *strategic management*.

Chapter 6 introduces the strategic management process and focuses on its initial stages. In these stages, the organization defines its mission and strategic goals, analyzes the environment and its own strengths and weaknesses, and then develops strategies to achieve the mission and goals.

Chapter 7 reviews the process of implementing the organization's strategies—turning its goals into action. This *operational planning* segment of strategic management entails identifying the actions, schedules, policies, and budgets needed for the successful implementation of strategy. Taken together, these two chapters describe how management sets the direction of the organization and implements plans to place the organization in a competitive position for success in a changing environment.

CHAPTER 6
Strategic Management

LEARNING OBJECTIVES

After studying this chapter, you should be able to:

- *Describe the overall strategic management process.*

- *Explain the key components of a mission statement.*

- *Discuss the various elements of the organization's environments as well as the key areas of its own competencies.*

- *Describe the process of SWOT analysis.*

- *Explain the concepts of strategy and strategic alternatives.*

- *Contrast corporate, business, and functional-level strategies.*

- *Explain how strategy implementation and strategic control are essential parts of the strategic management process.*

n the late 1980s, American Greetings found itself in a price war with Hallmark and other greeting card companies. The organization's profits suffered because of constant price-cutting as each company sought to underprice its competitors. Recognizing that it couldn't continue to cut its prices indefinitely, American Greetings developed a strategy to escape the price wars. It decided to differentiate itself from Hallmark and its other competitors by offering creative services as well as greeting cards. As a way to help increase customer traffic for the retailer in general, not just in the card area, American Greetings' creative services unit assisted retailers in designing seasonal displays throughout stores. The company also began offering information services to retailers through computer software that analyzed a store's sales and inventories. Lastly, American Greetings acquired Custom Expressions, Inc., a company that makes kiosks, called CreataCard, where customers design and create their own cards in a minute. By 1992, American Greetings' earnings were more than double what they were at the height of the price wars in 1987.[1]

In today's environment, with its constant and rapid changes, most organizations have learned what American Greetings learned: They can no longer simply react to circumstances around them. They must be proactive and take the initiative to develop strategies that minimize threats and maximize opportunities. Through planning, organizations are able to keep pace with changes in the environment, rather than simply react to them. Our focus in this chapter is on the strategic portion of the planning process: setting goals for the organization and developing strategies to achieve them. *Strategic planning* is the responsibility for understanding the mission of the organization, for anticipating and recognizing changes in the world outside the organization, and for developing strategies for positioning the organization to compete in the changing environment.

STRATEGIC PLANNING

Between 1965 and 1975, the concept and process of strategic planning came into wide use.[2] It was during that time that global competition first began to escalate, as the Japanese and European economies completed their recovery from World War II. Also, computers began to change the way business was done, and changes in transportation and communication began to have an impact. As the rate and magnitude of these changes in the environment increased, organizations began to pay more attention to changes in their environments and to how they affected market conditions and other key factors. They began to develop goals and plans reflecting these changes. This process of monitoring and analyzing key changes in the environment and developing strategies to increase the organization's effectiveness in response to those changes came to be known as "strategic planning."

Initially, the emphasis in strategic planning was on a top-down approach, where top-level managers and professional corporate planners analyzed the environment, developed very specific goals and highly detailed plans, and then passed them down to front-line managers.[3] Because a lack of communication often existed between those who developed the plans and those who were supposed to put them into action, these top-down strategic plans were almost never effectively implemented.

Companies also learned that there are problems when "experts" such as top managers and professional planners rely solely on their own judgment and opinions to analyze the environment or forecast the future. Tom Peters provides classic examples of the type of thinking that results when even highly qualified individuals rely only on their own analysis:[4]

"Who in the hell wants to hear actors talk?"—Harry Warner, founder of Warner Bros. Studio (1927).

"I think there is a world market for about five computers"—Thomas J. Watson, chairman of IBM (1943).

"There is no reason for any individual to have a computer in their home." —Ken Olsen, president of Digital Equipment (1977).

In an effort to avoid such tunnel vision, as well as the communications problems mentioned above, the top-down approach to planning began to change in the 1980s. To ensure both broader input into the planning process and more effective implementation once the plans were developed, organizations began to involve managers from all parts of the organization in the development and implementation of strategic goals and plans. This process of encouraging all managers, employees, and teams to think strategically and to focus on the organization's environment is called strategic management.

THE STRATEGIC MANAGEMENT APPROACH TO PLANNING

The major components of the strategic management approach to planning are summarized in Figure 6-1. As the figure shows, the strategic management process is a continuous one. Because the environment is continuously shifting and changing, strategic management must be an ongoing, continuous examination of how well the organization is aligned to that environment.

This chapter will focus primarily on the first three phases of the strategic management process: from defining the organization's mission and strategic goals to developing the strategies for achieving those goals.

Step 1: Establishing the Organization's Direction

As we noted in Chapter 4, the first responsibility of management is to provide vision, a clear sense of direction, and that vision is achieved in an organization through its overall network of goals. In terms of strategic management, an organization's general and enduring sense of direction is defined as its *mission*. At AT&T, for example, chairman Robert E. Allen sees the company's mission as providing "anytime, anywhere communication." He views the company as a high-tech communications system that will deliver a message to people no matter where they are by means of a digital information superhighway.[5] Similarly, the Sierra Club, an environmental organization, sees its mission in these terms: "To enjoy, explore and protect the environment."

A clear and compelling sense of direction is the starting point of the strategic management process; it is management's responsibility to give the organization

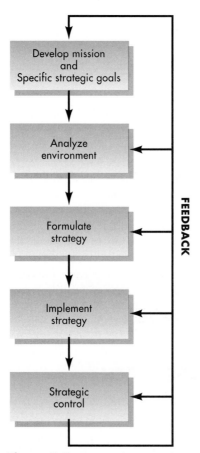

Figure 6-1 Strategic Management Process

this sense of its own enduring purpose.[6] The most common way that organizations attempt to communicate this sense of purpose or direction is through a mission statement.

The Mission Statement

The *mission statement* is a summary of what business the organization is in or seeks to be in, and often includes a statement of its philosophy and values. The mission statement reveals the organization's long-term vision—what it wants to be and whom it wants to serve. An effective mission statement provides a general sense of direction for every individual and group in an organization.

First, regarding the company's business, the mission statement should clearly answer the questions "What business are we in?" and "What business should we be in?" It is important that these questions be answered in terms of customer needs and not in terms of the products or services the company currently offers.[7] This focus on customer needs helps the company avoid being left behind by changes in technology or consumer preferences. Theodore Levitt described the decline of U.S. railroads in terms of a failure to have a customer-oriented mission:

> The railroads did not stop growing because the need for passenger and freight transportation declined. That grew. The railroads are in trouble today not because the need was filled by others (cars, trucks, airplanes, even telephones), but because it was not filled by the railroads themselves. They let others take customers away from them because they assumed themselves to be in the railroad business rather than in the transportation business. The reason they defined their industry wrong was because they were railroad oriented instead of transportation oriented; they were product oriented instead of customer oriented.[8]

Levitt's point is that railroad companies might have been more successful in the second half of the twentieth century if they had defined their mission in broader terms, in terms of meeting the transportation needs of their customers, rather than in terms of a particular technology—railroads. With a mission defined in terms of meeting the nation's transportation needs, they might have moved to include trucking and air transportation among their services.

The problem of defining an organization's mission too narrowly can be found in government and nonprofit organizations as well. At first glance, a city fire department might have as its mission "To put out fires." But a fire department's purpose goes beyond this definition. If a car is leaking gasoline or if a parent calls to say her child stopped breathing, the department will respond. Thus, a more realistic statement would be "To ensure the preparation of officers, men and equipment so that together we are prepared to provide cost effective resolution to emergencies that threaten or will threaten life and property in our community."[9]

It is because of its customer orientation that Apple Computer defines its mission in terms of making technology more user friendly and finds itself developing not only computers but all kinds of technology that might be easier for the customer to use. Similarly, McDonald's views itself, in part, as selling "fun" and continues to experiment with McDonald's Playlands as one of the ways to satisfy this mission.

First and foremost, then, a mission statement must clearly define what business an organization is in or seeks to be in, and this definition must be in terms of the customer needs it seeks to satisfy.

Philosophy and Values.   Beyond the business it is in or seeks to be in, a mission statement should also define the organization's philosophy—its basic beliefs, values, and priorities. It defines how the company intends to do business and often indicates the organization's understanding of its social responsibility.

Note the mission statement of Ben & Jerry's Homemade, Inc., shown in Figure 6-2. The company's beliefs and values come through loud and clear. They express strong support for Vermont dairy farmers, and emphasize Ben & Jerry's deep respect for individuals inside and outside the company.

Many companies establish a creed to highlight their distinctive outlook on business. Johnson & Johnson is noted for its summary of its business philosophy.

BEN & JERRY'S STATEMENT OF MISSION

Ben & Jerry's is dedicated to the creation and demonstration of a new corporate concept of linked prosperity. Our mission consists of three interrelated parts:

PRODUCT MISSION:	SOCIAL MISSION:	ECONOMIC MISSION:
To make, distribute and sell the finest quality all natural ice cream and related products in a wide variety of innovative flavors made from Vermont dairy products.	To operate the company in a way that actively recognizes the central role that business plays in the structure of society by initiating innovative ways to improve the quality of life of our employees and a broad community: local, national and international.	To operate the company on a sound financial basis of profitable growth, increasing value for our shareholders and creating career opportunities and financial rewards for our employees

Underlying the mission of Ben & Jerry's is the determination to seek new creative ways of addressing all three parts, while holding a deep respect for individuals, inside and outside the company, and for the communities of which they are a part.

Figure 6-2 Mission Statement for Ben & Jerry's *(Source: Company Reports)*

Its credo, shown in Figure 6-3, articulates the belief that the company's first responsibility is to the doctors, nurses, and patients who use its products, followed by the employees, communities in which employees live and work, and finally the company's shareholders. It was this credo that guided company decisions in the 1982 Tylenol crisis, mentioned in Chapter 5. By taking actions consistent with its values and philosophy, Johnson & Johnson presented itself as a company that was willing to do what was right regardless of the cost. As a consequence, the crisis enhanced rather than tarnished the Johnson & Johnson image.[10]

The mission statement, then, defines for employers, customers, and all stakeholders the organization's highest and most enduring goals in terms of the needs of the customers it is seeking to satisfy, and the organization's philosophy and values in pursuing those goals.

Specific Goals

While the mission statement points to the general and enduring purpose of the organization, it is corporate goals that provide more specific direction. For example, at Federal Express corporate goals are spelled out in three areas, as shown in Figure 6-4:[11]

Since these goals are stated in very specific terms, they are not actually part

OUR CREDO

We believe our first responsibility is to the doctors, nurses and patients,
to mothers and fathers and all others who use our products and services.
In meeting their needs everything we do must be of high quality.
We must constantly strive to reduce our costs
in order to maintain reasonable prices.
Customers' orders must be serviced promptly and accurately.
Our suppliers and distributors must have an opportunity
to make a fair profit.

We are responsible to our employees,
the men and women who work with us throughout the world.
Everyone must be considered as an individual.
We must respect their dignity and recognize their merit.
They must have a sense of security in their jobs.
Compensation must be fair and adequate,
and working conditions clean, orderly and safe.
We must be mindful of ways to help our employees fulfill
their family responsibilities.
Employees must feel free to make suggestions and complaints.
There must be equal opportunity for employment, development
and advancement for those qualified.
We must provide competent management,
and their actions must be just and ethical.

We are responsible to the communities in which we live and work
and to the world community as well.
We must be good citizens – support good works and charities
and bear our fair share of taxes.
We must encourage civic improvements and better health and education.
We must maintain in good order
the property we are privileged to use,
protecting the environment and natural resources.

Our final responsibility is to our stockholders.
Business must make a sound profit.
We must experiment with new ideas.
Research must be carried on, innovative programs developed
and mistakes paid for.
New equipment must be purchased, new facilities provided
and new products launched.
Reserves must be created to provide for adverse times.
When we operate according to these principles,
the stockholders should realize a fair return.

Johnson & Johnson

Figure 6-3 Johnson & Johnson Credo *(Source: Johnson & Johnson)*

of the mission statement. But translating the mission into specific corporate goals is an essential part of the planning process. As we noted in Chapter 4, only when goals are specific can they provide the kind of focus, direction, and understanding critical for effective performance.

General Electric understands the importance of corporate goals. GE operates 350 businesses in thirteen different industries and one of GE's corporate goals is

People: Improve the quality of leadership corporate-wide to achieve an overall SFA leadership index of 76 or better (SFA stands for Survey Feedback Action, which is a survey that is given internally to employees as a way of measuring their satisfaction with management).

Service: Service quality indicator (SQI) will be 125,000 daily points or better (SQI is a system designed by Federal Express to measure various facets of the service it provides).

Profit: Achieve a 5 percent pretax margin for the corporation.

Figure 6-4   Specific Goals at Federal Express

to be first or second in every industry in which it competes. By translating its mission into these kinds of specific corporate goals, GE has become a leader in most of the industries in which it competes. GE's success is just one example of the importance of translating clear mission statements into well-defined goals.

Once its mission and goals are clear, the organization is ready to turn its attention to the environment in which it must pursue these goals. Only when the organization fully understands its mission and goals can it begin to assess the potential impact of the changing environment on its goals.

Step 2: Analyzing the Situation: Comparing the Organization to Its Environment

In terms of planning, even organizations that have clear missions often tend to get so caught up in day-to-day problems that they fail to recognize and respond to what's happening around them. In the late 1960s and early 1970s, for example, local school systems throughout America were so busy building new schools for the baby-boom generation that they didn't even notice that the birth rate had begun to fall off dramatically. The decline was so drastic in the northeastern United States, for example, that the number of children born to families in that region had dropped by 40 percent in the ten years between 1970 and 1980. Most school administrators were so intent on making sure they had enough space for school-age children that they failed to recognize that the birth-rate trend had already begun to reverse itself. As a result of this inattention to the environment, by the early 1980s, schools were being closed that in some cases had been built only a few years earlier. This is the kind of experience that convinces organizations of the critical importance of monitoring the trends in their environment. In the strategic management view, an organization can be thought of as a sports team whose mission is to win. Before deciding on a game plan, or a strategy to achieve that mission, the team must analyze the situation: not only its own strengths and weaknesses but also those of the opposing team and the field the game is being played on.

Recognizing what is actually happening in the environment and evaluating the organization in terms of those trends is what a situation analysis is all about. *Situation analysis* examines the complex set of interactions between factors both inside and outside the organization. It begins with a review of conditions in the environment to see if they pose opportunities or threats and then uses this review as a basis for assessing the organization itself for potential strengths and weaknesses.

Figure 6-5 shows the relationship between the organization and its environment. The outer circle represents the *general environment*, which includes broad trends and conditions in society. These are factors outside the organization that tend to affect society and organizations in general. The middle circle represents the *task* or *specific environment*, which consists of individuals, groups, and organizations that directly affect a particular organization but are not part of it. The inner circle is the organization itself, the dimensions of the organization that impact performance. All three elements require management's constant attention.

The Two Environments

The first step in analyzing the organization's situation is to assess the environment for opportunities and threats. As we said, there are two categories of environments that must be monitored: the general environment, which is shared by

Figure 6-5 The Organization and Its Environment

every organization in a society; and the task or specific environment, which is unique to a particular organization.

General Environment. As Figure 6-5 shows, the general environment can be divided into five dimensions or subcategories of change: social, economic, political/legal, technological, and global.

Social change includes changes in social patterns, demographics, values, and institutions. The "graying" of the American population due to the aging of the post–World War II baby-boom generation, the increase in single-parent and two-income families, problems in public education, increased violence in our society, and increased life expectancy are all examples of important recent social changes. Changes in society and social values can affect everything from the goods and services customers are interested in, to the attitudes and work ethics of the workforce, to the standard of social responsibility to which organizations will be held.

Economic change refers to the overall status of the economy, which varies over time. Times of economic prosperity, when demand for services and goods is high and unemployment is low, as was the case for the United States during most of the 1980s, represent periods of tremendous opportunity for business organizations. Obviously, the situation is less positive during periods of low economic prosperity, when the demand for goods and services is low and unemployment is high, as was the case for most developed nations in the late 1980s and early 1990s. Economic factors such as changes in interest and inflation rates are other key elements of the economic environment that affect organizations.

Political and legal change includes the impact of governmental laws and the legal system, as well as the relationship between government and business. Changes in the laws regulating the banking industry in the United States, for example, impacted the entire American economy during the 1980s; and in the early 1990s organizations have paid the closest attention to how health care legislation might affect them. Changes in government policy regarding the trading status of China, North Korea, and Vietnam are also part of the political environment that companies have watched closely. And laws protecting the employment rights of the disabled and older workers have had a major impact on every kind of organization.

Technological change refers to the advances that create new products and new ways of producing goods and providing services. As we noted in Chapter 3, information technology has transformed every organization's environment with revolutions in manufacturing, communication, information processing, entertainment, and shopping. Major breakthroughs are occurring in bioengineering and space-age materials. Managers who ignore these kinds of technological changes not only risk missing important opportunities for improving performance; they risk seeing their existing products and processes become obsolete or extinct.

Global change has been perhaps the most volatile environmental factor in the 1990s. International politics and economic conditions have been dramatically altered by the sudden shift of whole geographic regions from communism, where the government once planned all of the production and distribution of goods and set prices, to capitalism. Now Poland, the Czech Republic, Bulgaria, Romania, and independent states from the former Soviet Union are becoming potential markets and sources of inexpensive labor. And these are only some of the most recent nations following in the steps of South Korea, Malaysia, and the other Pacific Rim countries that joined the global marketplace during the 1980s. Just as importing foreign goods has become commonplace in Europe, the United States, and Japan, exporting goods to these emerging free-market economies also provides enormous business opportunities.

Changes in the social, political, economic, technological, and global environment, then, can have a dramatic effect on any organization. It is the responsibility of management to monitor continuously these key dimensions of the general environment in order to recognize as early as possible the changes that might impact the organization. This responsibility extends also to the task environment.

Task Environment. The task, or immediate, environment includes the factors in the environment that directly impact a specific organization. Thus, in Figure 6-5 the elements of the task environment are located closer to the organization. Like the general environment, the task environment consists of a number of dimensions. Among the most important are customers, competition, suppliers, and regulators.

Customers are the individuals, groups, and other organizations which purchase the products and services that an organization provides. Changes in customers' needs or priorities can have a significant effect on an organization. Organizations can achieve a competitive advantage when they respond quickly to such changes. The Chrysler minivan was an on-target response to the shift in customer emphasis to family-based transportation. Federal Express correctly recognized the shift to an emphasis on speed in transporting business documents and filled the need. BMW, on the other hand, failed to recognize its customers' shift to a greater emphasis on value, and saw its share of the U.S. auto market plummet from a peak of 96,000 car sales in 1986 to a low of 53,300 in 1991.[12]

Competitors are other organizations that compete for an organization's customers. Companies such as Nike, L.A. Gear, and Reebok compete directly in the sports shoe market. Burger King, McDonald's, and Wendy's compete in the fast-food market. What each of these companies does in terms of pricing, marketing, or new product development has a direct effect on each of its competitors. When Perrier water was found to be tainted, for example, or when Nike spokesman Michael Jordan retired for a period from basketball, these events represented significant opportunities for those two companies' competitors.

Suppliers also can exert a strong outside influence on organizations. They may raise their prices, or the quality of the goods they provide may become a problem. The labor supply may be limited in its skills, thus requiring the organization to train new hires. In the late 1980s, banks in the United States entered a crisis period of their own, which in turn severely limited many organizations' access to the supply of the key resources of money and credit.

Increasingly, organizations are viewing suppliers as potential sources of competitive advantage. Rather than let a wire and cable supplier go out of business, Fujitsu Electronics Co. invested millions of dollars to transform the failing organization into a supplier of semiconductor chips. Fujitsu thereby obtained a loyal business partner and supplier.[13] Similarly, Nike has invested millions of dollars in the research and development efforts of its suppliers as a way to ensure a steady flow of new product ideas.

Regulators are the final component of the organization's task environment. These outside agencies have the ability to control or influence the internal workings of an organization. The State of California's requirement, for example, that one in every ten cars sold after the year 2002 must be electric will have a significant impact on car manufacturers. Governmental agencies such as OSHA (Occupational Safety and Health Administration) and the EEOC (Equal Employment Opportunity Commission), as well as state agencies that establish insurance rates are examples of government regulators that have a continuing impact on organizations.

Private interest groups also attempt to influence an organization's policies and procedures. Groups such as Mothers Against Drunk Drivers (MADD), for example, have pressured beer companies to put warning labels on beer cans. Similarly, the American Association of Retired Persons (AARP) has had a major impact on drugstore chains and their policies toward senior citizens.

Management's purpose in studying the general and task environments is to identify trends that represent opportunities or threats to the organization's ability to achieve its goals. This process of monitoring and evaluating puts the organization in a proactive rather than reactive position and reduces its likelihood of being caught off guard by shifts in the environment. This phase of the strategic management process can be thought of as a kind of early warning system that allows management to take the initiative either to maximize the opportunity or to minimize the threat in responding to change.

The Organization's Competencies

There is more to an organization than just its mission, philosophy, and goals. An organization consists of human, technological, and financial competencies as well. Once it is clear what changes are taking place in the environment, the next step is to analyze these competencies. A checklist of key areas of organizational competency might include the following.

Management. An analysis of business successes and failures of the past decade indicates that one crucial ingredient in virtually every case was management expertise. Does the organization possess the management skill and experience necessary to address a potential threat or to pursue a potential opportunity? General Motors, IBM, and American Express all changed CEOs in recent years in an effort to strengthen their management capabilities. Each company appointed a new CEO to provide the management expertise demanded by the changing environment.

Corporate Culture and Values. Is the value system of the organization consistent with the demands of the environment? For example, there is a problem if the organization values conservative decision-making and the environment requires risk taking. There is also a problem if the environment requires a focus on customer demands and the organization does not value customer input. If the environment demands speed and innovation, are these also valued inside the organization?

Human Resources.   Do the organization's employees have the skills necessary to respond effectively to changes in the environment? As technology becomes more complex, does the organization have people able to operate complex systems? As the environment requires competition on a global basis, does the organization have people with the language skills and cultural understanding necessary to compete?

Operational Systems.   Does the organization possess, or can it develop, the systems necessary for the business to succeed? Wal-Mart and other retail chains have developed information technology that allows corporate headquarters to keep track on a daily basis of the level of sales of every product it carries. UPS and Federal Express developed electronic tracking systems to satisfy customer demands for immediate location of any package. Only when Harley Davidson revamped its inventory system was it able to compete with Japanese motorcycle makers.

Marketing.   Does the organization have the ability to evaluate customer needs and to effectively price, promote, and advertise its products or services? Burger King continues to trail McDonald's in market share despite the fact that it consistently beats McDonald's in blind taste tests. One of the reasons: a series of failed advertising campaigns. Reebok and Nike define their marketing capability as the key to their success and contract with other companies to manufacture their products.

Financial Resources.   Does the organization have access to the financial resources necessary to effectively respond to the environment? Can it afford the management, human resources, technology, research, and marketing that will allow it to compete? Because Morton, a manufacturer of air bags sold to automakers, had the financial resources to invest in air-bag technology long before it was a viable business, it was able to position itself to be the leading competitor in the industry. Sales of air bags were $225 million in 1991, and Morton expects to sell $1 billion of the product by 1995, as new laws requiring air bags in automobiles go into effect.[14]

A clear and realistic understanding by the organization of its own competencies is essential to analyzing its situation. Only with an understanding of its competencies can the organization begin the process of determining its strategic strengths and weaknesses.

SWOT Analysis

The process of considering an organization's competencies in terms of changes in the environment is called a SWOT analysis.[15] (*SWOT* stands for the *S*trengths and *W*eaknesses of the organization and the *O*pportunities and *T*hreats in the environment.) Through a SWOT analysis, the organization determines whether its level of competencies represents strategic strengths or weaknesses given the current environment.

For example, the technical know-how and reputation of Mercedes Benz would represent a strength in light of an increased demand for luxury cars (environmental opportunity). However, in light of an increased demand for lower-priced, high-quality Japanese luxury cars such as Lexus (environment threat), Mercedes' own high-cost production system becomes a definite weakness. Similarly, the size of General Motors allowed it to dominate the automobile industry in the 1960s and 1970s, but that same size became a weakness in the 1980s and 1990s when the environment demanded more speed and flexibility for meeting the challenges of the competition and changing customer preferences.

Once a SWOT analysis has identified the organization's strengths and weaknesses in terms of opportunities and threats in the environment, the organization can begin to consider strategic alternatives for achieving its goals.

Step 3: Developing Strategy

The term *strategy* comes from the Greek words meaning "to lead an army." In that sense, a strategy is a kind of battle plan. In strategic management terms, strategy is the course of action an organization selects to minimize threats and maximize opportunities that emerge in the environment.

As shown in Figure 6-6, the strategies an organization selects must reflect its mission, the opportunities and threats in the environment, and its own strengths and weaknesses. The process of developing strategy, shown as the shaded area in Figure 6-6, helps the organization find the best fit among the three sets of forces.

■ Process of developing strategy.

Figure 6-6 Forces that Influence Strategy Development

Developing Strategic Alternatives

Strategic alternatives are the options management can select among as the possible courses of action for obtaining its goals. Strategic alternatives exist at three levels: corporate, business, and functional. *Corporate-level strategy* deals with the alternatives a company explores as it conducts business across several industries and several markets. For example, Philip Morris has separate divisions in the beer industry (Miller), the tobacco industry, and the food industry (General Foods). Similarly, Black & Decker has divisions in the power tool industry and the small-appliance industry. Organizations with businesses in more than one industry or more than one market require corporate strategies that lead its various divisions in a unified direction.

Business-level strategy deals with alternatives for a company operating in a single industry.[16] Examples include Southwest Airlines, Stroh Brewing Co., and McDonald's. Each of these is a large company, but only operates in a single industry and only requires a strategy for the success of that single business.

Functional-level strategy involves plans for each of the organization's functional areas. Key areas typically include research and development, operations, finance, marketing, and human resources. Strategies at the functional level are designed to implement the higher-level strategies at the corporate and business level. Figure 6-7 summarizes the characteristics of the three levels of strategic alternatives.

Corporate-Level Strategy

At the corporate level, strategy deals with an organization's decisions about either expanding or retreating, either itself or from industry to industry. These decisions are not made in a vacuum. The strategic alternative a corporation chooses depends on the environmental conditions of today and the forecasted trends of tomorrow.

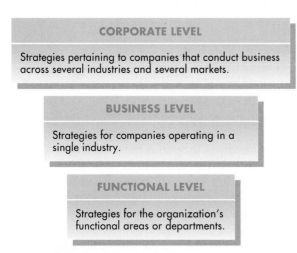

Figure 6-7 Different Levels of Strategic Alternatives

Merger and Acquisition. These strategies involve an organization's merging with or purchasing an organization in another industry to offset threats in its own environment and/or take advantage of opportunities in the environment of the other industry. A case in point is the tobacco industry, where increased public concern about smoking led many tobacco companies to acquire businesses in other industries. For example, Philip Morris acquired General Foods to move into food products, and R. J. Reynolds merged with Nabisco to form RJR Nabisco. In both cases, the parent corporation was following a growth strategy and chose to diversify as a way of minimizing the effect of threats in the tobacco industry.

Retrenchment. When an organization is not competing effectively, *retrenchment*, or turnaround, strategies are often needed. One retrenchment option involves *divesting*, selling off divisions in industries the company no longer wants to do business in. The other involves reducing the size of the organization (downsizing). During the late 1980s and into the 1990s, many large organizations sold off businesses they had acquired earlier as part of a growth strategy. In many cases these organizations found it difficult to compete in the industries they had become involved in. The Rite Aid drugstore chain, for example, decided to sell Adap, its auto-parts retailing division, as well as its Encore Books division, Concord Custom Cleaners, and Sera Tec Biologicals Corp. Rite Aid sold these other businesses in order to concentrate its resources on its core drugstore business. Although Rite Aid's drugstore business was its most profitable, it was facing strong competition from supermarkets selling health and beauty products.[17] Rite-Aid's management decided this core business needed full attention if it was going to continue to prosper in the face of such strong competition.

The other form of retrenchment, *downsizing*, typically involves a significant reduction in the size of the organization and the number of employees working for it. In 1993, for example, American corporations laid off 615,186 employees as a way to reduce costs.[18] The purpose of this strategy is to enable an organization to become more agile and cost effective as it competes in its environment.

Business-Level Strategy

The second level of strategy, as we said, deals with an organization or corporate business unit operating in a single industry. The purpose of defining a business-level strategy is to give the organization an advantage over its competition in the same industry. At the business level, there are three approaches for achieving a competitive advantage: differentiation, cost leader, and focus.[19]

Differentiation. When a firm attempts to gain a competitive advantage through a differentiation strategy, it strives to be unique in its industry or market segment by designing product characteristics to satisfy customer needs in ways that competitors find difficult to match. This uniqueness may come from physical characteristics of the product, such as quality or reliability, or it may lie in the product's appeal to customers' psychological needs, such as needs for prestige or status. Nike's Air Jordan shoes are perceived to be unique due to their high-technology air construction, and Honda automobiles are considered differentiated because of their high reliability. Heineken differentiates itself as an imported beer, and the stereo speaker manufacturer Bose positions itself as the quality leader.

Cost Leader. The alternative to differentiation is the cost leader strategy. A cost leader strategy is pursued by companies that strive to produce goods or services at the lowest cost in the industry, thereby enabling them to offer the lowest prices. While all companies, especially in the 1990s, are focused on containing costs, a cost leader takes an extreme position in this regard. In the service sector, Southwest Airlines keeps its costs the lowest in the airline industry, primarily because of its no-frills approach to service. In the retail area, Wal-Mart is the cost leader because of its sophisticated inventory management systems. In the manufacturing sector, BIC pens concentrates on cost-saving technological improvements to keep its competitive advantage.

Focus. In the focus strategy, a company targets a particular customer or geographical market. An organization following a focus strategy specializes in some way. For example, Porsche competes in the sports car market and targets the elite customer. In terms of geographical focus, many regional brewers, called *minibreweries,* have developed a competitive advantage by selling beer to local or regional markets only.

Functional-Level Strategy

Functional-level strategies deal with the plans that must be developed in each of the organization's key areas of functioning in order to support and implement corporate-level and business-level strategies. For example, members of the *research and development* area in an organization generate plans for new-product ideas as part of a growth strategy. Specialists in *operations* focus on strategies for ideal plant capacity, for improving manufacturing processes, and for managing inventory. *Financial* specialists are responsible for the financial strategies in terms of budget allocation and investment. Employees in the *marketing* area determine the appropriate markets for the organization's products and/or services and decide on pricing, product features, promotion, and channels of distribution. *Human resources* specialists are concerned with attracting, assessing, motivating, and retaining the employees required to run the organization effectively.

We will review many of the planning tools and techniques used by functional specialists to implement higher-level strategies in Chapter 7.

Steps 4 and 5: Implementing Strategy and Strategic Control

As important as it is, the development of strategy is not enough to ensure that an organization will achieve its mission and goals. For strategies to be effective, they must be translated into action. This brings us to the final two stages of the strategic management approach to planning: implementing strategy and strategic control. We will discuss each of these two stages only briefly in this chapter. Implementing strategy or operational planning is the focus of Chapter 7. Strategic control is an important focus in Chapter 12.

Implementing Strategy

The implementation of strategy is actually the first stage of what is called the operational planning phase of strategic management. Operational planning is the process of determining how the corporate- or business-level strategy will be put into action.

At Lincoln Electric, a maker of arc-welding products and electric motors, implementation of strategy is key. The company's business-level strategy is cost leader, a position it has maintained for eighty years. To carry out this strategy, an advisory board elected by workers meets with Lincoln's top management every two weeks to discuss plans for improving operations. Employees are trained internally, and the company's very generous incentive system is based on the quality of employee work, employee dependability, initiative, and output. To avoid paying interest on the money it needs, financing for company growth comes from within the company, through cash investment, retention of earnings, and employee stock ownership.[20] These policies and procedures in the organization's personnel and financial functions are critical for Lincoln's implementation of its cost leader strategy.

For strategy to work, as it does at Lincoln, it must be translated into programs, policies, and procedures that constitute "strategy in action."

Strategic Control

The last step in the strategic management process involves continuous monitoring of the organization's progress toward its long-range goals and mission. It involves evaluating the effectiveness of the organization's strategy on an ongoing basis. Is the strategy working, or should it be revised? Is it still consistent with current environmental conditions? Are there problems with implementation? Where are problems likely to occur?

At Kids "R" Us, the growing clothing subsidiary of Toys "R" Us, the strategy of expanding into Puerto Rico did not work. The company had ignored key customer characteristics, which should have been part of its environmental analysis. It also had ineffective strategic control measures, particularly in terms of early-warning systems. For example, the chain expected heavy back-to-school sales, but Puerto Rican students all wear uniforms. Also, a lot of the clothing in the Kids "R" Us inventory was considered too heavy for the climate. By the time the company realized this, it was too late to correct the situation. So the company closed its three outlets on the island and abandoned its plans for five more.[21] Based on its monitoring of the effectiveness of its strategy, Toys "R" Us changed course and avoided even more serious problems.

Financial controls, in the form of budgets, often provide warning signals that potential problem areas might exist. *Budgets* are statements of expected results in financial terms. Discrepancies between budget targets and actual results may be an indication of something happening that was unanticipated. Again, monitoring performance, in this case financial performance, allows the organization to stay in touch with whether or not its strategies are succeeding.

Nonfinancial controls are used for the same purpose and include areas such as productivity and quality controls and feedback from customers. Most organizations use a combination of financial and nonfinancial controls to provide early-warning systems.

Continuously evaluating and responding to internal and external environmental changes is what strategic management is all about. Through early-warning systems and continuous feedback, management ensures that the organization's strategy remains on target.

SUMMARY

One of the most powerful tools management has for ensuring an organization's long-term success is planning. This chapter describes the basic steps of the strategic management approach to planning, which emphasizes the organization's relationship to its environment.

The process begins with a review of the company's mission, which identifies the company's business and its goals. A detailed situational analysis follows, beginning with an assessment of trends in both the general and the task environment of the organization. The organization's competencies are then evaluated and assessed in terms of opportunities and threats in the environment. Referred to as a SWOT analysis, this process of assessing the organization's competencies in light of environmental conditions helps management to identify potential areas where the organization may be weak or strong, or where the environment is threatening or promising.

Based on the SWOT analysis, strategies at the corporate, business, and functional levels are formulated to maximize opportunities and minimize threats to the organization as it seeks to achieve its mission and goals. Corporate-level strategies consist of strategic choices made when organizations compete in *several industries.* At this level, organizations may pursue strategies of merger and acquisition as a way of growing, or may reduce the size of the organization by retrenching or downsizing.

Business-level strategy deals with strategic alternatives for a company operating in a *single industry.* The approaches available at the business level include differentiation, cost leader, and focus strategies. All three provide an organization the opportunity to achieve a strategic advantage over competitors in the same industry.

Functional-level strategies define the plans of action that are necessary in each of the organization's functional areas to carry out the corporate- and/or business-level strategies. This level of planning, operational planning, is part of the implementation stage of the strategic management process and is the focus of Chapter 7.

Finally, strategic control involves constantly monitoring the organization's progress toward its long-term goals and mission. Financial and nonfinancial controls provide information to the organization as to whether its strategies are working, whether they are consistent with the environment, and where problems are likely to occur.

The advantage of the strategic management process is that it puts the organization in an offensive, proactive position. Identifying shifts and trends in the environment enables management to respond more effectively to new technologies, new competition, social changes, and changes in the political and legal environment. When managers deal with challenges today by revising their mission, goals, and strategies, they are in a better position to avoid crises tomorrow and to take full advantage of tomorrow's opportunities.

QUESTIONS TO CHALLENGE YOUR UNDERSTANDING OF THE CHAPTER

1. One executive noted that her company's mission could be stated very briefly: to make a profit. She explained, "That is the only reason we are in business." Do you agree? Explain your answer.

2. Differentiate between the general environment and the task environment and provide two examples of each.

3. Explain SWOT analysis and how it improves the process of selecting strategy.

4. Describe the corporate strategy that many companies have followed in the 1990s. Explain their reasons for selecting this strategy.

5. Identify an organization, other than those mentioned in the chapter, that appears to be following a differentiation strategy. What functional-level strategy in the marketing area does this company follow to carry out the differentiation strategy?

6. What is the difference between strategy implementation and strategic control?

7. Explain whether the strategic management approach to planning can be used in government and nonprofit organizations.

MANAGEMENT EXERCISE

Strategic Thinking

1. Several years ago, a national hotel chain advertised itself as "Innkeeper to America's Travelers." Technically, this is not a mission statement. But based on the words in this phrase:

   a. Whom does this organization appear to define as its customers? Briefly list the various categories of travelers in America.

   b. By its choice of the word "innkeeper," what does this organization think its customers value? What qualities in terms of a hotel/motel stay might *you* associate with the term "innkeeper"?

2. Which business-level strategy is this organization pursuing? Discuss.

3. Through market research, this firm discovered that the fastest-growing category of travelers is women traveling both for business and for leisure.

   a. This represents a change in who this organization's customers are. Describe two things women as compared with men might value in their stays at a hotel or motel—i.e., two areas that women might be more concerned about than men.

   b. Satisfying these concerns now becomes part of this organization's strategic goals. For each of the two areas of concern you identified, state a strategic goal in terms of operations and identify some activities that might be included in the firm's plans to achieve it.

4. Surveys of potential travelers show that 25 percent indicate a preference for this hotel, but only 12 percent actually stay at this chain during their travels. Identify three possible explanations for this discrepancy.

REFERENCES

1. Laurel Touby, "Congratulations on Your Big Earnings Increase," *Business Week,* August 17, 1992, 58.

2. Dan E. Schendel and Charles W. Hofer, *Strategic Management: A New View of Business Policy and Planning* (Boston: Little, Brown, 1979), 10.

3. F. Gluck, "Strategic Management: An Overview," in *Handbook of Strategic Planning,* ed. J. Gardner, R. Rachlin, and A. Sweeny (New York: John Wiley & Sons, 1986), chap. 1.

4. Tom Peters, *Thriving on Chaos* (New York: Alfred A. Knopf, 1987), 199.

5. "AT&T's Bold Bet," *Business Week,* August 30, 1993, 26–30.

6. Collin Carlson-Thomas, "Strategic Vision or Strategic Con: Rhetoric or Reality?" *Long-Range Planning,* February, 1992, 81–89.

7. Derek F. Abell, *Defining the Business: The Starting Point of Strategic Planning* (Englewood Cliffs, N.J.: Prentice-Hall, 1980), 17.

8. Theodore Levitt, "Marketing Myopia," *Harvard Business Review* (July–August 1960), 45–56.

9. Jerry Knapp, "A Mission Statement," *Firehouse,* March 1992, 70–71.

10. For details, see the "Johnson & Johnson (A)" *Harvard Business School Case #384–053,* Harvard Business School.

11. Corporate Overview, Internal Publication of Federal Express Corporation, 1990, 19.

12. John Templeman and James B. Treece, "BMW's Comeback," *Business Week,* February 14, 1994, 42.

13. John Macmillan, "Managing Suppliers: Incentive Systems in Japanese and U.S. Industry," *California Management Review,* Summer, 1990, 38–55.

14. Jessica Skelly von Brachel, "A High Stakes Bet That Paid Off," *Fortune,* June 15, 1992, 121–22.

15. Kenneth R. Andrews, *The Concept of Corporate Strategy* (Homewood, Ill.: Dow Jones Irwin, 1971); Charles W. Hofer and Dan Schendel, *Strategy Formulation: Analytical Concepts* (St. Paul, Minn.: West Publishing, 1978).

16. Charles W. L. Hill and Gareth R. Jones, *Strategic Management Theory: An Integrated Approach,* 2d ed. (Boston: Houghton Mifflin, 1992).

17. Robin Goldwyn Blumenthal, "Rite Aid Drugstore Chain Plans to Sell Four Units, Take a $91 Million Charge," *Wall Street Journal,* January 10, 1994.

18. John A. Byrne, "The Pain of Downsizing," *Business Week,* May 9, 1994, 61.

19. Michael Porter, *Competitive Advantage* (New York: The Free Press, 1985), 11–14.

20. Fred R. David, *Cases in Strategic Management,* 4th ed. (New York: Macmillan, 1993), 344–64.

21. Douglas Zehr, "In Puerto Rico, Kids "R" Not Us," *Business Week,* February 28, 1994, 8.

CHAPTER 7
Operational Planning

LEARNING OBJECTIVES

After studying this chapter, you should be able to:

- *Define the management by objectives system and review its strengths and weaknesses.*

- *Distinguish between quantitative and qualitative forecasts.*

- *Compare flowcharts, Gantt charts, and PERT networks, and explain their role in scheduling.*

- *Discuss how policies and procedures assist the organization in achieving its strategic goals.*

- *Explain the concept of "loose/tight" in terms of policies and procedures.*

- *Compare zero-based budgeting techniques to the traditional budgeting process.*

- *Describe how budgets are used as strategic tools to involve managers and others in implementing strategy and improving the competitiveness of the organization.*

Once a strategy is chosen, management's next responsibility is to translate it into goals, plans, and operational systems at every level of the organization. This process is referred to as *operational planning.* It is the process of determining in each of the organization's key functional areas how strategy will be translated into action.

An example of the operational planning process is provided by the E. & J. Gallo Winery, which in the mid-1980s decided to diversify its product mix to include wine coolers, a product that is part wine and part soft drink. To translate this strategy into action, a comprehensive marketing plan was developed, which included the creation of the Bartles & Jaymes name, an extensive advertising campaign for the new product, and a sixteen-chapter, three-hundred-page manual of operational procedures for Gallo sales representatives to follow when they met with store owners.[1] Similarly, the production department at Gallo had to develop plans for producing the new beverage and for filling the new sized bottles, which were different from traditional wine bottles. Plans for hiring additional personnel and for training in the new production systems were also developed, and the finance department set projections for income based on the new product's sales and costs. Examples such as this one highlight the chain of events required to put strategies into action.

In essence, once a strategy is formulated or chosen, another planning cycle is set in motion. As shown in Figure 7-1, the operational planning cycle includes the plans, policies, procedures, and budgets that are part of the implementation and control steps of the strategic management process.

In this chapter we will review several techniques and planning tools that are essential for effective operational planning. The former include management by objectives, forecasting, and scheduling; the latter include policies, procedures, and budgets.

MBO: COLLABORATIVE GOAL-SETTING

Management by objectives (MBO) is a system whereby individuals in an organization set goals, identify plans to achieve them and are evaluated based on the results they have achieved. With so many departments, work groups, and individuals involved in implementing an organization's strategy, the potential exists for individuals to pursue goals that are not linked to the overall strategic-level goals. *MBO serves to connect the goals of individuals throughout the organization with the organization's overall strategic goals.*

General Motors is recognized as the first company to have used MBO, and Peter Drucker was the first to describe it.[2] In MBO, a cascade effect occurs as managers and subordinates set goals together. Managers explain the organization's higher-level goals, and subordinates are asked to think about how they can help achieve them. Each subordinate then meets one-to-one with his or her manager and together they identify a set of goals for the subordinate. The activities to achieve the goals are also stated, with needed resources spelled out, as shown in Figure 7-2.

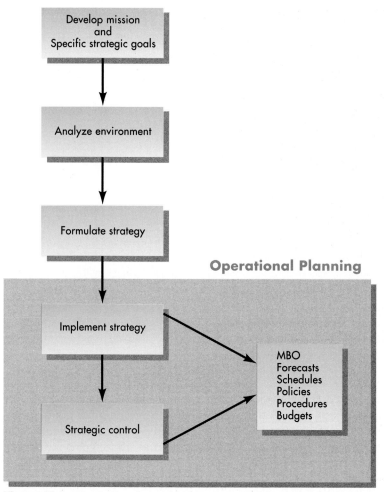

Figure 7-1 The Relationship of Operational Planning to the Strategic Management Process

Managers act as counselors in setting the goals and as coaches in periodically reviewing progress toward them. Finally, each employee's performance is assessed based on his or her level of goal attainment.[3]

The importance and effectiveness of an MBO system is evident in Cypress Semiconductor Corp., a San Jose, California, electronics firm. Cypress president T. J. Rodgers nicknamed his computerized goal system "Turbo MBO." According to Rodgers,

> All of Cypress's 1400 employees have goals, which, in theory, make them no different from employees at most other companies. What makes our people different is that every week they set their own goals, commit to achieving them by a specific date, enter them into a database, and report whether or

Strategic goal:

To reduce customer complaints about quality by 50% during the next 12 months.

Manufacturing goal:

To improve quality assurance skills on all manufacturing teams by having all team members complete training in statistical quality-control methods within 6 months.

To reduce quality problems attributed to raw materials defects by 50% during the next 9 months by instituting a program of inspecting all incoming raw materials at the time of delivery.

Human Resources Department goal:

To complete development of a training program in statistical quality control within 90 days by assigning 1 HR staff member to develop the program.

To complete statistical quality-control training for all manufacturing teams within 6 months by assigning 3 HR staff to provide training.

Figure 7-2 Examples of Goals in an MBO System

not they completed prior goals. Cypress's computerized goal system is an important part of our managerial infrastructure. It is a detailed guide to the future and an objective record of the past. In any given week, some 6000 goals in the database become due. Our ability to meet those goals ultimately determines our success or failure.[4]

When correctly carried out, MBO creates a clear, continuous sense of purpose and strategy throughout the organization by coordinating individual and unit goals with the overall goals of the organization. This enhances teamwork and effectiveness; it ensures that everyone is pulling in the same direction. Continuously evaluating individual goals and plans helps the organization stay on course toward its own long-term strategic goals.

While MBO is valuable for communicating and implementing a wide range of operational plans across a number of different organizational levels, problems do occur with this approach.[5] Basically, the problems arise in the same areas as in any goal-based system, as we discussed in Chapter 4: in management's willingness and ability to negotiate and articulate fully developed goals; in measuring performance where the results or outcomes aren't easily quantified.

In addition to these problems, critics argue that MBO places such great emphasis on goal attainment that it results in employees cutting corners and bending rules just so they can "make their numbers." One example of this might be an account representative at a bank approving loan applicants with questionable credit as a way to reach an MBO goal for new loans. Another might be a production supervisor approving a shipment including some defective units that are likely to be returned just to meet an MBO goal in terms of "on-time" delivery of orders.

It is because of these kinds of problems that W. Edwards Deming, mentioned in Chapter 2 as one of the founders of the quality movement, opposes the use of goal systems such as MBO. Deming says organizations should eliminate management by numbers or numerical goals and should instead substitute leadership. His point is a good one. Without strong leadership to emphasize the importance of goals as a means to improve performance, even simple numerical goals can generate unwanted behavior.

Nevertheless, the evidence is clear that an MBO-type approach to operational planning does help ensure employees' coordinated involvement at every level in developing goals to implement organizational strategy. The challenge for management is to design and operate an MBO system that coordinates individual goals with organizational goals without focusing entirely on "making the numbers."

Finally, MBO works best when employees are both able and willing to participate effectively in this kind of joint goal-setting process. It is essential that employees perceive MBO as a genuine collaborative effort to improve the organization's performance.

FORECASTING

Beyond goal setting and action planning, operational planning also includes forecasting. *Forecasts* are predictions, projections, or estimates about future events. Organizations need to understand as well as they can the future events or conditions that might impact their strategies and plans. There are two kinds of forecasts; quantitative, and qualitative or judgmental.

Quantitative Forecasts

Quantitative forecasts use numerical data and mathematical formulas to project information about future events. This type of forecasting is based on the assumption that the past is a good predictor of the future.

Time Series Analysis

One method of quantitative forecasting is *time series analysis,* which estimates future values based on a sequence of statistical data. For example, organizations often base their sales forecasts on how much was sold during a similar period in the past. Figure 7-3 shows a time series analysis of pizzas sold at a pizza shop. Assuming that the future will be much like the past, the forecast in Figure 7-3 is that sales are expected to increase 11 percent in 1996 over 1995.

Based on this method of predicting future sales, an organization implementing a growth strategy, for example, would be able to plan at what rate to hire more workers, to order supplies, or to expand the operation.

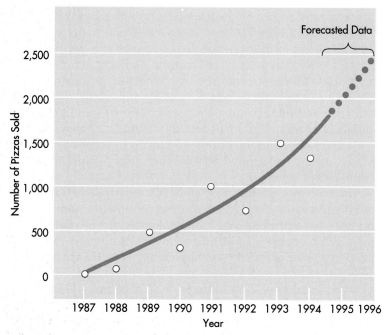

Figure 7-3   Time Series Analysis

Linear Regression

Another quantitative method of forecasting is *linear regression,* which predicts how changes in one variable might be related to changes in another variable. Suppose that sales from the pizza shop are highly dependent on one variable (the student population within a certain area) and on another variable (the total number of employees working at area businesses). Using a mathematical equation and sales information from the existing pizza shop, managers can forecast sales for a proposed new store based on the population of students and the number of employees at businesses in the vicinity.

Figure 7-4 shows a mathematical formula used by McDonald's to forecast, or estimate, the total number of restaurants it could build in a foreign country. The

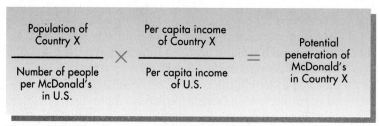

$$\frac{\text{Population of Country X}}{\text{Number of people per McDonald's in U.S.}} \times \frac{\text{Per capita income of Country X}}{\text{Per capita income of U.S.}} = \begin{array}{c}\text{Potential penetration of McDonald's in Country X}\end{array}$$

Figure 7-4   Quantitative Forecasting at McDonald's

formula divides a country's population by the number of people per store and adjusts for differences in per capita income.[6]

Qualitative Forecasts

When the past is not a good predictor of the future, as when many environmental variables are changing, or when time does not permit the gathering and analyzing of quantitative data, qualitative forecasting methods are frequently used.[7] *Qualitative techniques* rely more on individual or group judgment or opinion to predict future events, rather than mathematical or statistical analysis.

The *Delphi Method* is one such qualitative technique. In the Delphi Method, input is solicited from a variety of experts who provide opinions on an individual basis. Their separate opinions are then gathered, evaluated and summarized, and form the basis of a forecast. Suppose a timetable is being forecasted for the sale of high-density televisions to consumers nationwide. High-density televisions (HDTV) are not widely available yet, but they provide a significantly better picture image than conventional televisions. For this situation, participants in the Delphi forecast might include experts in HDTV technology, executives in the television industry, and university market researchers. The experts are asked anonymously to predict a time frame for when HDTV is likely to become widely available for sale to customers. Persons coordinating the Delphi group collect the responses, average them, and ask for another opinion. Those experts who provide predictions in the first round that are significantly different from the others are asked to justify them. When the predictions get more and more similar, the average prediction is taken and becomes the group's forecast.

Other qualitative techniques for forecasting future events include opinion surveys of executives, sales forces, and consumers. In each case, individual judgments are combined to generate information about the timing and other details of future events and about conditions in the environment essential to the organization's strategy.

Frequently, qualitative and quantitative forecasts are combined. At L'Eggs Products, for example, forecasts reflect both the marketing group's qualitative opinions and observations and statistical (quantitative) analysis of past trends.[8] Together, quantitative and qualitative forecasting are important tools for organizations desiring to develop detailed plans to implement larger strategies.

SCHEDULING

In addition to forecasting techniques, which are used to anticipate future conditions, a number of other tools are available for use in actually planning future activities. Flowcharts, Gantt charts, and PERT charts are three widely used tools for scheduling the activities that must be accomplished to implement an organization's strategies.

Flowcharts

Flowcharts were once thought to be the tool only of computer programmers, who used them for sequencing the instructions required to allow the computer program to operate correctly. Increasingly, flowcharts are being used as visual aids for analyzing and planning the sequence of significant events that must occur if a series of activities is to be successful in achieving its goals. Flowcharting assures that the key events and options are all provided for and that they are designed to take place in the order or sequence that makes the most sense. For example, the event "Shop for a new car" would come before the event "Purchase a new car" in a flowchart sequence. As shown in Figure 7-5, a flowchart consists of boxes that signify events and diamonds that indicate a yes or no decision. Start or stop ovals are also part of the diagram. In Figure 7-5, the sequence of events for sending a patient from the emergency department of a hospital for X-rays is shown.

Flowcharting is a good way to look closely at what is actually going on at each step or stage of a particular operation. At each stage, the question "Why?" is asked. Why is a step performed? Could the process be more efficient? For example, in Figure 7-5, if a computer form is not available for the patient, the information must be recorded by hand. Could this be corrected to include direct computer processing at this point? Managers at all levels can identify and sequence important events and decisions with flowcharts. Since all relevant links in a process are spelled out, flowcharts can encourage analytical thinking by everyone in an organization.

However, flowcharts do not include time dimensions. They show only the order or sequence of the activities to be completed, not the time required to complete them. The key variable of time is added to the scheduling process through the Gantt chart.

Gantt Charts

Gantt charts are one of the most commonly used graphic scheduling tools. Developed by Henry L. Gantt,[9] these charts show the significant activities required to meet an objective or to complete a project, with the events arranged in chronological order and the amount of time allotted for each activity.

The application of Gantt charts is widespread, from coordinating large projects to scheduling everyday activities. Figure 7-6 is a sample Gantt chart for a company building tennis rackets. The shaded areas indicate completed activities. Managers also can use Gantt charts for progress reports. In this example, note that steps 8 through 10 are yet to be finished.

Like flowcharts, Gantt charts require analytical thinking, as they reduce projects or jobs to separate steps. They have the additional advantages of allowing planners to specify the time to be spent on each activity and of tracking the progress toward completion of activities. Gantt charts are especially useful for scheduling activities that happen sequentially.

The disadvantage of both flowcharts and Gantt charts is that they are not effective for scheduling complex situations where hundreds of activities, some occurring simultaneously, must be scheduled and monitored. For these kinds of more complex applications, PERT charts are more effective.

PERT Charts

PERT, which stands for program evaluation and review technique, is a graphic scheduling tool for large, complex, nonroutine projects. The technique was devel-

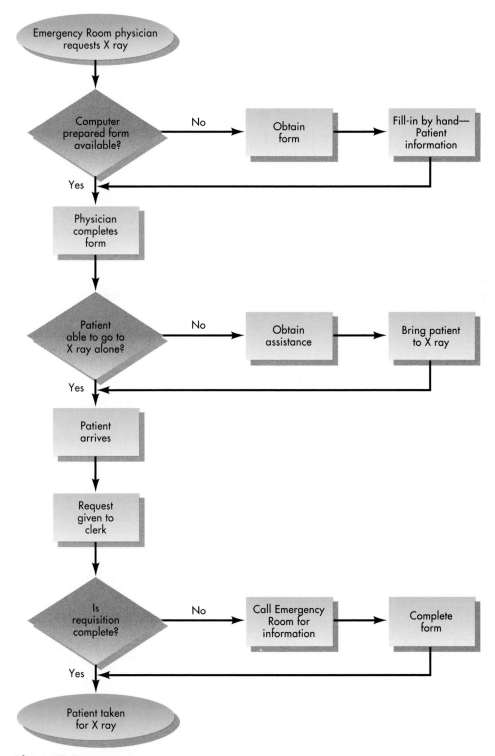

Figure 7-5 Emergency Room Radiology Process

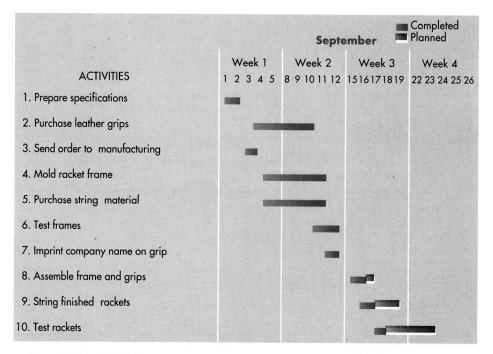

Figure 7-6 GANTT Chart for Manufacturing 100 Tennis Rackets

oped in 1958 by a team of management consultants for the U.S. Navy. Not only did this technique contribute to the development of the Polaris submarine project, but it caught the attention of managers around the world for use in their organizations.[10]

The PERT symbols and terminology are slightly different from those shown in the flowchart system. In PERT, an event that represents the start or finish of an activity is a circle. A square represents work in progress. Activities are thus time-consuming jobs that begin and end with an event. Figure 7-7 shows the activities

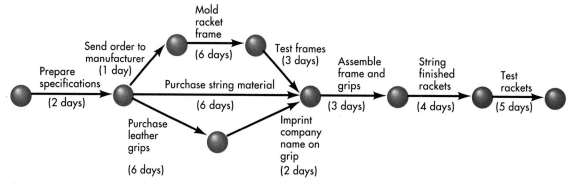

Figure 7-7 A Simplified PERT Chart for Manufacturing Tennis Rackets

involved in the manufacture of tennis rackets using a PERT chart. Note that there are time estimates for each PERT activity. Planners pinpoint the *critical path,* or most time-consuming chain of activities and events in the network. The longest path is the most critical because any delays will cause a delay of the entire project. In Figure 7-7, the longest path is twenty-four days. Any delays in that path will affect the scheduled completion date of the project.

This example is intentionally simplified for instructional purposes. PERT charts are actually most often utilized, as we said, for projects with hundreds of activities. They allow management to predict resource needs, identify potential problem areas, and assess the impact of delays at any given point in one project that might affect the other project phases and the overall project completion time.

THE COMPUTER AS A PLANNING TOOL

Computer software packages that can be loaded on a personal computer are making the job of forecasting and scheduling easier. Data for time series forecasts and regression equations can be stored on computer spreadsheets, such as LOTUS, Quattro Pro, and Excel. Many of these spreadsheets not only generate the forecasts for future periods but also transform the data into graphics, such as the chart shown in Figure 7-3. The dBase package is another software option that allows the user to store and retrieve large quantities of data for use in forecasting.

In terms of scheduling, computer software packages now enable the user simply to input events, activities, and timetables, depending on the type of schedule desired. The computer then generates the flowchart, GANTT chart, or PERT network of projects and activities as needed. An excellent example of computer-assisted planning is at the International Benchmarking Clearinghouse in Houston, which uses its database to store benchmarks of the best practices and how-to guidelines of businesses in every industry. Members of the Clearinghouse can then obtain these benchmark standards directly from the database, and either adopt or modify these benchmarks for their own plans. Similarly, as noted earlier in the chapter, Cypress Semiconductor Corporation uses a database to keep track of its fourteen hundred employees' goals that are stored and retrieved from the database on a weekly basis.

As software for computers becomes more user friendly and as personal computers become more portable, these computerized tools will greatly enhance management's ability to forecast and monitor key activities and work processes throughout the organization.

DEVELOPING GUIDELINES FOR IMPLEMENTING ORGANIZATIONAL STRATEGY

The first steps, then, in the implementation phase of the planning process are to identify and schedule the essential events and activities necessary to implement the organization's strategy. Once this is done, management's attention turns to developing the policies, procedures, and budgets that are the organization's guidelines as it implements its strategies.

Policies and procedures, and even budgets to a certain extent, are often viewed simply as the "rules" of the organization. In fact, however, each is a goal, a standard, or a target in terms of how the organization and its members should conduct themselves in order to achieve the organization's overall strategic goals.

Policies

Policies are guidelines for decisions. They provide standards for how decisions should be made in key areas throughout the organization. Policies in the human resources area, for example, guide decision making in hiring, compensation, promotion, and other key areas. Policies for customer service may guide decisions regarding the return of merchandise or the method of handling customer complaints.

Policies serve two purposes. One, as we have already indicated, is to ensure that decisions in the organization are consistent with the organization's strategic goals. Strategies heading in one direction, when combined with decisions reflecting a different course, are a disaster for an organization. For this reason large Japanese companies, for example, traditionally supported their strategy of high worker commitment with a policy of lifetime employment for their workers. They knew that to achieve their strategic goal of a highly committed, highly involved workforce, their employment decisions must reflect the high commitment of the company to the worker. More recently, however, as companies in Japan have shifted their strategic goals to focus more on greater flexibility and a smaller workforce, the policy of lifetime employment has also changed. For the first time in generations, workers at large Japanese corporations are being laid off.

Similarly, when the Bay City, Michigan, General Motors parts assembly plant shifted to a high-worker-involvement strategy, one policy it developed to implement this plan was that workers would move into self-managing teams only on a volunteer basis. The manager of that facility knew that a policy that forced people onto teams would be contrary to the strategic goal of obtaining the workers' genuine commitment to their work. This consistency between the unit's strategic goals and operating policies was an important part of the dramatic turnaround that resulted in that facility remaining in operation rather than closing down, as had been feared, for poor quality and inefficiency.

The other purpose of policies is to ensure a reasonable degree of consistency throughout the organization in the ways decisions are made. In the chapter on decision making we pointed our that decisions tend to reflect the personality, values and experience level of the decision maker. Policies can offset this built-in idiosyncratic tendency by establishing guidelines to ensure consistency regardless of who is making the decision. Policies increase the likelihood that decisions will reflect the larger strategic goals of the organization rather than just the personality or individual goals of the decision maker.

Finally, it bears repeating that policies are intended to serve as *guidelines* for decisions, not as absolute rules. In their research on America's excellent companies, Peters and Waterman found that one key characteristic of these companies was the property they described as "loose/tight." According to Tom Peters and Robert H. Waterman, America's most successful corporations tend to be very specific, very "tight," in terms of goals for various units throughout the organization and in terms of how they measure performance toward these goals. But they also tend to be very "loose" in terms of defining how these goals should be achieved.[11] Managers throughout the organization tend to be allowed a fair degree of flexibility in how they interpret and implement decision policies.

As the rate of change continues to accelerate for organizations, it seems reasonable to expect that the importance of this "loose/tight" duality in terms of policies will increase. The challenge for managers in the area of policies will be to balance the need for consistency in decisions with the need for flexibility to ensure that decisions truly support and further the organization's strategic goals.

Procedures

Procedures are guidelines for how tasks in the organizations are to be performed. You may remember that for Frederick Taylor and scientific management, the focus was on management's defining and training workers in the most effective procedure for performing each task. A well-developed set of work procedures can serve as a kind of road map guiding the efforts of individuals throughout the organization.

UPS, the package shipping giant, is a strong believer in the importance of procedures. Drivers for UPS receive rigorous training in the procedures the company has developed to maximize their efficiency. The procedure for every drop-off or pickup is the same: The driver is to unbuckle the seat belt, sound the horn, and turn off the engine as the truck glides to a stop. The emergency brake is then secured and the gearshift is slipped into first gear so the truck is ready for departure after the stop. The driver steps to the ground right foot first, clipboard under the right arm and the package under the left. Keys are carried teeth up on the middle finger of the right hand. Only one look is permitted at the address on the package, and the driver moves at three feet per second. This may be an example of procedure taken to the extreme, but UPS views these procedures as essential to its strategy of efficient, consistent quality service.[12]

In fact, operational procedures have come to be viewed more and more not just as guidelines to ensure efficiency in the way tasks are done, but as a potential source of strategic advantage as well. McDonald's, for example, has a six-hundred-page operating manual detailing the procedures for preparing, cooking, and serving every item on its menu.[13] A hamburger, for example, is always prepared the same way: After the hamburger is placed on the bun, first mustard is applied, then ketchup, then onions and two pickles. These highly detailed procedures assure McDonald's the consistency of product and speed of service that allow them to maintain their significant edge over Burger King and the rest of the fast-food competition.

The Saturn division of General Motors has demonstrated just how powerful appropriate procedures can be. To implement its strategy of becoming "a different kind of automobile company," Saturn instituted a procedure of "no haggling" over the price of its automobiles. The price is posted on each automobile, and unlike the procedure for every other nameplate in the United States, the sales procedure for Saturn allows for no negotiation in terms of price. The haggling over price had become such an unpleasant part of the car-buying experience for Americans that when Saturn implemented its policy of no haggling, it achieved a significant strategic advantage over its competitors. People began to go to Saturn simply because they knew they would not be forced to negotiate a final price.

Not surprisingly, the challenge in terms of developing effective procedures is not a simple one. Management's job is not, as Frederick Taylor suggested, just to define the most efficient way to perform each task. Today's environment is too complicated for such a simplistic approach. First and foremost, tasks are becoming increasingly complex. Fewer and fewer tasks are of the assembly-line variety of years ago that lent themselves to the "step 1, step 2, step 3" approach. How, for example, can management define the most appropriate procedures for solving a customer's problem or for building creativity into a group decision?

Second, in developing procedures as in developing policies, flexibility is key. As increased speed and improved customer service become important strategic goals, individuals need to have the flexibility to perform the required tasks in whatever way is most appropriate to meet the needs of the particular customer or situation. To be effective in the emerging environment, procedures must be viewed as guidelines supporting the efforts of individuals and groups to do their work, not as obstacles preventing them from responding to the special requirements of customers and conditions. It appears that procedures, like policies, must be "loose/tight"—specific enough for consistency and efficiency, flexible enough for responsiveness to nontypical situations. Nordstrom, the department store chain, provides an interesting example of the "loose/tight" approach in the statement it issues to all new employees, shown in Figure 7-8.[14]

Like policies, procedures or work rules must point the individual in the right direction, but leave room for creativity and judgment in terms of the details of how to get there.

Budgets

Budgets are guidelines indicating how an organization intends to allocate its financial resources. Budgets are plans that spell out in what areas an organization expects to spend its money, and how much. Like policies and procedures, to be most effective budgets need to reflect the strategic goals of the organization. Sam Walton, for example, the founder of Wal-Mart, always set a budget limit of 2 percent of sales to be spent on operating the company's corporate offices. This meant that the salaries and expenses involved in running the company were intended to be no more than 2 percent of the company's revenues. An important part of Wal-Mart's low-cost strategy is to compete on the basis of price, and Walton was convinced an important element of that strategy was to keep expenses as low as possible in every area of the budget.

Similarly, the Saturn division of GM knew that reaching its strategic goals would require a team-based work design. Saturn also realized that this kind of work design required a highly trained workforce. To make sure it has the resources required to complete this training, Saturn's budget allocation for training

- Our number one goal is to provide outstanding customer service.

- Nordstrom Rules

    Rule #1: Use your good judgment in all situations.

    There will be no additional rules.

Figure 7-8 Nordstrom's Statement to New Employees

is much higher than the industry average. Saturn's budget for management positions, on the other hand, is probably much lower, reflecting its strategy of using self-managing teams.

Zero-Based Budgeting and Budgets as Strategic Tools

One of the techniques used to ensure that budgets reflect the most current strategic goals is called "zero-based budgeting."[15] In the traditional approach to budgeting for an upcoming year, managers begin with the existing budget, justify any changes that might be needed, and then add or subtract from the existing budget amounts. In *zero-based budgeting*, on the other hand, managers start each year from zero and justify each expenditure in terms of its contribution to the organization's strategic plan, rather than simply explaining changes from the previous budget.

This approach of starting with a "blank sheet of paper" ensures that budgets remain focused and timely tools for implementing strategy.

In addition to reflecting and supporting strategy, budgets—like policies and procedures—can also be an important source of strategic advantage. In the early 1990s, more and more organizations began to be forced to compete on the basis of lower cost. To implement this strategy, organization leaders reduced budgets drastically and then left it to the discretion of managers in the affected units to determine how to do the same work with significantly fewer financial resources. For example, a manager might receive a budget for next year that is 20 percent lower than the budget for the current year. It is up to the manager to meet that budget, by either reducing the number of people working in the unit or in some other way reducing the unit's expenses. One benefit of this approach is that it results in much greater discipline on the part of managers in allocating their financial resources. In previous years, managers could avoid having to choose between funding two positions or two projects—they would do both. Now, with budgets being used as cost-cutting tools, managers must choose one—hopefully, the better—option.

Strategic budgeting also tends to result in more creative solutions that accomplish the same work with reduced funding. Managers looking to avoid completely eliminating positions or projects that they consider essential find ways of continuing them by combining or sharing resources.

The strategic budgeting approach has been criticized for resulting in planning that is more budget driven than strategy driven. The concern is that managers are forced to choose alternatives that may be unwise in the long run in order to meet the reduced budget goals for a given year. Costs may be lowered by reducing a company's research and development budget, for example. But in the long term that may leave the company without the new products or innovations that are critical to its future.

While this criticism is certainly understandable, the fact remains that most organizations must find ways to become more cost-effective if they are to compete in the changing environment. Management's challenge is one of balance: to intelligently reduce budgets while at the same time ensuring that the decisions made to meet the strict budget targets are consistent with the organization's longer-term strategic goals.

We should also point out that budgets have begun to have strategic value beyond their impact on management discipline and creativity. Organizations that have shared budget information with their workforces have found it to be a powerful tool for increasing worker understanding of the financial condition of the business. More importantly, as their understanding of the organization's finances increases, the workforce in general begins to display the same discipline and creativity in terms of spending that we have seen in managers.

An example of the power of sharing budgetary and other financial information is seen at Springfield Remanufacturing Corp. SRC was once the engine-rebuilding unit of International Harvester. Since 1983, SRC has been owned by its employees and run by a system it calls "The Great Game of Business." Employees are trained to understand every aspect of the company's budgets and other financial information. This enables them to closely follow weekly financial statements and to compare actual figures to projections. Jack Stack, the CEO of SRC, who also invented the game, is convinced of the value of sharing budgetary and other financial information throughout the organization. "The more people understand, the more they want to see the results."[16] The experience at SRC is clear: Workers who understand and can see how costs affect the organization's profitability become aggressive waste-cutters and rich sources of creative ideas for reducing costs and expenditures.

SUMMARY

This chapter focuses on the implementation phase of the strategic management process: on translating strategy into action. A number of the elements of this process are discussed.

Management by objectives (MBO) is a system used to translate the strategic goals of an organization into more specific goals for managers, teams, and individuals. Operated effectively, MBO ensures that efforts throughout the organization are targeted toward the achievement of the organization's strategic goals.

Once more-specific goals have been targeted through processes like MBO, forecasting and scheduling become critical activities for understanding and planning the conditions and activities necessary for implementing strategy. Forecasting generates predictions and projections about when key events might take place in the organization's environment. Scheduling ensures the effective identification and sequencing of key activities within the organization. Together, forecasting and scheduling address the timing concerns in terms of implementing strategy. Computer-assisted forecasting and scheduling make both these processes even easier and more effective.

Finally, policies, procedures, and budgets are important tools for ensuring that behavior throughout the organization is consistent with the organization's strategic goal. Policies are guidelines for decisions, procedures are guidelines for action, and budgets are guidelines for the allocation of financial resources. Each must be specific enough to ensure consistency with strategic goals, yet flexible enough to allow responsiveness to changing conditions. Policies, procedures, and budgets each make a unique contribution in terms of keeping the organization on course as it implements its strategy for achieving its mission.

QUESTIONS TO CHALLENGE YOUR UNDERSTANDING OF THE CHAPTER

1. Your professor has established an average grade of B for students on the next test. Using Figure 7-2 as a model, develop a set of MBO-type goals that would help you achieve this target grade.

2. Compare the strengths and weaknesses of the MBO system.

3. Whom would you place on a Delphi panel of experts predicting what features will be included on automobiles ten years from now? Explain your selections.

4. What product's sales could be forecast on a quantitative basis? Identify two variables that might be used in a linear regression equation to forecast sales of this product. Summarize the difference between quantitative and qualitative forecasts.

5. Describe the attendance or test makeup policy for one of your courses. Does it satisfy the need for consistency and flexibility?

6. Explain zero-based budgeting. How does it differ from the traditional budgeting process?

7. Describe the Great Game of Business developed by Springfield Remanufacturing Corp., and explain its effect on the organization's performance.

MANAGEMENT EXERCISE

Flowchart Diagram

1. Using the diagram in Figure 7-5 as a guide, draw a flowchart that depicts the process for registering for courses at your school. Begin with the notification you receive about the upcoming registration period and continue through the steps until your courses are confirmed.

2. Are there any parts of the process that could be improved? Does the flowchart help to identify areas for improvement?

REFERENCES

1. J. Fierman, "How Gallo Crushes the Competition," *Fortune*, September 1, 1986, 24–31.

2. Peter F. Drucker, *The Practice of Management* (New York: Harper & Bros., 1954).

3. For readings on MBO, see George Odiorne, Heinz Weihrich, and Jack Mendleson, *Executive Skills: A Management by Objective Approach* (Dubuque, Iowa: Wm. C. Brown, 1980).

4. T. J. Rodgers, "No Excuses Management," *Harvard Business Review* 68, (July–August 1990): 87, 89.

5. The negative and positive aspects of MBO are discussed in Robert C. Ford and Frank S. McLaughlin, "Avoiding Disappointment in MBO Programs," *Human Resource Management* 21 (Summer 1982): 44–49. Also, see Robert C. Ford, Frank S. McLaughlin, and James Nixdorf, "Ten Questions about MBO," *California Management Review*, Winter 1980, 84–89; and Jack N. Kondrasuk, "Studies in MBO Effectiveness," *Academy of Management Review*, July 1981, 265–339.

6. Andrew E. Serwer, "McDonald's Conquers the World," *Fortune*, October 17, 1994, 104.

7. Nada R. Sanders and Larry P. Ritzman, "On Knowing When to Switch from Quantitative to Judgmental Forecasts," *Interfaces International Journal of Operations and Production Management* 6 (1991): 27–37.

8. Barbara R. Michel, "Improving the Forecasting Process at L'Eggs Products," *Journal of Business Forecasting*, Winter 1991–1992, 26, 30.

9. Henry L. Gantt, *Organizing for Work* (New York: Harcourt, Brace & Howe, 1919), chap. 8.

10. Ivars Avots, "The Management Side of PERT," *California Management Review* 41 (Winter 1962): 16–27.

11. Thomas J. Peters and Robert H. Waterman, Jr., *In Search of Excellence* (New York: Harper & Row, 1982).

12. Todd Vogel and Chuck Hawking, "Can UPS Deliver the Goods in a New World?" *Business Week*, June 4, 1990, 80–82.

13. Lois Therrien, "McRisky," *Business Week,* October 21, 1991, 115.

14. Thomas J. Peters and Nancy Austin, *A Passion for Excellence* (New York: Random House, 1985).

15. Peter A. Phyrr, "Zero-Base Budgeting," *Harvard Business Review* (November/December 1970), 111–21; Linda J. Shinn and M. Sue Sturgeon, "Budgeting from Ground Zero," *Association Management,* September 1990, 45–48.

16. John Case, *"A Company of Businesspeople,"* INC, April 1993, 86.

FROM THE MANAGER'S E-MAIL
The "Pay for Skills" Program at Granger Foods

It's decision time. You are the owner of Granger Foods, a specialty meats company that produces gourmet hams, sausages, and other meat specialties. For the past several years your goal has been to get all of the people who work for Granger to become more personally involved in making the company successful. You are convinced that only when your workforce is fully involved will Granger be able to achieve the level of quality, price, and customer service that will allow the company to succeed in the highly competitive gourmet meats business.

The decision that confronts you is how to make Granger's pay policy consistent with this strategy. One option you have been considering is called "pay for skills." In this approach, an individual can receive a pay increase only by successfully completing training in a specific skill area. Your hourly wage workers—for example, your meat processors and packagers—would increase their pay by 50 cents an hour for completing training in statistical quality control, 50 cents an hour for training in group problem solving, 50 cents an hour for training in team leadership, 50 cents an hour for training in reading financial statements, and so on.

In two weeks, you are to announce the annual increase, so if you're going to make any changes now is the time. You have set a deadline of next Monday for deciding about a pay system, and you will start today by reviewing the E-mail you have received from two of your most trusted managers.

Date:	November 14, 1995
From:	LOCALSYS (John Starks, Manager of Human Resources)
Subject:	Pay-for-Skills Program

I reviewed your pay-for-skills proposal with great interest. As you know, our people are used to getting an across-the-board increase each year, so it would take some getting used to on their part. In my judgment, your plan has at least four major advantages:

1. First and foremost, it provides a strong incentive for our people to increase their skills. You and I both know that we're going to demand continuously improving performance from our people just to maintain our market share. I suppose we could just require the training for everyone, but I know that's not consistent with your goals, and I also don't think we'd get what we want in terms of motivation during the training.

2. I know that not everyone will need all of the training immediately. But as enough people complete enough of the training, we can begin to have our teams become self-managing. I know that's part of your goal, and over the long term we won't have to pay a separate group of individuals to do the managing. So from that perspective, I think it's important to view the new system as a long-term investment.

3. Even if everyone doesn't use all of the skills they've been trained in, just having the skills will allow them to participate more fully in making this company productive.

4. Frankly, I just don't think any company can afford to give raises to everyone anymore just because it's been a year since the last increase.

I know there are good arguments against pay-for-skills, but I just believe the pluses far outweigh the minuses. Let me know if there's anything more I can do to help with your thinking about this.

Date: November 13, 1995

From: LOCALSYS (Maria Ruiz, Manager of Accounting and Finance)

Subject: Pay-for-Skills Proposal

I completed reading your pay-for-skills proposal last week, but
I wanted to take some time to think about it. You asked for my
reaction, and I want to be totally honest with you. You make
excellent arguments for the proposal, but I think pay-for-skills
would be a mistake for Granger. My conclusion is based on
research I've done on other companies that have tried this
approach. My research suggests that there have been at least
three problems with what you're suggesting:

1. You'll be paying for skills that won't necessarily be used.
Even under your long-term plan to move to self-managing teams,
not everyone will need all of these skills. But everyone will
take the training because that's the only way to get a raise.
All that will happen is we'll increase payroll and training
costs unnecessarily.

2. People will become frustrated having new skills that they
might never have the opportunity to use. It could be years
before many of our people have the chance to apply even some of
this training.

3. Most of these skills are exactly what we're paying our
managers for. I'm not really sure we can afford to pay two
groups of people for the same set of skills, especially when one
group isn't even using the skills.

I apologize for seeming so negative about this, but I feel I owe
it to you to play devil's advocate on this issue. I just think

---

it sends the wrong message when we preach employee involvement.

We provide the training for that involvement, and then there

are limited opportunities to actually get involved and use the

skills developed. Obviously, though, you have my support either

way.

Both of these managers make good arguments. As you consider your decision, your only concerns are (a) how best to implement your strategy of high employee involvement, and (b) how most responsibly to utilize the financial and human resources of the company.

1. Would you implement pay-for-skills at Granger Foods? Explain the reasons for your decision.

2. If you answered yes to question 1, what procedures might you suggest to minimize the potential negative effects of pay-for-skills described in the E-mail memo from Maria Ruiz?

3. If you answered no to question 1, what alternatives might you suggest so that the pay policy at Granger is consistent with the strategy of high employee involvement in making the company successful?

SECTION

IV

Organizing for Performance

The planning process is only the beginning of the management responsibility. Once the organization has achieved a clear sense of direction and developed strategies for pursuing its goals, management needs to structure the organization to implement these strategies. How the organization arranges and groups its people and how the actual work of the organization is designed are critical factors in the success or failure of its strategies. Designing or structuring the organization to effectively implement its strategies is the "organizing" responsibility of management.

There are two dimensions to the organizing responsibility. The first has to do with creating and coordinating the various work units necessary to implement the organization's strategies. This includes creating the different departments or divisions necessary to do the various kinds of work the organization needs done—sales and marketing, for example, or finance and accounting. **Chapter 8** describes the elements of this responsibility and traces how organizations have continually redesigned their structures in response to the performance challenges of the twentieth century and beyond.

The other dimension of the organizing responsibility has to do with the way work is performed within the different departments and work units of the organization. **Chapter 9** describes how task specialization came to be the dominant model for the design of work during the twentieth century, and how, as we indicated in Chapter 1, teamwork has begun to replace task specialization in the changing workplace.

Together, these chapters show the continuing impact of the changing environment on the organizing responsibility, both in terms of how organizations are designed and how work is performed. Together, they make clear just how important the organizing responsibility is for the successful performance of organizations.

CHAPTER 8
Designing the Organization

LEARNING OBJECTIVES

After studying this chapter, you should be able to:

- *Discuss Edgar Schein's four essential elements of organizational design.*

- *Explain the fifth element of effective design: Structure follows strategy.*

- *Describe the bureaucracy model of organizational design, how it contributes to organizational performance, and its limitations.*

- *Compare the functional organizational model to the various forms of divisional organization structure.*

- *Define a conglomerate structure and discuss its advantages and disadvantages.*

- *Differentiate among the three different models of flexible organizational structure: matrix organization, horizontal organization, network organization.*

- *Discuss the contingency view of organizational design.*

Perhaps no development in the business world in the early 1990s was more surprising than the possibility that IBM might no longer be able to compete. For more than a generation IBM had been one of the most successful and admired companies in the world. Yet in a single year, IBM went from a $6 billion profit to a loss of nearly $3 billion.[1] It appeared that IBM had become too big and too slow to meet the challenges of the changing environment. And it wasn't just IBM. Similar patterns had already been seen at Sears and at General Motors and at any number of other one-time stars of the American economy. IBM was just the brightest star at the time, and it seemed to have dimmed most quickly.

Most interesting from a management studies point of view was the fact that nearly all of the solutions being suggested for IBM were organizational design solutions. The consensus was that IBM was too large to be flexible and responsive in a rapidly changing market, and the solution most often suggested was that IBM should reorganize itself, perhaps into nine or ten smaller companies.

In fact, much of the effort of organizations to prepare themselves for the challenges of the changing environment and the twenty-first century have centered around reorganization. The 1990s have seen organizations of every kind seeking to improve performance by improving the way they define and coordinate the units that do the work necessary for their success. We will take a more detailed look at these most recent efforts to organize for performance, but first some background is necessary.

THE ESSENTIAL ELEMENTS IN THE DESIGN OF ORGANIZATIONS

Edgar Schein, a prominent organizational theorist, suggests that four essential elements must be present for an organization to function effectively: common goals, division of work, coordination of effort, and authority structure.[2] According to Schein's model, if any of these elements are missing or poorly designed, the organization is unlikely to be successful in implementing its strategies and pursuing its mission.

Common Goals

Common goals, as we have seen in Chapter 4, provide the sense of direction, the target to aim for, and the basis of cooperation that are critical for the success of any organization. Without goals as a focus for its efforts, the energy of the organization would be wasted on random activities toward no particular end. It would be like playing football without goalposts or end zones.

And as we have seen in Chapters 6 and 7, planning is the process of developing goals and strategies to achieve the organization's mission. Schein's point is that you have to know where you are going (mission and goals) and how you're going to get there (strategy) before you can design a structure to take you there. To use an analogy, you need to know which event you're trying to win in a track meet and your strategy for winning that event before you can design a training program to prepare you for the race. The first essential element, then, in designing an effective organization is shared or common goals—from mission to strategic goals to policies and procedures.

Division of Work

Common goals alone, however, are not enough. Once the organization's mission and strategic and operational goals are clear, the work necessary to achieve those goals must be divided up in the most productive way possible. This is what management has been struggling with for more than one hundred years: how to group and divide all of the tasks, all of the work done in the organization for maximum productivity.

Following this overview of Schein's four key elements of organization, much of the chapter focuses on what management has learned during the past century about how most effectively to divide up work in organizations.

Coordination of Effort

Logically speaking, if the work of an organization is divided among several separate units or departments, it is essential that there be effective coordination among them. Coordination is critical to ensure that the work being done within each unit is consistent with the overall goals of the organization.

It is also important to ensure that these units are not working at cross-purposes with one another. For example, it makes no sense for the research and development unit to design a product which the sales and marketing unit knows will be difficult to sell and which the production unit knows will be very expensive to manufacture. Coordination is necessary among all three units to ensure that the product which is developed both is appealing to the customer and can be produced profitably.

A comprehensive network of goals is the starting point for this kind of coordination, but goals are not enough. There must also be a steady flow of communication among the various units of an organization to ensure that the coordination of efforts is continuous and effective. Later in the chapter we will describe a number of approaches taken by management to achieve and maintain effective coordination.

Authority Structure

The fourth of Schein's elements of effective organization is authority structure. *Authority* is often defined as the right to direct the actions of others.[3] Organizations, as we have said, are collections of individuals who share common goals. However, sharing common goals does not mean that they will also agree on what must be done in order to achieve them, or on who must do it. For this reason, authority—the right to direct the actions of others—is a key element in designing an organization. For an organization to succeed there must be an authority structure, what Fayol would call a "chain of command," to define the goals, to divide the work, and to require coordination to the extent that others will accept and follow this direction. An organization without an effective authority structure is like an individual without discipline: the goals and plans may be in place, but without the ability to require action, not much is likely to get accomplished.

For most of this century, authority was assumed to be most effective when it rested in the hands of managers at the top of the organization, the executives. It was assumed that only the people at the highest levels of the organization had the education and information necessary to exercise authority responsibly. Over the past twenty years, however, there has been a variety of efforts to move authority out across the organization and to distribute it among the managers of the various departments and divisions. More recently, authority has begun to move down through the organization as well, in some cases to teams of workers who now have the right to direct their own actions. For example, at the General Electric factory at Bayamon, Puerto Rico, every hourly worker is on a ten-person team. Teams are responsible for assembly, shipping, and receiving, as they have always been. However, now they have been given authority to make decisions on how to improve performance in these areas as well. A supervisor-advisor remains available but participates only if the team needs help.[4] This pattern of distributing authority throughout the organization is called *decentralization.*

Decentralization

As shown in Figure 8-1, there is a range of options available in terms of decentralization. The overall trend, however, has been toward greater decentralization. As we will see in the sections ahead, in response to the increasing demands of the changing environment, organizations have expanded and become much more complex, with increasing numbers of departments and divisions. For such complex organizations to be effective, authority cannot remain in the hands only of the top-level executives. Authority to make decisions must be distributed throughout the organization so that decisions can be made on a timely and focused basis. General Electric, as we said earlier, operates 350 business units in thirteen different industries or business groups, and each unit is required to be

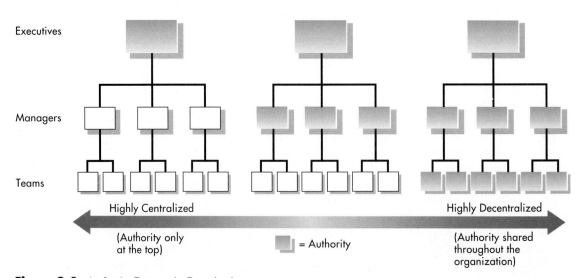

Figure 8-1 Authority Patterns in Organizations

either first or second in terms of market share in its field. To pursue that strategic goal, the managers of each of these 350 units are given the authority necessary to make their units responsive to the changing environment. For GE, the results of this decentralization of authority have been very positive. Motorola, AT&T, UPS, and many other organizations have achieved similar results, all using a highly decentralized authority structure.[5]

There can be problems with decentralization, however. The more authority distributed among the organization's various departments and divisions, the more difficult it is to ensure coordination and consistency throughout the organization. In the 1980s, for example, in an effort to encourage creativity and innovation, Apple Computer took a highly decentralized approach, delegating broad levels of authority to each of its various units and divisions. Unfortunately, these various units failed to coordinate their efforts, which in turn resulted in overspent budgets and missed delivery deadlines.

One solution to the problem of coordination and consistency is an approach practiced by many of America's most successful businesses. They are highly centralized in terms of setting goals for the organization's many units, but decentralized when it comes to deciding how the goals are achieved.[6] This is consistent with the "loose/tight" principle discussed in Chapter 7. The key to developing an effective authority structure is balance: Authority must be centralized enough to ensure consistency and coordination, and decentralized enough to provide for timely and focused decisions and action by managers in the various units of the organization. It is management's responsibility in designing the organization to ensure that this balance in terms of authority is effectively achieved and maintained.

Schein's four elements of organizational design clearly are essential for the success of an organization. Without common goals, effective division of work, coordination of effort, and authority structure, an organization is unlikely to achieve its purpose. In a sense, Schein's elements are like a chain that is only as strong as its weakest link.

But while these four elements are essential, more is needed to ensure that the design of an organization will be effective. Management historian Alfred D. Chandler suggests what might be termed a fifth element of effective organizational design: Structure follows strategy.

A Fifth Element of Design: Structure Follows Strategy

Early in the 1960s, after studying such successful (at that time) U.S. corporations as Sears, GM, DuPont, and others, management historian Alfred Chandler identified what appeared to be a pattern common to all these companies: Management had designed the organization to pursue specific strategies. This pattern he described as "structure follows strategy."[7] Chandler also found evidence that when these companies changed their strategies, they changed their structures. Chandler cited the classic example of GM in the 1920s.

For most of the first part of the twentieth century, Ford dominated the automobile industry. Fully 55 percent of the cars sold in the United States were Fords.

In order to compete with Ford, five other car manufacturers—Chevrolet, Pontiac, Buick, Oldsmobile, and Cadillac—agreed to join forces. Their strategy was to pool their financial resources while offering the customer a variety of different models that Ford could not match. The structure they created to implement that strategy was a single organization with five separate divisions. The organization was to be centralized for all financial and budget decisions, but each division was to make its own decisions on such issues as design and marketing, for example. From 1924 to 1927, GM's share of the motor vehicle market rose from 18.8 percent to 43.3 percent. With the right structure in place to effectively implement its strategy of co-operation, GM surpassed Ford to become the largest manufacturer of automobiles in America.

So, to Schein's four elements of effective organizational design, we add a fifth: To be effective, organizations must be structured to implement their strategies. The relationship between strategy and structure can be thought of thus: Structure *follows* strategy, structure *reflects* strategy, structure *implements* strategy, structure *supports* strategy. We will now consider the models of organizational design consistent with these five elements.

TRADITIONAL MODELS OF ORGANIZATION DESIGN

Bureaucratic Structure

One of the first models of organizational design was bureaucracy, which the German sociologist Max Weber described almost a century ago.[8] Weber was deeply concerned that many of Germany's governmental organizations were managed primarily on the basis of self-interest and favoritism rather than efficiency and reason. Decisions about whom to hire and whom to promote, for example, were based more on whom a person knew rather than on his or her competency or qualifications for the position. Weber feared that this kind of favoritism would significantly reduce the efficiency of Germany's rapidly expanding business and governmental organizations. He was convinced that organizations could be productive only if they were operated on principles of efficiency and reason, not favoritism.

At that time, the most efficient organization in the world was the highly respected Prussian army. Not surprisingly, the structure Weber prescribed for an efficient and rational organization—which he called a "bureaucracy"—very much reflected the principles which governed the Prussian army. Weber's bureaucracy included the four important characteristics described in Figure 8-2.

Colleges provide excellent examples of Weber's model of *bureaucracy,* or organization based on rules. There are rules in terms of degree requirements, in terms of course requirements, in terms of course registration procedures, and so on. Colleges can sometimes seem to be a maze of rules. But the purpose of this design is to ensure fair and consistent treatment for all students, and the rational and efficient operation of the organization.

In recent years, problems have arisen with the bureaucratic model of organizational design, and we will discuss them later in the chapter. But for nearly a

1. A clear-cut division of labor to ensure efficiency. Individuals were to be trained to perform specific tasks so that they could perform them well.

2. Staffing and promotion on the basis of tests to ensure that these decisions would be made on the basis of what individuals know, rather than who they know.

3. A formal system of well-defined rules and policies to ensure fairness and consistency, and to reduce bias and subjectivity in decision making.

4. A clearly identified hierarchy of authority to ensure that rules and policies are followed.

Figure 8-2 Characteristics of a Bureaucracy

century, Weber's bureaucracy has been the dominant model of organizational design. Virtually every formal organization that has emerged since the end of the nineteenth century has relied on rules and policies to improve performance.

Functional Structure

Like many organizational changes, the next major advance in the design of organizations came in response to changes in the internal and external environment. Remember, most large organizations at the beginning of the twentieth century were business organizations. Most of these were involved in some form of mass production. Typically, this involved the operation of a large facility filled with a variety of machines, employing large numbers of people to perform many specific and relatively simple tasks. To ensure that a steady flow of products from these factories was being matched by a steady supply of customers, sales became an important function. Sales work was different from manufacturing, and yet the sales tasks were essential to the success of the organization. A similar pattern can be seen for engineering, for accounting and finance, and for the other kinds of work that become essential in large-scale organizations.

No individual or group of individuals could be expected to perform all of the different kinds of work that now needed to be done. Different people were required to specialize in each area. The organizational structure that emerged to implement this specialization strategy is called the *functional organization.* The organization is divided into units, with each unit performing one of the specialized functions essential to the operation of the business.

Organizational structures are usually shown on organization charts. The chart of an organization designed according to the functional model is shown in Figure 8-3.

While the functional organization has been divided into an ever-increasing number of units as organizations have become more complex, the basis for dividing the work remains the same: A separate unit or department of specialists is created to perform each function essential for achieving the organization's strategic goals.

The functional model is most effective for organizations producing a single

Figure 8-3 A Functional Organization

product or service for a single market, such as the Golden Bear Corporation example shown in Figure 8-3. For organizations producing more than one product or service and/or operating in more than one market, a different model is typically used as a basis for structuring the organization. This model is called the divisional structure.

Divisional Structure

In the *divisional structure,* the work of the organization is divided according to the kind of products or services being provided, the type of customer being served, or the geographic areas in which the organization competes. Figure 8-4 illustrates Golden Bear Corporation structured according to the three different versions of the divisional model.

For many complex organizations providing many kinds of products and/or serving many markets or customer categories, the structure might actually combine the functional and divisional models. Separate divisions are created to focus on the organization's different types of customers or products, and functional departments provide services to these various divisions. For Golden Bear Corporation, this mixed divisional and functional structure might look like the structure shown in Figure 8-5.

In each of the preceding examples there is a common thread: The organization is divided into separate units to focus more effectively on the factor that is most essential to the organization's success. In Chandler's terms—structure follows strategy—the divisional model allows the organization to respond more effectively to the special needs and requirements of different kinds of products, customers, or markets, whichever of these factors is the focus of its strategy.

Conglomerate Structure

During the 1980s, there was a significant increase in what has come to be known as the conglomerate structure. Organizations with a *conglomerate structure* have separate divisions operating in entirely different industries. For example, General Motors' Hughes Aircraft division operates in the aerospace industry, and its Elec-

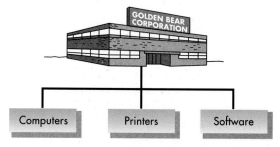

Product Division Structure

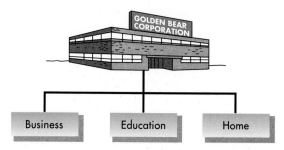

Customer Division Structure

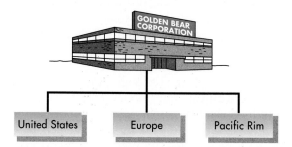

Geographic Division Structure

Figure 8-4 Golden Bear Corporation Organized in Product, Customer, and Geographic Divisions

tronic Data Services (EDS) division operates in the information systems industry. Similarly, Pepsico's divisions operate in the beverage industry (Pepsi-Cola), the restaurant industry (KFC), and the snack-food industry (Frito Lay). Most companies that form conglomerates do so either to expand their overall capabilities, as GM did, or to broaden their range of opportunities, as Pepsico has done. Figure 8-6 shows Golden Bear Corporation in terms of a conglomerate structure. The conglomerate model provides organizations with the ability to expand themselves almost indefinitely.

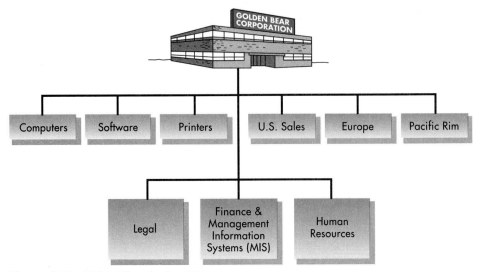

Figure 8-5 A Mixed Organizational Structure

Problems with Organization Design

As we said earlier, virtually every organization that has emerged during the twentieth century has been bureaucratic in design. Whether the design of the organization has been functional, divisional, conglomerate, or some combination of all three, the model has been organization by rules with a fully developed chain of command (authority structure) to ensure that the organization's decisions follow the rules. And for most of the twentieth century these bureaucratic organizations have been impressive in terms of their efficiency and effectiveness.

In recent years, however, the bureaucratic design has begun to show signs of being less effective. It now appears that the bureaucratic model works well when the environment changes very slowly, because rules can be gradually modified to reflect these changes. As the rate of change begins to speed up, however, changes in rules begin to fall behind changes in technology, the competition, and customer

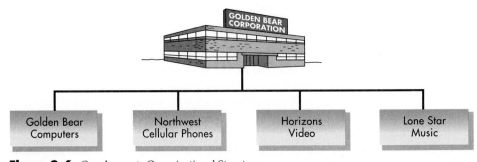

Figure 8-6 Conglomerate Organizational Structure

demands. At some point, the rules and structure that were intended to make the organization more efficient become obstacles that slow the organization down, as IBM and a number of other large organizations have discovered.

Harry Quadracci, CEO of Quad/Graphics Inc., printer of such publications as *Time, Playboy,* and L. L. Bean's catalogs, describes the problem this way: Managing by rules, he says, "is like firing a cannonball. It's fine if you are shooting at a castle. But today's markets are moving targets. The only way to hit them is to launch your business like a cruise missile." You fire it in the direction of your target market, he says, and it makes its own adjustments. According to Quadracci, organizations are in trouble if they rigidly follow rules rather than finding ways rapidly to respond to change. "Today's successful business is fast, nimble and strikes first."[9]

Rosabeth Moss Kanter, a leading management scholar and consultant, agrees with Quadracci: "The organizations now emerging as successful will be, above all, flexible."[10] To be effective in the changing environment, organizations must now satisfy a sixth requirement for effective organizational design. In addition to common goals, division of work, coordination of effort, authority structure, and designing the structure to reflect the organization's strategies, the design of the organization must also be flexible. A structure that enables the organization to adapt quickly to changes in the environment and to respond rapidly to new opportunities is the sixth requirement of organizational design.

FLEXIBLE MODELS OF ORGANIZATION DESIGN

Futurist Alvin Toffler, in his book *Powershift,* uses interesting language to describe the need to move beyond bureaucracy. In Toffler's word's, bureaucracies consist of what he terms "cubbyholes" and "channels."[11] The "cubbyholes" are occupied by the functional specialists in organizations—the engineers, the marketing and sales specialists, the accountants, and so on. Each specialist performs his or her specialty in relative isolation from the others.

The "channel" function is performed by managers who receive information from the cubbyholes in their departments and transmit that information up, down, or across the organization as needed. The beauty of the cubbyholes and channels structure, as we have seen, is that new cubbyholes and channels—called departments or divisions—can be added whenever it becomes necessary for the organization to engage in new types of work.

The problem with the cubbyholes and channels structure is that it requires time to function effectively. For departments to communicate with one another, information must move from each department up to the department manager, then across channels from manager to manager, and then from the manager down to the cubbyholes in another department or division.

In Chapter 1 we pointed out that speed is a function of flexibility. For Toffler, the solution to the speed problem in organizations is "flex-firms," organizations capable of rapid information-processing, whether in a crisis such as the Tylenol scare mentioned earlier, or on a continuing basis such as new-product development. *Flex-firms* attempt to build flexibility into their structures. Matrix, horizontal, and network organizations are three examples of Toffler's flex-firms, organizations designed for flexibility and speed.

Matrix Organization

One of the early forms of flexible organization was the *matrix organization*, in which specialists are assigned to a specific project or product or customer account. In a traditional organization, a marketing or accounting specialist, for example, works only with other marketing or accounting specialists in a marketing or accounting department. In a matrix organization, these specialists work directly with specialists from other areas in finance, for example, or with specialists from computer information systems as part of an ongoing group or team assigned to a long-term project or to develop a new product. Golden Bear Corporation organized according to a matrix structure as shown in Figure 8-7.

One advantage of the matrix model is that specialists from each functional area can focus their expertise on a specific project or product area. Another advantage is that it facilitates communication and coordination among specialists. Instead of having to communicate through channels, specialists communicate directly with one another, dramatically increasing their ability to respond quickly to problems or opportunities.

Finally, the matrix structure also increases an organization's flexibility and

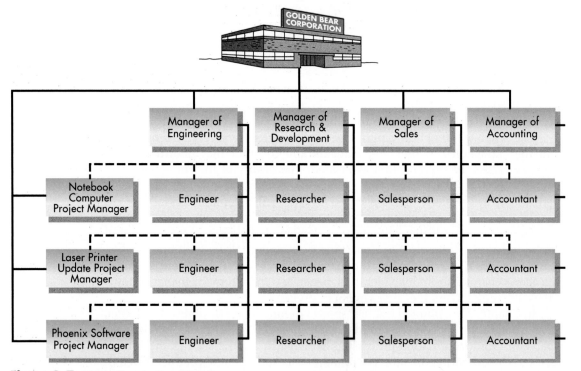

Figure 8-7 Matrix Organizational Structure

speed by allowing it to create a new group of specialists drawn from existing departments to respond to a crisis or to a rapidly developing opportunity. For example, when Golden Bear Corporation decided to update its laser printer product, it formed a project group made up of specialists from all of the functional areas. This enabled the organization not only to maximize the expertise and coordination around the project but also to ensure maximum speed in a fast-moving field.

One weakness of matrix organization is that the authority structure can be confusing. Most people in a matrix organization have two superiors to answer to instead of the one superior prescribed by Fayol's unity of command principle noted in Chapter 2. People are responsible both to the manager of their functional department (accounting, sales, engineering, CIS, etc.) and to the group manager in the area or project to which they are assigned. When an individual's managers fail to communicate and coordinate with one another, this can lead to conflicting demands being made on the subordinate, and can leave the individual in the middle, not knowing which manager's directions to follow. One of the keys to an effective matrix structure, then, is to train managers in effective communication and coordination skills to enhance their ability to provide clear and unified direction.

Horizontal Organization

A second form of flexible organization is the horizontal organization. The objective of the horizontal corporation is to expand the focus of everyone in the organization beyond their own narrow area of functional expertise, and even beyond their specific product or project team. The horizontal organization is one response to the problem of what DuPont's Terry Ennis calls the problem of "disconnects." *Disconnects* are the problems that occur whenever there is a "handoff"—that is, whenever work moves from one department to another or from one functional specialist to another. Every handoff is a chance for a fumble. According to Ennis, "The bigger the organization, the bigger the functions, and the more disconnects you get."[12]

The problem, of course, is not just the disconnects that occur between departments. There are also disconnects as work moves up and down through the various levels of management in the organization. Ennis's point is that every time work moves across a boundary, either between functions or between levels of management, there is the likelihood that key information will be lost or distorted.

To minimize the number of disconnects, the *horizontal organization* attempts to reduce the levels of management in the organization, and to eliminate the boundaries between departments. To accomplish this, the horizontal, or "flat," organization begins by identifying the three to five key processes necessary for the success of the organization, and by defining performance goals in each of those areas.

Once these three to five key processes have been identified, teams are created consisting of members who together possess all of the expertise necessary to achieve the performance goals in these areas. To eliminate the need to hand off work to managers for review, the teams are made *self-managing*—that is, the members of the team share responsibility for the team's achieving its goals. In the hori-

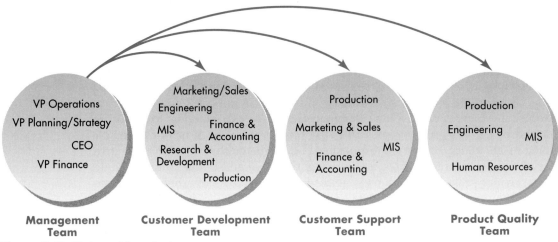

Figure 8-8 Horizontal Organization

zontal organization, teams report directly to top management, as shown in Figure 8-8. Because the teams are self-managing and report directly to top management, this eliminates the problem that matrix organizations have of team members reporting to more than one manager.

The horizontal approach to organizational design forces team members to move beyond their functional areas of expertise as accountants or marketers or engineers and to develop skills and expertise in a variety of areas needed for the team's success. But the key contribution of the horizontal organization is that it attempts to reduce the levels of authority—and thus the number of disconnects—that can slow down the organization. By reducing the number of layers of management through which decisions and questions must filter, the horizontal organization reduces the number of opportunities for an issue to be fumbled. It also increases the speed with which the organization can respond to challenges and opportunities.

Network Organization

A third design option for meeting the organization's need for speed and flexibility is the network organization.[13] The *network organization* is not really an organization in the traditional sense, but rather a temporary alliance of organizations that come together to take advantage of a strategic opportunity. Most organizations do not have all of the in-house expertise needed to respond to every opportunity or challenge—and by the time they developed the necessary expertise, it might be too late to take advantage of the opportunity. The network organization brings together independent companies with different areas of expertise to function as a temporary organization.

Consider this example: To take advantage of the rapidly developing market for notebook computers, AT&T worked with Japan's Marubeni Trading Co. and with Matsushita Electric Industrial Co. to move as quickly as possible into the production of its Safari notebook computer, designed by Henry Dreyfuss Associates.[14] Traditionally, this computer would have been designed, manufactured, and marketed by a single corporation. Increasingly, there just isn't time for this approach. The network organization created by AT&T accomplished the same task in a shorter period of time, and with a higher level of quality, by integrating the areas of expertise of several different companies.

Sometimes the network organization actually creates alliances between rivals. Again to take advantage of the rapidly developing market for notebook computers, Apple Computers actually contracted with rival Sony to manufacture its Power Book computer. Sony already possessed the ability to manufacture these units, and it would have taken Apple months or even years to develop the same kind of capability.

Even rock groups are adopting the network organization model. The Rolling Stones *Voodoo Lounge* tour in the summer of 1994, for example, consisted of three organizations that came together exclusively for the purpose of creating the tour. Toronto-based Concert Productions International marketed and promoted the tour, RZO Productions created the huge stage and transported it and two hundred stagehands in fifty-six trucks to concert sites around the United States, and the Rolling Stones provided the music. *Voodoo Lounge, Inc.,* generated more than $300 million in revenue, and simply disbanded once the tour was finished.[15]

The network organization is also known by other names. British management philosopher Charles Handy created the term *shamrock organization* to reflect the ever-changing nature of the new-style structure.[16] He chose the shamrock to symbolize the fact that the organization combines three key forces: core employees, external contractors (the independent companies the organization combines with), and temporary or part-time employees.

Jan Hopland, a Digital Equipment Corp. executive, is credited with having coined the term *virtual corporation* to describe an enterprise that may seem to be a single organization when in fact it is the collaboration of a number of organizations combining their strengths to achieve results more quickly and with greater expertise than any of the individual companies possess alone.[17] Figure 8-9 shows Golden Bear Corporation as a member of a network or virtual organization.

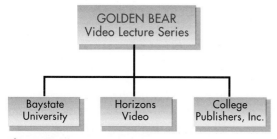

Figure 8-9 Network Organization

The potential weaknesses of the network or virtual model of organization are in the areas of common goals, coordination of effort, and authority structure. Obviously, in an organization consisting of several different independent companies, the managements will have to take great care to define common goals and an authority structure, and to develop effective means of coordination. And even if all of these challenges can be worked out, there is still an increased number of handoffs and consequently increased potential for disconnects when more than one company is involved in manufacturing a product or providing a service.

Still, it is clear that when managed effectively, network organizations give their constituent organizations more speed, expertise, and flexibility than each possesses individually. Both Nike and Reebok recognize the potential of network organizations. Neither actually manufactures very much of the billions of dollars' worth of products they sell annually. Both have created networks of manufacturers that allows them to concentrate their resources on the marketing and product development at which they excel. With such success stories, we can expect a steady increase in the number and variety of organizations moving into network structures.

THE CONTINGENCY VIEW OF STRUCTURE

Earlier in the chapter we discussed Chandler's point that structure follows strategy. It is important to note, however, that important as it is, strategy is not the only consideration in designing organizations for performance. The design of an organization needs to reflect other factors as well, among them the organization's size, the technology of production, and management's philosophy and style.[18] In other words, the question of how most effectively to design an organization is a complicated one, and there are no simple answers.

This relates back to the contingency view of management discussed in Chapter 2. This view requires management to adapt to the demands and characteristics of the situation. Clearly this is the case with the design and structure of organizations. As Toffler points out, we actually have "an immense repertoire of organizational forms to draw on—from jazz combos to espionage networks, from tribes and clans and councils of elders, to monasteries and soccer teams. Each is good at some things and bad at others."[19] It is just as the contingency view says: There is no one best way to organize or structure a company. It depends on the overall situation. Management's task is both to recognize that there is no one best form of design and at the same time to work to develop a structure that enhances the organization's ability to achieve its particular strategic goals.

SUMMARY

Management's organizing responsibility is to effectively implement the organization's strategic direction. The design of the organization's structure is a critical factor in how effectively the organization will achieve its strategic goals.

Edgar Schein has suggested four elements that must be present for the design of an organization to be effective: common goals, division of work, coordination of effort, and authority structure. The careful development of each of these elements is essential for the organization to function effectively.

A number of models for designing organizations have emerged over the course of the twentieth century. Each of these models is bureaucratic, in the sense that each is designed around plans and policies to ensure efficiency and objectivity in decision making. The functional, divisional, and conglomerate models are all bureaucratic, and each has specific advantages.

As the rate of change has accelerated in organizations' environments, management has been challenged to develop organizational designs that are faster to respond and more flexible than the traditional bureaucratic models. Organizational structures based primarily on plans and policies can be slow to adapt to rapidly developing threats and opportunities in the environment. Matrix, horizontal, and network or virtual structures have emerged to give organizations greater flexibility for adapting to the realities of the changing environment.

Finally, there is no one best way to design or structure organizations. The best way always depends on the situation. Each of Schein's elements for effective design must be satisfied, and there is a need for adaptability as well. But the specific design of a particular organization should ultimately reflect a range of variables. The manager's responsibility, as in any design task, is to satisfy the design requirements in the most effective structure possible to enable the organization to pursue its strategic goals.

It is highly unlikely that the bureaucratic organizational structure will ever disappear. Within every organization there is today a difficult tension. On the one hand there is the need for the kind of rules and clear authority structure that bureaucracy provides. On the other there is the need for speed and flexibility. It is management's responsibility to recognize both these needs, and to exercise creativity and judgment in structuring the organization for optimum performance and for effective response to change.

QUESTIONS TO CHALLENGE YOUR UNDERSTANDING OF THE CHAPTER

1. List and briefly explain Schein's four elements of effective organizational design.

2. Select an organization with which you are familiar (athletic team, student club, business organization), and discuss which of the characteristics of Weber's bureaucracy it has.

3. Discuss the differences between a functional organizational structure and a divisional organizational structure.

4. Discuss the organizational structure of your college or university. Is it organized according to the functional model? Divisional? A combination? Some other model?

5. Explain why a conglomerate structure increases an organization's ability to adapt to a changing environment.

6. Describe the advantages and disadvantages of a matrix structure.

7. Explain why the Golden Bear Corporation shown in Figure 8-9 is considered a network organization.

8. Explain why the concept "structure follows strategy" is consistent with the contingency view of organizational design.

MANAGEMENT EXERCISE

A Lesson in Disorganization

Tonya Ward recently graduated from college with a degree in management and was hired by the owner of a small residential real estate firm as the company's first assistant manager. Prior to her arrival, the company consisted of the owner and about a dozen part-time real estate agents.

Tonya's first major project as part of her new job was to organize a series of meetings with the company's agents to develop recommendations for improving the firm's overall performance. When Tonya asked the owner for details about the kind of recommendations he was looking for, he said only that he wanted to leave it "wide open" and not impose his ideas on the members of the group. He reminded Tonya that it was her responsibility to organize the group's meetings and to make them as productive as possible.

At the group's first meeting, Tonya explained the purpose of the group was to develop a set of recommendations for improving the firm's performance. She explained that while it was her responsibility to get the ball rolling and to prepare the group's final report, she hoped everyone would share in leading the group.

Tonya then suggested breaking up into subcommittees to review different areas of the firm and come back to the larger group with recommendations for improvement. One of the other group members disagreed and suggested that everyone work together on all of the tasks so that the entire group would move through all phases of the process together. There was a lot of support for this approach, so Tonya did not press the group to form subcommittees.

The group then moved on to discuss what its purpose should be. Some felt the focus should be on improving customer service, others felt the goal was to improve the operation of the office, and still others thought the group should be concerned primarily with how to better market the company. Tonya suggested using a group decision technique she had learned in college as a way to arrive at a consensus on what the group's purpose should be, but there was little support for her suggestion, and the discussion continued to go back and forth, reaching no conclusion. By the time the one-hour meeting time had elapsed, the question of what the group's purpose should be still had not been agreed upon, and Tonya was beginning to wonder whether this group would ever become productive.

1. How well would this group score in terms of Schein's four elements of an effective organization? For each element, give the group a 1 (poor), 2 (fair), or 3 (good) rating. The highest rating would be a 12 (four elements x 3 rating).

2. If you were Tonya, what would you attempt to do at the next meeting to increase Schein's effectiveness factors in this group?

REFERENCES

1. Laurence Hooper, "IBM's 4th-Quarter Deficit Hit a Record $5.46 Billion," *Wall Street Journal,* January 20, 1993, A3.

2. Edgar H. Schein, *Organizational Psychology,* 3d ed. (Englewood Cliffs, N.J.: Prentice-Hall, 1980), 12–15.

3. Max Weber, *The Theory of Social and Economic Organization,* trans. and ed. A. M. Henderson and Talcott Parsons (New York: The Free Press, 1947), 324–58.

4. Thomas A. Stewart, "The Search for the Organization of Tomorrow," *Fortune,* May 18, 1992, 93–94.

5. G. Christian Hill and Ken Yamarda, "Motorola Illustrates How an Aged Giant Can Remain Vibrant," *The Wall Street Journal,* December 9, 1992, A1, A14.

6. Thomas J. Peters and Robert H. Waterman, Jr., *In Search of Excellence* (New York: Harper & Row, 1982).

7. Alfred D. Chandler, *Strategy and Structure* (Cambridge, Mass.: MIT Press, 1962).

8. Weber, *Theory of Social and Economic Organization.*

9. Thomas J. Peters, "Cannonball to Cruise Missile," *Springfield Union News,* January 26, 1989.

10. Rosabeth Moss Kanter and John D. Buck, "Reorganizing Part of Honeywell: From Strategy to Structure," *Organizational Dynamics* 13 (Winter 1985): 6.

11. Alvin Toffler, *Power Shift* (New York: Bantam Books, 1990).

12. John A. Byrne, "The Horizontal Corporation," *Business Week,* December 20, 1993, 79.

13. Charles C. Snow, Raymond E. Miles, and Henry J. Coleman, Jr., "Managing 21st Century Network Organizations," *Organizational Dynamics,* Winter 1992, 5–20.

14. John A. Byrne, Richard Brandt, and Otis Port, "The Virtual Corporation," *Business Week,* February 8, 1993, 99–103.

15. Mark Landler, "It's Not Only Rock 'N' Roll," *Business Week,* October 10, 1994, 83–84.

16. Byrne, "The Horizontal Corporation," 80–81.

17. John A. Byrne, "The Futurists Who Fathered the Ideas," *Business Week,* February 8, 1993, 103.

18. For a discussion of these factors affecting organizational structure, see Mariann Jelinek, Joseph A. Litterer, and Raymond E. Miles, *Organization by Design: Theory and Practice,* 2d ed. (Plano, Tex: Business Publications, Inc., 1986).

19. Toffler, *Power Shift,* 182–183.

CHAPTER 9
The Design of Work

LEARNING OBJECTIVES

After studying this chapter, you should be able to:

- *Explain the advantages and disadvantages of task specialization.*

- *Review how Herzberg describes the relationship between work design and worker satisfaction.*

- *Discuss the concepts of job enlargement and job enrichment.*

- *Identify the key points of the job characteristics model.*

- *Describe the concept of team-based work design and identify the management activities and tasks that can be performed by self-managed work teams.*

- *Discuss the essential conditions for effective work teams.*

- *Explain the difference between work redesign and reengineering.*

- *Discuss the impact of technology on work design.*

- *Explain how both the logic of the work and the logic of the worker can be satisfied by teamwork designs in today's organizations.*

Designing an effective organization structure is one half of the organizing responsibility of management. The other half has to do with the design of the work itself. Once the units—the divisions, the departments, the teams—have been created that are needed to perform the essential work of the organization, it is management's responsibility to organize how the work will be done within those units to make it as productive as possible.

TASK SPECIALIZATION

You may recall that Adam Smith was one of the early commentators on the design of work. Writing in the late 1700s, Smith chronicled the advantages of task specialization. In his classic example of pin making, he described how breaking complex work into smaller, simpler tasks and having each worker perform only one of the separate tasks resulted in the work's being many times more productive than when each worker performed all of the tasks required to complete the finished product. Task specialization, as we said earlier, allows each worker to focus only on a single part of the overall work and to become a specialist at that task.

Two advantages result from the task specialization model of work design. First, usually very little training is required to perform each of the various tasks. Because the tasks are broken down to be relatively simple, it is relatively easy to learn how to perform them. Second, focusing on a single task usually allows the worker to perform the task more quickly. An individual continuously repeating a specific task can work faster than an individual moving from task to task to complete the overall product or service. For both of these reasons, task specialization is an extremely effective work design for work that can be divided into simpler subtasks.

While Adam Smith was an earlier commentator on the design of work, Frederick Taylor is credited as the first man in history who actually studied the design of work systematically.[1] While Smith recognized the power of dividing work into simpler subtasks, Frederick Taylor's focus was on *how* the work should be divided, and how each task should be designed. You may recall that a key element of Taylor's scientific management approach involved observing and experimenting with the design of work to make it as productive as possible.

In many ways, the dominant design of work for most of the twentieth century has been the kind of scientific task specialization emphasized by both Smith and Taylor. For almost one hundred years, the work done in units has been divided into specialized tasks performed by experts trained in those tasks. The marketing work of the organization, for example, has been divided from the production work, the accounting work, and so on. In addition, the marketing work itself has also been divided into the subtasks of market research, advertising and promotion, and sales. And each of these subtasks has been performed by specialists who are experts at that task.

So effective has the task specialization model been that it is the most common work design in every kind of organization, from businesses to colleges and universities to hospitals and government organizations. In every case, work has been made more productive by dividing it into ever more specialized tasks. In many ways, the tremendous economic advances during the twentieth century in the United States, Western Europe, Japan and the Pacific Rim countries, and most recently Mexico are striking testimony to the power of task specialization to make work more productive.

Problems with Task Specialization

As effective as task specialization has been as a work design, it is not without problems. One is boredom. Taken to the extreme, task specialization can result in work that consists of tasks so simple and repetitive that the person doing them has no sense of meaning or satisfaction. Almost forty years ago, management researcher Chris Argyris reported the boredom, daydreaming, absenteeism, negativism, and lower productivity of workers who were assigned highly specialized tasks.[2]

Ben Hamper, in his book *Rivethead: Tales from the Assembly Line,* gives a first-hand account of the monotony of an automobile assembly line:

> The one thing that was impossible to escape was the monotony of our new jobs. Every minute, every hour, every truck and every movement was a plodding replica of the one that had gone before. The monotony gnawed away at Roy. His behavior began to verge on the desperate. The only way he saw to deal with the monotony was to numb himself to it.[3]

Obviously, this is not as much of a problem for professionals doing specialized work—for physicians and accountants and scientists, for example. But for people on assembly lines, claims processors in insurance agencies, data entry specialists for telemarketing firms, and so on—for the people on the front lines in manufacturing and service industries—there is a point at which task specialization can actually result in less productivity. As the general level of education in a society rises, worker dissatisfaction increases when tasks are so simplified and repetitive that they become boring and meaningless. At that point, task specialization becomes part of the problem in terms of task design instead of part of the solution.

Herzberg and Job Satisfaction

Frederick Herzberg's two-factor theory provides a framework for better understanding the relationship between work design and worker satisfaction.[4] Herzberg's research suggests that there are two kinds of factors influencing how people feel about their work. One category of factors is called "hygiene factors"; the other is called "motivators."

Hygiene Factors and Motivators

When Herzberg surveyed workers in the 1960s about the things they didn't like about their jobs, he noticed an interesting pattern in their responses: People generally talked about different aspects of the workplace, or the conditions surrounding the job, rather than about the job itself. Examples of these *working conditions* or *hygiene factors,* as Herzberg calls them, are shown in Figure 9-1.

For Herzberg, hygiene factors are important primarily because if workers

HYGIENE FACTORS

- Working conditions such as temperature or lighting
- Interpersonal relations with other workers
- Company policies relating to vacations, sick time, and benefits
- Effectiveness of superiors as supervisors
- Basic wage or salary

MOTIVATORS

- Sense of achievement
- Sense of recognition
- Sense of responsibility
- Opportunity for advancement
- Sense of personal growth

Figure 9-1 Herzberg's Hygiene Factors and Motivators

are not satisfied with these basic conditions in the workplace, productivity will suffer. But as you can see, hygiene factors are not directly related to the design of the work itself.

The factors that are more closely related to the design of the work are what Herzberg calls *motivators.* He uses this term for the kinds of factors people mention when they are asked about what motivates them to do a better job. This list of motivators that emerged from Herzberg's research are also shown in Figure 9-1. Unlike hygiene factors, motivators can increase someone's satisfaction with the work he or she is doing. Also unlike hygiene factors, motivators are strongly affected by the design of the work itself.

The Herzberg model provides a theoretical explanation of why task specialization is sometimes less effective as a work design. Doing extremely simple and repetitive tasks makes work so routine and boring that it lacks the motivators necessary to allow the individual to be productive: opportunity for a sense of achievement, recognition, responsibility, and personal growth.

For years, it was acceptable for organizations to focus on hygiene factors in the workplace, on eliminating or at least minimizing those things which were sources of worker dissatisfaction. In the changing environment and the changing workplace, it is no longer enough to minimize people's dissatisfaction with the work they are doing. Now it is essential to design work to allow people to be as productive as possible. The challenge for management is to move beyond task specialization to work designs that incorporate Herzberg's motivators—to design work so that it yields the sense of achievement, growth, and recognition that can lead to better performance.

JOB REDESIGN

Job redesign is the term used to describe the effort of organizations to improve job satisfaction by improving the way work is designed or organized. It recognizes that most jobs have traditionally been divided into simpler subtasks, and for this kind of work to become more satisfying it is necessary to redesign how the work is done. Two redesign options that have emerged in this effort are job rotation and job enlargement.

Job Rotation and Job Enlargement

Job rotation is the practice of periodically moving individuals from task to task within a work area. For example, at a McDonald's an individual might move from working the grill, to staffing the drive-up window, to refilling stock that is running low, to working the front counter, and so on. Or in a factory, workers may exchange places from time to time, taking turns operating the various machines involved in the production process. The intent of job rotation is to increase the variety of tasks any one person is performing, and to reduce the boredom that occurs from doing the same thing over and over. Job rotation can also increase the individual's sense of achievement, because it requires the mastery of a variety of skills rather than the constant repetition of a single skill.

Rotating among a variety of tasks has the added advantage of giving each individual an increased understanding of how the various tasks of the organization fit together. Even managers and other professionals seem to gain a greater sense of the overall operation of the organization when they rotate through a variety of managerial or professional positions, moving from manufacturing to marketing to finance, for example. In fact, the Japanese have used job rotation for years as a way to develop their managers.

Job enlargement goes beyond job rotation to combine simpler tasks into a larger series of tasks, all performed as part of one individual's job. An assembly line worker, for example, without job redesign, might have the task of installing a component and tightening the same four screws every ninety seconds, for eight hours every day. With job enlargement, the same individual might actually install a number of different components and repeat these same tasks only every eight or ten minutes.

Aetna Life & Casualty uses job enlargement to give some of its employees relief from staring at a computer terminal all day. Now, no one in a data entry job spends more than 70 percent of the day working in front of a computer screen. Instead, the job has been enlarged to involve paperwork and telephoning as well.[5]

By combining tasks, job enlargement attempts to increase worker satisfaction and performance by increasing the variety of tasks performed as well as the sense of achievement that can come from mastering a variety of tasks and from being more meaningfully involved in the overall task.

Both job rotation and job enlargement are intended to improve performance by improving work design, but the results are not always positive. This is especially true when the initial tasks that are being redesigned are extremely simplified to begin with. Herzberg himself questions why anyone would be more motivated just from rotating through a variety of low-skill jobs, or just from having their job enlarged to include a larger number of low-skill tasks. Both these approaches may represent steps in the right direction, but for genuine improvement in terms of work design, Herzberg suggests a redesign approach he calls "job enrichment."

Job Enrichment

Job enrichment is the redesign of work to incorporate as fully as possible an increased sense of achievement and responsibility and expanded opportunities for growth and recognition. The differences between job rotation, job enlargement, and job enrichment are summarized in Figure 9-2.

For Herzberg, the key to job enrichment is to redesign the work to include not only the core tasks but other significant functions as well. For example, sales clerks at Montgomery Ward are also authorized to approve checks and to handle merchandise return problems, functions that previously were performed only by store managers.[6] In Herzberg's view, by giving workers not only different tasks to perform but also different kinds of responsibility produces the motivators that can result in improved performance.

As organizations reduce their workforces in an effort to cut costs and become more competitive, an ever-increasing number are following Herzberg's advice and designing greater responsibility into every level of task. At the General Motors parts manufacturing plant in Bay City, Michigan, plant manager Pat Carrigan has essentially made the workforce partners in the effort to save jobs by making that facility profitable. Carrigan's approach is one Herzberg would applaud. The workers at Bay City form volunteer teams that not only run the machines in their area but also plan the week's production, inspect the quality of their own work, train each other on the different tasks, and in general manage themselves. These are individuals who formerly would simply operate their machines or perform other routine, simplified tasks. Bay City is a prime example of

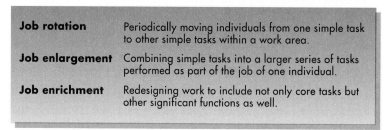

Job rotation	Periodically moving individuals from one simple task to other simple tasks within a work area.
Job enlargement	Combining simple tasks into a larger series of tasks performed as part of the job of one individual.
Job enrichment	Redesigning work to include not only core tasks but other significant functions as well.

Figure 9-2 Job Redesign Definitions

how organizations are working successfully to enrich ordinary jobs by giving people the kinds of responsibility once reserved for managers.

Management theorists Richard Hackman and Greg Oldham have suggested a model of work design that actually expands and clarifies Herzberg's definition of job enrichment. They call their model the Job Characteristics Model.[7]

Job Characteristics Model

The Hackman and Oldham model suggests that more can be done to improve work design than just giving workers some of the planning, problem solving, and inspection responsibilities. The five key characteristics of fully enriched jobs are shown in Figure 9-3.

According to the Job Characteristics Model, these five elements—skill variety, task identity and significance, autonomy and feedback—greatly enhance Herzberg's motivators—the sense of personal growth, of achievement, of recognition, and of responsibility. And from the evidence, the Job Characteristics Model has produced favorable results. For example, work at the New Castle, Indiana, Chrysler plant is designed according to this model. Workers (all members of the UAW) are now called "technicians" and their line supervisors are called "team advisors." The seventy-seven teams at the plant assign tasks, talk with customers, order repairs, and even do hiring for their teams. Absenteeism is under 3 percent (from over 7 percent); even more impressively, defects are down to 20 per million, from 300.[8] Chrysler has reaped the benefits of designing jobs in ways that respond to people's need for meaningful work. And similar results have been reported by Volvo, Monsanto, and others. By designing work to include the characteristics identified by Hackman and Oldham, these companies have achieved significant improvements in performance.

Difficulties with Job Redesign

Full-scale job enrichment is not the answer in every situation. Not every worker is ready for the kind of expanded responsibilities that job enrichment offers. Not

Skill variety	The job requires or involves multiple skills, activities, and abilities to complete the work.
Task identity	The job allows the completion of an identifiable "whole," rather than just a very minor part of a much larger task.
Task significance	The job is important enough to have a substantial impact on the lives or well-being of others.
Autonomy	The people doing the job have the authority to make decisions on how to organize and do the work.
Feedback	People doing the job receive clear and regular information about how well they are performing.

Figure 9-3 Five Characteristics of Fully Enriched Jobs

everyone, for example, possesses the skills necessary for planning and inspecting his or her own work, or for dealing directly with customers. Some workers might also prefer not to participate in the decision-making responsibilities.

For these reasons, the Job Characteristics Model is actually a contingency model. The effectiveness of job enrichment may depend on the workers' need for growth. In fact, Hackman and Oldham specifically suggest that job enrichment is more appropriate in situations where workers have a strong desire for increased opportunities for growth, responsibility, and achievement. The theory is that workers with greater personal growth needs are likely to respond more positively to the increased opportunities afforded by enriched jobs. Workers with greater security needs, on the other hand, are likely to feel more threatened by what they view not as increased opportunities but as increased demands. For this reason, research on the relationship between job redesign efforts and performance has revealed mixed results.[9]

Besides the effect of level of worker needs on how well workers react to job redesign, there is the fact that the task or redesign is extremely difficult. Change does not come easily to organizations that for decades have been designed around task specialization. Job redesign is not simply a potentially better way of organizing work; it can also represent a drastic change in the way an organization does business. Like all such changes, job redesign of any kind can be extremely threatening to an organization that has been operating in a certain way for generations. The resistance to this kind of change can be a critical factor in the success or failure of efforts at job redesign.

Yet despite resistance and mixed results, organizations continue to press forward in their search for improved work designs. The challenges of global competition require that designs be developed to make work and workers ever more productive. One approach to job redesign has become so important that we discuss it separately in the next section. That approach is teamwork.

TEAMWORK

A *work team* is a designated group of individuals who together are responsible for a significant unit of work—a product or service that is delivered to a customer either inside or outside the organization. Work teams are known by various other names, including *autonomous work groups* and *self-managing teams.* Work teams are more like departments than they are like project teams, because the members of the teams work together on a long-term day-to-day basis. In its most advanced form, the work team essentially replaces the manager by taking on responsibility for most of the tasks traditionally performed by management: planning and scheduling the work, hiring and training team members, and providing discipline and resolving conflicts among team members or with other teams.

Work teams initially appeared as part of the job enrichment efforts we've been discussing in this chapter. With changing performance standards of greater speed and flexibility, the move toward work teams gained real momentum. The experience of successful teams at Ford (Taurus), IBM (PC), General Motors (Saturn), and Motorola (cellular phones) made clear the potential of teams for improving performance. Organizations discovered that by bringing skilled individuals together on teams, and by eliminating the need to go to management for every decision, the speed of virtually every process in the organization could be increased significantly. The new-product-design work team at Mattel, for example, reduced the time it takes to develop and bring to market a new toy from eighteen months to five months. Similarly, the time required for credit and approval at American Express was shortened by quality teams from twenty-two days to eleven days. And production teams at Titeflex, a Teflon hose manufacturer, can now fabricate and ship a piece of hose requested on an emergency basis in six hours rather than six days.[10]

The experience at Titeflex is a fairly typical example of the switch to work teams. Literally over a single weekend, Titeflex eliminated one whole level of management, organized its employees into teams, and gave the teams responsibility and authority for whatever changes were necessary in their areas to improve speed and productivity. The results were dramatic. The simple act of processing a customer's order, for example, used to require as long as five or six weeks as the paperwork moved from the inventory department (to see if the parts for the product were already in stock) to the engineering department (to provide specifications for producing the product) to the purchasing department (to order the materials necessary to produce the product) to the production planning department (to schedule the order for production). And this was before even a single inch of the hose could be manufactured. Under the team approach, members from each of these departments now have their desks together in one place and work together on each order to complete it in a matter of days, and sometimes hours.

Besides increased speed, there are other advantages of work teams. General Electric, for example, reported an increase in productivity of 250 percent at its Salisbury, North Carolina, plant as a result of combining work teams with computer technology. Northern Telecom reports that its self-directed work teams are achieving a 60 percent improvement in quality with 40 percent fewer quality inspectors. Food products giant General Mills has experienced such productivity gains through self-managing teams that by 1992, 60 percent of its plants had been converted to teamwork, and plans were in place to spread the team-based approach to all of the company's operations.[11]

While the move toward work teams has gained momentum in recent years, the use of them has not spread as quickly as expected. A survey conducted by the Center for Effective Organizations at the University of Southern California in 1994 showed that 68 percent of Fortune 1000 companies used work teams, but only 10 percent of workers were in such teams.[12] Increasing the number of workers involved in teams is an important challenge for management.

Making Teams Work

The potential effectiveness of the team-based work design is clear. It is also clear that making a team design work effectively can be a challenging task for management. Earlier we mentioned the natural human resistance to change. During the first two years of its changeover to work teams; the GE plant at Salisbury experienced a 14 percent turnover rate: nearly one out of every seven workers left rather than accept the increased responsibilities of the team-based approach.

One strategy for reducing resistance to team-based work is training. If people feel they possess the skills to be successful in the new team environment, they are more likely to be willing to stay with the transition to teams. On the other hand, it is important to realize that even with training, some workers are likely to leave for a work situation that is less demanding. Management consultant Michael Hammer puts it this way: "Getting people to accept the idea that their work lives—their jobs—will undergo radical change is not a war won in a single battle. It is an educational and communications campaign that runs from reengineering's start to its finish."[13] Even with an effective campaign of worker education and training, a period of time will probably be required for an organization to allow less willing employees to leave and to recruit new workers who are more comfortable with the demands of working in teams.

It is also important to realize that individual workers are not the only source of resistance to the work team design. Organizations designed around highly managed departments of experts can have great difficulty learning how to function as self-managing teams. Issues of chain of command (who reports to whom) and channels of information (who tells who what) take time to redefine. Organizations, like individuals, often require a period of training and education to learn to do their work through teams.

Self-Managed Teams

Research suggests that self-managed work teams can be involved in a wide variety of management activities and tasks, including those listed in Figure 9-4.[14]

Not every team design includes responsibility for all of the tasks shown in Figure 9-4, but it is reasonable to suggest that any truly self-managed work team will perform a significant number of these responsibilities. One of the key chal-

- Recording quality control statistics
- Making scheduling assignments
- Solving technical problems
- Setting group or team goals
- Resolving internal conflicts
- Assessing group or team performance
- Delegating assignments to team members
- Preparing a budget
- Training members
- Selecting new members
- Allocating pay raises for members

Figure 9-4   Activities Often Performed by Self-Managed Teams

lenges for management, then, is to provide team members with training in each activity for which they are responsible. Some of this training will be technical, in the areas of accounting and finance, for example, or statistical quality control or inventory management. But much of the training must be managerial, in the areas of planning, organizing, providing feedback, group decision-making and problem-solving, managing conflicts, and so on. Work teams will be effective in managing themselves only if their members possess managerial skills and understanding.

This is an important point. You may recall Henri Fayol's caution from early in the century: To improve performance, train management in the functions of the manager; provide managers with the training and skills needed to manage effectively. In the work team design, teams share in the responsibilities that are part of management. For teams to fully achieve their potential in this area, work teams must receive the kind of training they need to allow them to perform their management responsibilities effectively.

Teamwork: The Bottom Line

Teams enhance the speed of work processes in the organization; they have the potential to increase quality and productivity; and where workers are motivated by growth needs, teamwork can increase job satisfaction. The barriers to effective teamwork are also apparent. They include the natural human resistance to major change, the inherent difficulty of organizations learning to operate in new ways, and the need for work teams to develop the skills necessary to manage themselves effectively.

Management's task is to have the patience and commitment necessary to develop a workforce and an organization capable of achieving the improved performance team-based work design makes possible. An important part of this task is understanding what it takes for teams to be effective. If team members have the necessary training and the organization has the required commitment and patience, management still needs to ensure that the conditions are in place for teamwork to be effective.

Conditions for Effective Teams

McKinsey & Co. consultants Jon R. Katzenbach and Douglas K. Smith studied the differences between teams that perform well and other groups that don't. They interviewed hundreds of people, on fifty different teams in thirty organizations, from Motorola and Hewlett-Packard to Operation Desert Storm and the Girl Scouts. Based on these interviews, Katzenbach and Smith have offered the following definition of high-performance teams:[15]

> A team is a small number of people with complementary skills who are committed to a common purpose, set of performance goals, and approach for which they hold themselves mutually accountable.

Complementary skills, common purpose, common performance goals and approach, and mutual accountability: these appear to be the essential conditions for teamwork to be effective.

Complementary Skills

Team sports such as basketball and softball require collective effort. Katzenbach and Smith point out that these kinds of collective efforts are likely to be most effective where team members possess complementary skills—that is, where each team member contributes some of the skills needed for the team's success. Just as a baseball team benefits from having pitchers, hitters, and people who can catch and throw the ball, work teams benefit when team members contribute different skills and when their skills are complementary. It is not essential that each member possess all of the skills required for the work of the team. It is essential that the team members together possess all of the skills required for their work to be performed well.

Common Purpose

The second key ingredient for successful teamwork is the commitment of team members to a common purpose. Without this shared commitment, groups are likely to be little more than collections of individuals each performing independently. With shared commitment to a common purpose, groups become genuine teams, performance units capable of the kind of productivity improvements achieved by General Electric, Northern Telecom, General Mills, and others.

Shared commitment requires a purpose all team members can believe in. This sense of purpose is much like the sense of mission discussed in Chapter 6. Katzenbach and Smith suggest that the sense of common purpose is most powerful when it raises the sights of the team members: ". . . Credible team purposes have an element related to winning, being first, revolutionizing, or being on the cutting edge."[16] Tom Peters says the same thing differently: Everyone, Peters says, wants to be part of something bigger, something more important.

It is interesting to note that this essential element of a meaningful common purpose does not have to emerge entirely from within the group itself. Katzenbach and Smith found that management is most often the source of the group's initial purpose or mission. The most effective teams, however, are continuously involved in refining and reshaping that initial purpose. For example, a team brought together by management simply to improve customer service may come to redefine its purpose as excelling at that service, or as exceeding all of the traditional standards defining that service. In effective teams, the emphasis seems to be on expanding the assigned purpose to one of greater meaning.

Performance Goals

Complementary skills and strong commitment to a meaningful common purpose are just the starting point for effective teams. Consistent with our discussion of goals in Chapter 4, the best teams translate their common purpose into specific goals. Such goals might be defined in terms of getting a new product to market in less than half the normal time, or responding to all customers within twenty-four hours, or achieving a zero-defect rate while cutting costs by 40 percent. Such goals provide a clear target to aim for as well as the possibility of feedback.

It is the combination of shared purpose and clear performance goals that is essential. According to Katzenbach and Smith, "Clear performance goals help a team keep track of progress, while a broader purpose supplies meaning and emotional energy."[17]

Mutual Accountability

The final ingredient in the recipe for effective teams is a sense of shared responsibility for the team and for its work. In the best teams, members hold themselves accountable for the team's performance. They may receive their initial direction from management, but the most effective teams eventually define their own purpose and their own goals, and hold themselves responsible for achieving them. We have defined management as responsibility for performance. It should not be surprising that the most effective teams are self-managing—that is, they take responsibility for their own performance.

According to Katzenbach and Smith, the sense of mutual or shared responsibility produces a unique satisfaction for team members. "What we heard over and over from members of effective teams is that they found the experience motivating in ways that their normal jobs never could match."[18]

The four conditions for effective teamwork are summarized in Figure 9-5.

While effective teams are a powerful tool for improving performance, teamwork is not necessarily the right work design in every situation. For tasks in which *individual* talent or insight or intuition is the most important element, a team-based work design might only complicate or undermine the effort. The task for managers is to recognize the kind of work that can best be done by teams, and in those situations to create and support the conditions necessary for teams to be effective.

REENGINEERING

Organizations around the world now recognize that effective work design can bring a critical competitive advantage. There is also an emerging consensus that teamwork offers a potentially effective alternative to traditional task specialization. Beyond these realizations, however, there is a growing sense that simply taking the same work and redesigning it for teams may not be enough. Former MIT

Complementary skills	Each team member contributes some of the skills needed for the team's success.
Common purpose	The team commits to a shared mission or purpose.
Performance goal	The team sets specific targets for its performance.
Mutual accountability	The team has a sense of shared responsibility for the team and its work.

Figure 9-5 Conditions for Effective Teamwork

computer science professor Michael Hammer suggests that merely teaming people around the same tasks may amount to little more than improving on the way a task has always been done. While there is always some value in improving the design of a task, Hammer suggests that the question organizations should be asking is whether the task *needs to be performed at all. Reengineering* is the term he coined to describe the process of identifying the tasks that are essential to the success of the organization and eliminating those that are not.

John Herold, Jr., executive vice president of ITT Sheraton Corp., is a believer in reengineering. He tells the story of how Sheraton invented a "new hotel" through reengineering. According to Herold, the typical 300-room Sheraton Hotel required as many as 40 managers and a staff of up to 200 employees. Through reengineering, ITT found that many of the tasks being performed at its hotels were simply unnecessary. For example, many managers were spending much of their time filling out reports for other managers. By eliminating all of the tasks that didn't need doing, ITT was able to reengineer the hotel to operate 250 suites with only 14 managers and 120 staff members.[20]

As might be expected, reengineering is a difficult process for an organization to undertake effectively. Managers and employees understandably are reluctant to involve themselves wholeheartedly in a process that can result in the elimination of their own jobs. Researchers concede that for this reason as many as seven out of ten reengineering efforts achieve no significant results.[21]

Still, the questions posed by reengineering are important: To achieve success, does an organization really need to do everything it is currently doing? Might performance even be improved by eliminating some of these tasks? And as organizations' experience with reengineering increases, another question needs to be asked: At what point does reengineering result in so large an expansion of job responsibilities that it threatens to overwhelm the individuals and teams performing the work? The difficult side of reengineering is that it often results in fewer and fewer people in the organization being assigned greater and greater responsibilities. In the case of ITT, for example, the number of suites in the hotel was reduced by 17 percent. But the number of staff members was reduced by 40 percent, and the number of managers by more than 60 percent. While some of the tasks being performed at this hotel were eliminated through reengineering, undoubtedly each of the remaining staff and managers was left with significantly greater responsibilities than they'd had previously. This kind of increased workload can have a negative effect on workers' attitudes and performance.

Research suggests that when reengineering results in significant downsizing of an organization's workforce, potential is increased for stress and morale problems. A recent survey of managers by the American Management Association reports significantly increased levels of stress and widespread erosion of morale at companies where major job cuts have left employees who have kept their jobs with no choice but to cope with the mounds of work still remaining.[22] Economists and managers are concerned about just how far organizations can go with reengineering and still sustain the benefits in terms of performance over the long run.

Once again, the challenge for management is one of balance. The key in reengineering is to identify and maintain the tasks that are essential to the organization's success and at the same time to maintain a workforce large enough to perform those tasks well. This balance will probably be achieved only as organizations gain extensive experience with the reengineering process and its consequences.

TECHNOLOGY AND JOB DESIGN

Throughout this text, technology has been emphasized as a dynamic and important part of both the changing environment and the changing workplace. Technology also affects the design of work. As the use of technology grows—for example, information technology—more people than ever, from the factory floor to managers' offices, are finding the way they do their jobs dramatically changed. Two examples of technology impacting the design of work are robotics and office automation.

Technology on the Factory Floor

Robots are machines that perform highly specialized tasks through a mechanical arm controlled by a computer. They are highly efficient in welding, assembly, spray painting, filling containers, and other similar tasks. Robots can work non-stop and are very reliable. For these reasons, many manufacturing companies have installed robots as a way to cut labor costs in response to foreign competition. According to David Packard, former chairman of Hewlett Packard, "We have no choice but to automate because foreign competitors are doing so."[23]

However, the rate of robotization is not as high as was once predicted. One reason for this has been the discovery that *total* robotization is less productive than a combination of automation and a team-oriented workforce. For example, when GM and Toyota formed a joint venture to produce compact cars in the United States, the GM Fremont, California plant became its most efficient facility. The work design of the Fremont plant included some robots but stressed team-based work as well.[24] Examples such as this emphasize that it is management's task to discover the mix of automation and human factors that will be most effective in improving the performance of the organization.

Technology in the Office

As computer technology continues to advance, it is predicted that eventually every employee will have access to a personal computer, work station, or laptop computer. The presence of this technology in turn affects how work is designed and how people interact.[25] As a result of information technology, workers who once had only limited access to information and data can now participate in the decision-making process. And group members can now "meet" to exchange ideas and information over electronic communication systems without ever leaving their offices.

In fact, the portability of PC technology is also changing not just the design of work, but the work space itself. Jay Chiat of Chiat/Day advertising agency plans to make use of the new portable technology to completely revamp the traditional work environment of the firm's Los Angeles facility. Work that was once performed only in an office can now be done at home, entirely changing the way workers interact. People will come to the office only for essential face-to-face meetings. Brainstorming will be done by electronic mail and video conferencing rather than in an office where employees work from nine to five. "Sitting in your office moving papers is not our idea of creative work," he explains. Instead, Chiat/Day's eight hundred employees will have individual cellular phones and E-mail-equipped notebook computers so they can work and interact wherever they are in the world. The "office" will now be made up of elegant common areas and technically sophisticated meeting, editing, and screening rooms where people will meet when these kinds of meetings are needed.[26]

It is estimated that by the year 2000, as much as one-third of the workforce will be working at home,[27] all because of advanced technology. Such changes make it clear that advances in technology will continue to have a significant impact on the design of work and the way people do their jobs.

LOGIC OF THE WORK VERSUS LOGIC OF THE WORKER

Peter Drucker has used the terms "logic of the work" and "logic of the worker" in discussing how to make work more productive.[28] For Drucker, the logic of the work refers to the nature of the work or the tasks to be accomplished. Frederick Taylor and scientific management were concerned primarily with the logic of the work in focusing on the most effective way to design the task to make it as efficient as possible.

On the other hand, the logic of the worker refers to the needs of the people performing the work. The logic of the worker refers to how tasks might be designed to satisfy not only the requirements of efficiency, but the human needs of the worker.

For most of the twentieth century, with its emphasis on task specialization, the focus has been on the logic of the work. The assumption has been that work will be most productive if it is broken down into increasingly smaller tasks performed by specialists. This has been as true for hospitals and research laboratories as for factories and insurance companies. Work has been assumed to become more productive the more specialized it becomes. As a consequence of this emphasis on the logic of the work, not much attention has been paid to the logic of the worker. Because organizations had been able to succeed primarily through task specialization alone, they took little interest in the logic or needs of the worker or in the workers' perspective on their own productivity. Even Herzberg's concepts of job enrichment and Hackman and Oldham's Job Characteristics Model had very little actual impact until fairly recently.

Today organizations face new challenges in balancing the logic of the work and the logic of the worker. On the positive side, teamwork can provide a closer alignment of the two logics. It satisfies the demand for a work design that is efficient, flexible, fast, and yields high quality. It also satisfies workers' needs for work that is challenging and meaningful. On the negative side, when teams are given more responsibilities than they can perform well, as can happen with downsizing and reengineering, it is the logic of the worker that loses ground.

As the changing environment continues to alter the alignment between the logic of the work and the logic of the worker, it is management's responsibility to explore the common ground to find ways of dramatically improving productivity and performance.

SUMMARY

Since the time of Frederick Taylor and before, the design of work has been a key responsibility of management. It has been management's job to determine how work should be organized so that workers can be as productive as possible.

The earliest and most enduring work design was task specialization, the process of breaking down a large, complex task into a series of simpler tasks. The advantage of task specialization is that when a group of individuals each focus on a single task they can be significantly more productive than when each individual must master and perform all of the tasks required in the production process. Task specialization becomes a problem, however, when tasks become so simple that they are meaningless to the people performing them; at this point the workers actually become less productive.

Job redesign is the name that has been given to the overall effort to counteract the negative effects of task specialization. One form of job redesign is job rotation, which allows people to move among a number of tasks to avoid the boredom of performing the same task indefinitely. Another form of job redesign is job enlargement, which combines a number of similar tasks to allow the individual worker to complete a more significant portion of the overall task. A third form of job redesign is job enrichment. In job enrichment, teams are formed and are given both greater freedom and greater responsibility in determining how the work will be completed.

In Chapter 1 we briefly discussed the growing emphasis on teamwork in the changing workplace. In this chapter on the design of work, we note that with this greater emphasis on teamwork has come a corresponding increase in management effort to understand the conditions for effective teamwork. Early indications are that complementary skills, a commonly shared purpose, specific performance goals, and a sense of mutual responsibility are all essential for team-based work to be effective.

Beyond teamwork, reengineering has been suggested as a process not for improving the way tasks are performed, but for evaluating which tasks are essential to the work of the organization and which tasks should be eliminated altogether. All of these approaches to improving the design of work, including reengineering, have been supported and enhanced by the application of computer-based technology, from robots in the lab and factory to automation in the office.

Finally, management's efforts toward improved work designs have begun to restore the balance between the logic of the work and the logic of the worker. In particular, teamwork is a work design that is responsive both to the new performance standards and to the needs of workers for autonomy, responsibility, and challenge.

QUESTIONS TO CHALLENGE YOUR UNDERSTANDING OF THE CHAPTER

1   Explain two advantages and the major disadvantage of highly specialized tasks.

2. Discuss a job you are familiar with in terms of hygiene factors and motivators.

3. Explain the difference between job enlargement and job enrichment.

4. Describe how a job you are familiar with can be improved according to the job characteristics model.

5. Discuss why some individuals might prefer not to work in a team-based performance unit.

6. Discuss a performance unit you have been a member of (student club or organization, sports team, work organization, etc.) in terms of how well it satisfied the conditions for an effective team.

7. Compare the concepts of work redesign and reengineering and discuss how the work of classroom teaching might be reengineered to eliminate any unnecessary tasks.

8. Describe how technology has been used to make work more productive.

9. Contrast the logic of the work and the logic of the worker, and explain how both can be satisfied through teamwork.

MANAGEMENT EXERCISE

Practice in Job Redesign

This exercise is designed to provide you with experience in applying the principles of Hackman and Oldham's Job Characteristics Model, discussed in this chapter. In the first part of the exercise you will calculate the "motivating potential" of a job with which you are familiar. In the second part, you will develop suggestions for enriching this job to increase its motivating potential.

1. Think of a job with which you are familiar—one that you yourself or someone you know has held.

2. Using the scale provided, rate this job on each of the five following core job dimensions:

7 = very high	*3 = somewhat low*
6 = high	*2 = low*
5 = somewhat high	*1 = very low*
4 = moderate	

CORE JOB DIMENSIONS

_____ _Skill variety_	_(Consider all of the skills required for this job: technical, mental, physical, social, etc.)_
_____ _Task identity_	_(Does the job allow for the completion of a specific product or service [high], or of just a small portion of the completed product or service [low]?)_
_____ _Task significance_	_(How important is the performance in this job to the satisfaction of the customer or to the overall success of the work unit?)_
_____ _Autonomy_	_(How much control does the person doing this have? How much freedom to make decisions about how the job will be done?)_
_____ _Feedback_	_(How much feedback is there from the job itself, from customers, peers and superiors?)_

3. Using your ratings of the five core job dimensions above and the following formula, calculate the "motivating potential score" of the job you are analyzing.

$$\text{Motivating Potential Score} = \frac{\text{Skill variety} + \text{Task identity} + \text{Task significance}}{3} \times \text{Autonomy} \times \text{Feedback}$$

A score higher than 200 suggests a job with high motivating potential. A score lower than 100 suggests a job that would benefit significantly from redesign.

4. Develop a plan for improving the motivating potential of this job by listing specific suggestions for improving the rating on each of the five core job dimensions.

REFERENCES

1. Peter F. Drucker, *Management: Tasks, Responsibilities, Practices* (New York: Harper & Row, 1973).

2. Chris Argyris, *Personality and Organization* (New York: Harper & Bros. 1957).

3. Ben Hamper, *Rivethead: Tales from the Assembly Line* (New York: Warner Books, 1991), 41.

4. Frederick Herzberg, *Work and the Nature of Man* (Cleveland, Ohio: World Publishing Company, 1966); "One More Time: How Do You Motivate Employees?" *Harvard Business Review*, January/February 1968, 53–62.

5. David Kirkpatrick, "How Safe Are Video Terminals?" *Fortune*, August 29, 1988, 71.

6. Stephen Phillips and Amy Dunkin, "King Customer," *Business Week*, March 12, 1990, 91.

7. John Richard Hackman and Greg R. Oldham, *Work Redesign* (Reading, Mass.: Addison-Wesley, 1980).

8. H. John Bernardin and Joyce E. A. Russell, *Human Resource Management* (New York: McGraw-Hill, 1993), 129.

9. William E. Reif and Fred Luthans, "Does Job Enrichment Really Pay Off?" *California Management Review*, Fall 1972, 30–37; J. K. White, "Individual Differences and the Job Quality–Worker Response Relationships: Review, Integration Comments," *Academy of Management Review*, July 1978, 267–80.

10. See, for example, Eric Schine, "Mattel's Wild Race to Market," *Business Week*, February 21, 1994, 62–63; Thomas J. Peters, *Liberation Management: Necessary Disorganization for the Nanosecond Nineties* (New York: Alfred A. Knopf, 1992); and Aaron Bernstein, "Quality is Becoming Job One in the Office, Too," *Business Week*, April 29, 1991, 52–56.

11. Jana Schilder, "Work Teams Boost Productivity," *Personnel Journal*, February 1992, 67; John A. Byrne, "Management's New Gurus," *Business Week*, August 31, 1992, 50.

12. Brian Dumaine, "The Trouble with Teams," *Fortune*, September 5, 1994, 86–92.

13. Michael Hammer and James Champy, *Reengineering the Corporation* (New York: Harper Business, 1993), 148.

14. E. E. Lawler III and S. A. Mohrman, "Quality Circles: After the Honeymoon," *Organizational Dynamics* 15(4) (1987): 42–54.

15. Jon R. Katzenbach and Douglas K. Smith, "The Discipline of Teams," *Harvard Business Review*, March/April 1993, 112.

16. Ibid., 112.

17. Ibid., 114.

18. Ibid., 116.

19. Michael Hammer, "Reengineering Work: Don't Automate, Obliterate," *Harvard Business Review*, July/August 1990, 104–112.

20. Byrne, "Management's New Gurus."

21. Hammer and Champy, *Reengineering the Corporation*, 200.

22. Keith H. Hammonds, Kevin Kelly, and Karen Thurston, "Rethinking Work," *Business Week*, October 17, 1994, 84.

23. "High Tech: Blessing or Curse?" *U.S. News and World Report*, January 16, 1984, 38.

24. William J. Hampton and James R. Norman, "General Motors: What Went Wrong," *Business Review*, March 16, 1987, 106–7.

25. Peter Coy, "The New Realism in Office Systems," *Business Week*, June 15, 1992, 128–33.

26. Richard Rapaport "Jay Chiat Tears Down the Walls," *Forbes*, October 25, 1993, 25–28.

27. Luva K. Romei, "Telecommuting: A Workstyle Revolution," *Modern Office Technology*, May 1992, 38–40.

28. Drucker, *Management: Tasks, Responsibilities, Practices*.

FROM THE MANAGER'S E-MAIL

Reorganization at Adworks

You are the president of Adworks, an advertising agency that employs 150 people. Adworks designs advertising campaigns and provides marketing research for its clients. Adworks' clients are mostly large corporations primarily in three industries: regional grocery chains, regional pharmacy chains, and national motel chains. These companies hire Adworks to develop large advertising campaigns consisting of slogans and newspaper, magazine, radio, and TV ads. Adworks also conducts marketing research for these clients to test whether their advertising campaigns are working.

Adworks presently has a functional organizational structure as follows:

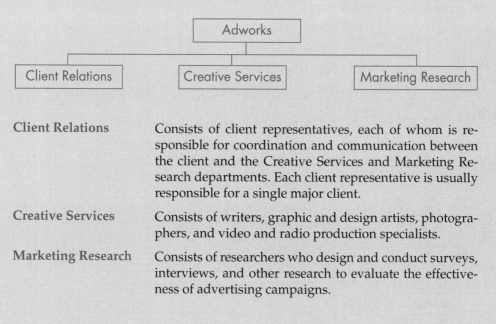

Client Relations   Consists of client representatives, each of whom is responsible for coordination and communication between the client and the Creative Services and Marketing Research departments. Each client representative is usually responsible for a single major client.

Creative Services   Consists of writers, graphic and design artists, photographers, and video and radio production specialists.

Marketing Research   Consists of researchers who design and conduct surveys, interviews, and other research to evaluate the effectiveness of advertising campaigns.

In this structure, the client representatives serve as the intermediaries, matching the client's advertising needs with the creative and marketing research services of Adworks. All communication with the client is supposed to be coordinated through the client representative. At least that is the way it is intended to work. Lately, however, problems have begun to surface. The following two E-mail memos are typical of these problems.

Date: February 6, 1996
From: LOCALSYS (George Higgins, V.P., Client Relations)
Subject: Communication Problems

It is time to do something about our channels of communication.
As you know, anyone from Adworks is supposed to communicate with
our client companies only through the client representative.
This is intended to ensure that our clients are receiving a consistent and coordinated message from us, and that they are not
receiving phone calls from 100 different Adworks people. What we
have begun seeing over the past year or so is a complete break-
down of this system. It is becoming more and more common for the
people from our Creative Services and Marketing Research departments to call and meet directly with our clients' marketing and
advertising managers. They say it takes too much time to coordinate every communication through the client representative, and
that direct communication is the only way they can meet the
clients' deadlines.

The client representatives are furious when this happens. They
say they're flying blind when they aren't made aware of what's
happening with the client, and that there's no way they can
coordinate when there's so much communication from so many
different sources.

But this is becoming more than just an internal problem for us.
The fact of the matter is that two of our largest clients are
threatening to take their business elsewhere if we don't get our
act together.

In my opinion, we've got to find a way to put the client representatives in charge so that they can ensure that communication
with our clients happens the way it's supposed to. I'll wait to
here from you on this, but I think we've got to make a move soon.

Date:	February 14, 1996
From:	LOCALSYS (Tashanda Wright, V.P. Marketing Research)
Subject:	Research Department Results

We are getting increasing pressure from our client representatives to show more positive results of our market research. One of my research supervisors told me of a situation where a research study we conducted found that the advertising campaign we designed for one of our clients is having no positive effect on that client's sales. The client representative went crazy, as if the results we found were our fault.

We are getting more and more calls from our client representatives pushing us to reword the results of our surveys to show some type of positive results, even when we find none. These people have got to learn that the Marketing Research Department's job is not to make up results that make the company look good. I think the Client Services Department needs to be reminded that they are not in charge here.

These tensions between Client Services and the Creative Services and Marketing Research departments have reached a crisis situation, particularly since major clients are now threatening to change advertising agencies. In addition, there seems to be a general change in clients' needs. What was once a relatively stable environment now is changing rapidly. Clients change advertising agencies more rapidly, and even longtime clients' needs change almost continuously, requiring the more rapid development of new advertising campaigns. This environment requires more speed and flexibility, and you are concerned that the current structure of Adworks cannot provide it.

1. Based on the models of organizational structure discussed in Chapter 8, select the design you think would be most effective in implementing Adworks' goals of speed, flexibility, and a coordinated response to customers' needs.

2. Prepare a chart showing how Adworks would be organized according to this design.

3. Prepare a brief memo describing how the new design works, and explain your reasons for selecting the new design.

SECTION

V

People and Performance

The impact of human performance on an organization's overall success is sometimes called the "people factor." The most carefully developed plans, organizational structure, and work design are little more than good ideas unless the people of the organization are able and ready to transform them into effective performance.

In the decades before the new aggressively competitive environment, the people factor was often taken for granted. As long as the workforce was able to produce products and services of an acceptable level of quality, at an acceptable level of cost, and reasonably on time, people were considered to be doing their job. It was only when the Japanese and other world competitors began providing superior products, often at lower prices, that the people factor became a major concern of management. The challenge, especially in American organizations, was to transform people from Adam Smith's "factor of production" into a genuine competitive advantage.

Chapter 10 presents five questions that reflect the concerns people have about their work in organizations. This chapter reviews the theories and concepts that clarify the meaning of each of these key performance questions. It also discusses the essential steps in creating a high-performance work environment, and the role of human resource management in developing a high-performance workforce.

In **Chapter 11** the focus is on the indispensable role of leadership in the highest-performing organizations. The chapter reviews the evolution of leadership theory from emphasis on the leader's personality to the contingency view of leadership. It describes the increasing importance of two more-recent leadership forms: the transformational leader and the team leader. Communication, perhaps the most essential ingredient for effective leadership, is also discussed.

Together these chapters emphasize the critical role that people play in the performance of organizations. As important as effective planning and organizing are to improving performance, it is still people—workers and leaders—who ultimately determine the success of organizations.

CHAPTER 10
Performance Motivation

LEARNING OBJECTIVES

After reading this chapter, you should be able to:

● *Identify the five questions people have about their work in organizations.*

● *Explain how the theories of human performance help managers to understand the issues and concerns behind these questions.*

● *Identify the four conditions required to achieve motivation in the high-performance work environment.*

● *Discuss the human resource management systems that assist in the development of a high-performance workforce.*

● *Distinguish between equal opportunity employment, affirmative action, and managing diversity.*

S outhwest Airlines, a regional airline based in Dallas, is a high-performance organization. Southwest averages 2,443 passengers per employee, which is twice the productivity rate of other airlines, including American, Delta, and USAir. In 1993 the U.S. Department of Transportation recognized Southwest as the dominant airline in the nation's busiest air-travel markets.[1] In one of the most competitive industries in the United States, in the early 1990s, Southwest Airlines outperformed virtually every other airline.

According to experts, the reason for Southwest's success during these years was its people. Southwest had created an environment in which employees were motivated to perform at levels that allowed them to succeed personally and to secure their own futures while also enabling the company to compete and prosper in its markets. In other words, the people of Southwest Airlines constituted a *high-performance workforce*. Creating this kind of workforce has become an essential management responsibility. Even the most carefully developed strategies and structures are not enough to make an organization competitive unless its people are highly motivated to perform.

PERFORMANCE IN THE CHANGING ENVIRONMENT

With the increased level and intensity of global competition, merely acceptable performance is no longer sufficient. To become more competitive, organizations have begun to focus on every factor affecting their performance, including the human factor. Increasingly, the goal is to develop a high-performance workforce.

Interestingly, one of the first steps many organizations have taken to make their workforce more competitive has been to reduce the number of people doing the work. That means having two people doing the work of three, for example, or eight thousand doing the work of twelve thousand. This approach to making people more productive is termed "downsizing" or "restructuring." Downsizing is often a result of the reengineering process described in Chapter 9.

Since downsizing and restructuring began in the early 1980s, millions of jobs have been eliminated in an effort to make organizations more competitive. Figure 10-1 offers a snapshot view of this trend by listing the number of jobs eliminated at twenty-five of the largest U.S. corporations since the early 1990s.[2]

There is no clear consensus as to what the ultimate impact of downsizing will be on the overall competitiveness of organizations.[3] But there is little doubt that the effect on workers has not been positive. Research suggests that 80 percent of downsized organizations admitted their employees' morale was significantly lowered by the elimination of so many jobs.[4] There are a number of reasons for this falloff in morale. First of all, as we mentioned in Chapter 9, those remaining after downsizing are expected to pick up the slack and do the work of the people who were let go as well as their own. Then, too, the remaining employees have often lost good friends when jobs were eliminated, people they had worked with in some cases for twenty years or longer. And finally, the remaining employees are given no assurance that their own jobs will be safe in the future.

For all these reasons, while downsizing was intended in part to make people more productive in their work, its effect in many cases has been to reduce the re-

COMPANY	STAFF CUTBACKS
IBM	85,000
AT&T	83,500
General Motors	74,000
U.S. Postal Service	55,000
Sears	50,000
Boeing	30,000
NYNEX	22,000
Hughes Aircraft	21,000
GTE	17,000
Martin Marietta	15,000
DuPont	14,800
Eastman Kodak	14,000
Philip Morris	14,000
Procter & Gamble	13,000
Phar Mor	13,000
Bank of America	12,000
Aetna	11,800
GE Aircraft Engines	10,250
McDonnell Douglas	10,200
Bellsouth	10,200
Ford Motor	10,000
Xerox	10,000
Pacific Telesis	10,000
Honeywell	9,000
U.S. West	9,000

Figure 10-1 Downsizing Jobs Eliminated at 25 Large Corporations *(Source:* Business Week Magazine, *May 9, 1994, pg. 61)*

maining employees to what one commentator called "shell-shocked survivors."[5] In these cases, the challenge for management is somehow to convert these "shell-shocked survivors" into world-class competitors.

Thus, after downsizing or restructuring, the management task of creating a high-performance workforce often becomes even more difficult. Not only must people work harder and with less job security than ever before, they must also work to a standard of quality and overall performance that the organization may have never before achieved. The task of creating a high-performance workforce, then, begins with understanding what it takes to achieve high levels of individual and team performance in an ever more challenging work environment.

THE KEY PERFORMANCE QUESTIONS

For more than fifty years, scientists, researchers, and theorists, primarily in the field of psychology, have worked to develop a clearer understanding of human motivation, of the factors that affect individual and group performance. The results of their efforts strongly suggest that human performance reflects a highly complex set of dynamics involving people's needs and goals, their skills and abilities, and the demands and challenges of the task itself. One way of understanding this complex set of factors is to examine five key questions that reflect fundamental concerns people have about their work in organizations.

1. Is the task well defined?

2. If I try to perform the task, will I succeed?

3. If I succeed, will I be rewarded?

4. Is the reward something I value?

5. Is the reward fair?

Given the importance of these questions, the challenge for managers is to create a work environment in which the answer to each question is yes. Each of these concerns must be satisfied for individuals and teams to perform well.

We will begin our discussion of these key performance questions with a review of certain theories and concepts that help clarify their meaning. We will then discuss the steps management can take to ensure that the answer to these questions will support the development of a high-performance workforce.

Question 1: Is the Task Well Defined?

The first thing people want to know about their work is what task is to be performed. Whether on a sports team, in schoolwork, or in the workplace, we are much more likely to perform better when we understand what the task is and how we are expected to perform it.

Goal Theory

Goal theory, as presented in Chapter 4, can help managers understand more clearly what individuals and teams want in terms of task definition. To perform well, people need their work defined in the same way that effective goals are defined. That is, the work must be described in terms that are specific, meaningful, accepted, realistic and time-framed, in other words "SMART."

Expecting people to perform well when they are uncertain about the task is like expecting someone to play a sport or a card game with which they are unfamiliar: Even if they try very hard, they are unlikely to perform well unless they have a natural ability for the game. Without a clear understanding of what the task is, no level of motivation may be high enough to result in successful performance. This is true whether the task is preparing a sales report, serving on a problem-solving team, or working with a customer. Goal theory provides management with both an understanding of the importance of defining the task well and the means for defining tasks in specific terms so that higher levels of performance become much more possible.

Question 2: If I Try, Will I Succeed?

This second question has to do with confidence and competence. It is the question of whether an individual feels capable of performing the required tasks.

Competence Motivation

According to Robert W. White, one of the strongest sources of motivation in human action is the desire for competence.[6] From the very first years of life, we see the efforts of individuals to succeed at the tasks that confront them in their environment, from passing a spoon from one hand to another, to learning to walk, to learning to write their name. At every stage of life there is a powerful desire to succeed at the tasks required in situations of all types. It is this desire for mastery or success in our environment that White characterizes as the motivation for competence.

The concept of competence motivation suggests that we are all drawn most strongly to the tasks at which we feel we can succeed. Nowhere is this more evident than in the workplace. People are quick to recognize the tasks which they feel they are competent to perform and to avoid or hesitate on those for which they do not feel competent. Only when people have full confidence in their skills are they likely to commit themselves to the full effort needed to achieve success on a task. Often, an individual's lack of confidence can lead to lack of effort, which in turn results in performance problems.

Working in performance teams, for example, requires skills in terms of conflict management and group decision-making that many individuals have never had the opportunity to develop. It is not unusual to see individuals give up or sit back in situations, not because they don't care but because they know they don't have the skills to be successful as fully participating team members.

Because of this link between competence, confidence, and level of effort, management must ensure that people possess the skills to be successful in the tasks they are asked to perform.

Question 3: If I Succeed, Will I Be Rewarded?

As we said earlier, the new competition requires consistently higher levels of individual and team performance than organizations have been achieving in the past. Naturally, these increased levels of performance require greater effort on the part of workers. Therefore, the question "Will I be rewarded?" is really asking, "Will I be rewarded for putting in more effort rather than the same amount or less?" Obviously, the challenge for management is to create a work environment in which this question too will be answered yes.

Reinforcement Theory

Reinforcement theory provides a very useful explanation for both understanding and answering the question of rewards. B. F. Skinner, perhaps the most famous reinforcement theorist, suggested that performance is influenced more than anything else by the consequences of performance, by what happens after people perform.[7] In other words, the amount of effort people put into a task depends on what happens to them once they complete the task. Figure 10-2 outlines the four types or categories of consequences of performance Skinner suggested.

An illustration of the kinds of consequences described in reinforcement theory can be seen in *The Soul of a New Machine* by Tracy Kidder. This book tells the story of a group of engineers and software programmers who worked twelve- and fifteen-hour days, six and seven days a week for more than a year, to complete the development of a computer called "Eagle."[8]

According to Kidder, one reason for this team's superior effort was a reward called "pinball," the term used in that company to describe the fact that if you were successful, as in pinball, you got to play again. This is an example of *positive reinforcement,* and on the Eagle team, the assumption was that if you succeeded on one major project you would be allowed to work on the next one.

A second explanation for the high level of performance by the Eagle team is *negative reinforcement.* According to this explanation, the Eagle team worked as hard as they did to avoid being assigned to minor, less interesting projects, as they almost certainly would be if the Eagle project failed. This high level of performance to avoid negative consequences is exactly what Skinner meant by negative reinforcement.

What actually appears to have happened in the case of the Eagle project team is described in reinforcement theory as *extinction.* Despite having successfully completed their work on the Eagle project, there was no "pinball" reward; most team members were not reassigned to the kinds of major projects they had hoped for. There was no reinforcement, and just as Skinner might have predicted, in the years following Eagle most of the team members did not continue their high level of effort but instead drifted away to other companies.

CONSEQUENCES THAT STRENGTHEN BEHAVIOR		
POSITIVE REINFORCEMENT	= BEHAVIOR + POSITIVE CONSEQUENCE	
NEGATIVE REINFORCEMENT	= BEHAVIOR + AVOIDANCE OF NEGATIVE CONSEQUENCE	
CONSEQUENCES THAT WEAKEN BEHAVIOR		
PUNISHMENT	= BEHAVIOR + NEGATIVE CONSEQUENCE	
EXTINCTION	= BEHAVIOR + NO CONSEQUENCE	

Figure 10-2 Types of Consequences in Reinforcement Theory

The "killer software" at Cypress Semiconductor, which we discussed in Chapter 4, provides a clear example of *punishment*, the fourth category of consequences in reinforcement theory. You will remember that Cypress CEO T. J. Rodgers used software programs to shut down the computers of any department that was falling behind its schedules or that in any other way was not keeping pace with performance standards. According to Skinner, the effect of punishment is almost always to reduce the likelihood of repetition of the punished behavior in the future. Obviously, this was exactly the intent of Rodgers with his "killer software."

As with the other key performance questions, the challenge for management is to ensure a positive answer to the question "If I succeed, will I be rewarded?" People generally are not looking to be punished or ignored for their performance; they are looking to be rewarded (positively reinforced). Management's job is to ensure that high levels of work performance result directly in the most positive consequences possible.

Question 4: Is the Reward Something I Value?

It is not enough simply to reward people for their performance; it is also essential that the reward be of value to them. Another way to ask this question is, "Is the reward something I *need*?" People tend to value most the things which they need most. Understanding how to provide rewards that people value, then, can begin with an understanding of human needs.

Needs Theory

Some of the most important contributions to our understanding of human needs have come from psychologist Abraham Maslow.[9] Maslow suggested that most of our needs can be grouped into five categories and arranged in levels, as shown in Figure 10-3.

Maslow suggested a number of interesting things about human needs. He began with the assumption that in any given situation human behavior, or performance (we will use the two terms interchangeably), tends to reflect the particular need level of the individual in the particular situation. For example, he points out that different individuals in exactly the same situation might behave or perform totally differently depending on their needs at the time. Someone at the esteem-need level, for example, might work extremely hard to receive recognition. Someone at the social-need level, on the other hand, might only work hard enough to be accepted by the group he or she is working in. And someone at the security-need level might purposely perform only well enough to keep his or her job, while avoiding receiving any attention at all.

There are a number of other needs theories that overlap and expand on Maslow's hierarchy. David McClelland, for example, has talked about the need for power and the need for achievement, and the need for affiliation which is similar to Maslow's social need.[10] Clayton Alderfer has described three levels of needs: existence needs, which correspond to Maslow's physiological and security needs; relatedness needs, similar to Maslow's social need; and growth needs, which would include Maslow's needs for esteem and self-actualization.[11] The

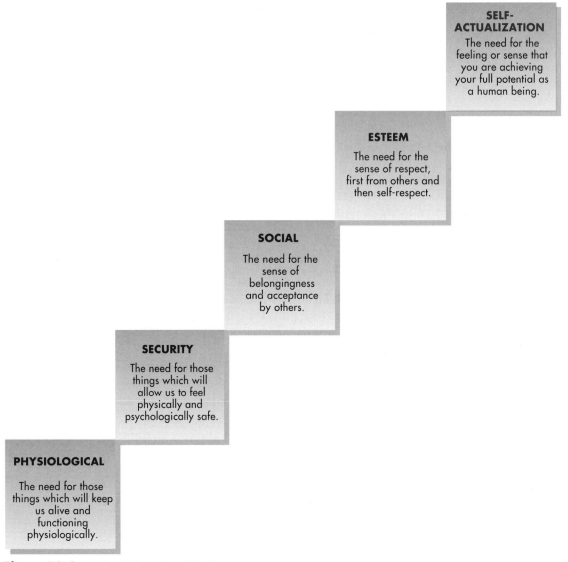

Figure 10-3 Maslow's Hierarchy of Needs

message for management from all of these needs theorists is the same: Management must recognize and understand the need levels of employees, and create opportunities for them to pursue the satisfaction of these needs through the work that they do.

Expectancy Theory

The last three questions we have considered—If I try, will I succeed? If I succeed, will I be rewarded? Is the reward something I value?—together form the focus of what is called expectancy theory. *Expectancy theory,* which was developed by Victor Vroom, suggests that the effort an individual puts into a task will be greater if he or she expects to succeed at the task, to be rewarded for the task, and that the reward is something he or she values.[12] If any one of these elements is missing, the theory emphasizes—if the answer to any of these questions is no—high levels of effort, and therefore high levels of performance, become much less likely.

For example, expectancy theory would predict a low level of effort by team members trying to complete a project by a specific deadline if they expected that (a) no matter how many hours they spent working each day, they still could not meet the deadline, or (b) even if they met the deadline, there would be no reward, or (c) there would be a reward, but not one the team members valued.

The point of Vroom's expectancy model, summarized in Figure 10-4, is in emphasizing the importance of positive expectations and how quickly motivation falls when the individual's expectations are less positive or when the outcome is less valued.

The expectancy model makes clear how important it is for managers to create and support the highest possible expectations in their people. Management must give workers confidence that high levels of effort will lead to high levels of success, and that successful performance will result in rewards that their people genuinely value.

Question 5: Is the Reward Fair?

To perform at their best, people want to know not only that they will be rewarded and that the reward is something they value, but also that the reward is fair. According to the equity theory developed by J. Stacy Adams, when people perceive the reward as fair, performance will be stronger. When they perceive the reward as unfair, performance becomes a problem. This theory about the impact of fairness on performance is called *equity theory.*

Equity Theory

Equity theory suggests that people view the equity or fairness of rewards on two levels. The first has to do with whether the reward is proportionate to the effort required. Most people, for example, would not view as fair the offer to have one day off during the week in return for having to work both days of the weekend. Most people would expect at least two days off during the week for giving up their weekend; many would expect three days off. The point is that if people view the reward as not equal to or worth the effort required, their performance will not be as strong.

The other level of equity has to do with whether the reward is similar or

Figure 10-4 Expectancy Theory: Calculation of the Motivation to Perform a Task

comparable to what others are getting for similar or comparable efforts. Most people will be satisfied with a reward for performance until they discover that someone else is receiving a larger reward for performing the same task, or the same reward for doing less.[13] It appears to be human nature for an individual to be pleased with a 4 percent salary increase, for example, until he or she hears of a coworker performing at the same level getting a 6 percent increase.

The final question people have about performance, then—Is the reward for performance fair?—really has two parts: Is the reward proportionate to the effort, and is it comparable to what others are getting? If the answer to these questions is yes, the effort needed for high performance is much more likely.

Goal theory, reinforcement theory, needs theory, and expectancy and equity theories each can help managers understand the questions people ask in the high-performance work environment, to know what the questions mean and the answers that are needed. Figure 10-5 summarizes the key performance questions and the theories that shed light on the issues they raise.

THEORY INTO PRACTICE: CREATING A HIGH-PERFORMANCE WORK ENVIRONMENT

Over the past ten years, organizations of every size and kind have been experimenting with different approaches to create a high-performance work environment. From these experiments, it appears that there are at least four essential requirements for creating such an environment. Figure 10-6 briefly describes these four elements. In the sections that follow, we will consider these requirements in some detail, as well as what management has learned as it has begun to put theory into practice in pursuit of high performance.

Goals: A Target to Aim For

To the question "Is the task well defined?" management's response must be a set of fully developed goals and standards that define exactly what the task is. There

PERFORMANCE QUESTIONS/CONCERNS	CLARIFYING THEORY
Is the task well defined?	Goal theory
If I try, will I succeed?	Competence motivation Expectancy theory
If I succeed, will I be rewarded?	Reinforcement theory Expectancy theory
Is the reward something I value?	Needs theory Expectancy theory
Is the reward fair?	Equity theory

Figure 10-5 Performance Questions/Concerns and the Theories that Clarify These Concerns

- Clearly defined goals
- Continuous training
- A stake in performance
- Employee involvement

Figure 10-6 Requirements for the High Performance Work Environment

is not much sense in seeking high levels of performance without carefully defining what high-level performance means. It does no good, for example, as we said in Chapter 4, simply to direct a team leader to "communicate more effectively" with his or her team members. Goals must be developed that define what is meant by more effective communication. These goals might include meeting with team members for at least twenty minutes every morning, providing team members printed copies of all important information, speaking with every team member at least once a day, requesting input and ideas from team members at least once a week, providing complete responses to inquiries and suggestions within forty-eight hours, and so on. With such specific goals, the team leader knows exactly what is expected in terms of the communication task he or she is expected to perform. Clearly defined goals are among management's most effective tools for clarifying tasks. High performance requires clear targets.

Training: Ensuring the Ability to Perform

As important as a clear target is, having the skills to achieve it is obviously also essential for success. People need to have confidence that they possess the skills necessary for success. Training is the essential management tool for ensuring that people develop the skills they need to perform. Surveys indicate that the vast majority of training programs presently being provided in organizations are not targeted for specific jobs or tasks. They focus on higher-level skills that an individual can transfer or use for whatever task she or he is performing—skills such as time management, performance appraisal, word processing, and leadership.[14]

Evidence of organizations' growing commitment to developing the skills needed for competitiveness is everywhere. By the late 1980s, expenditures related to training in U.S. organizations were exceeding $40 billion a year.[15] Spending for training at IBM alone began to exceed $1 billion a year.[16] In companies like Motorola, Corning, and GM's Saturn division, 5 percent of total expenditures are for educating, training, and developing their people.[17]

Although it is difficult to tie specific training programs to specific performance achievements, some organizations do attribute their higher productivity to employee training. Motorola estimates its return on investment for employee training at 30 to 1.[18] In other words, Motorola estimates that for every $1,000 it invests in the education and training of its people, it achieves a $30,000 improvement in performance.

With expenditures and results such as these, it is clear that organizations now recognize the essential place of training in creating high-performance work environments. Continuous training is a critical element of the organization's answer to the question "If I try, will I succeed?" It is also the answer to the organization's needs for a workforce with skills equal to the challenges of the changing environment.

Incentives: Creating a Stake in Performance

A third key element in creating a high-performance environment is incentives or rewards. For people to perform at consistently high levels, they must have a stake or an interest in doing so. They must have a reason for improving their performance. They must in some way be rewarded.

Increasingly, there is concern that well-defined goals and standards and continuous training may not be enough to sustain high levels of work performance over the long term. According to Massachusetts Institute of Technology professor Paul Osterman, ". . . you can't expect workers to keep contributing their ideas when they don't get rewarded for them."[19]

Two incentives which organizations can offer employees as rewards for improved performance are the opportunity to develop their skills and the promise of higher levels of pay for higher levels of performance.

The Opportunity for Development

In an environment where job security is not as readily available as it once was, workers need to develop and expand themselves, to learn the broadest possible range of skills to become increasingly more qualified for a wider and wider range of positions in the job market. Given this newly emerging need for skill development, the opportunity for training and experience in a high-performance work environment becomes more valuable to the worker and therefore a more powerful incentive.

Consider the case of computer programmers. The organization is convinced that individuals in this position would be even more effective if they received training in teamwork and group decision-making. Their incentive for learning these skills is not just to improve performance on their present job, but to increase their overall skills should they ever decide—or be required—to reenter the job market. In other words, the individual programmers' own professional development is the stake or interest they have for learning the skills that lead to higher performance.

Organizations must recognize and develop the opportunity for workers to learn and increase skills as one of the important incentives in a high-performance work environment. Increased levels of skills are a reward with a payoff for both the individual and the organization.

Pay for Performance (PFP)

Pay for performance, or *PFP,* is a strategy of linking pay directly to the key areas of performance in people's jobs. For service representatives, pay is linked to the speed and satisfaction with which they can resolve customer complaints or questions. For manufacturing workers, pay is linked to achieving quality standards. For managers, pay is linked to how well their people perform. In every application, the basic strategy of PFP is the same: Do not base pay simply on adequate performance. Provide people with a reason to perform better. Set goals, establish targets, and reward people for achieving them.

There are many different types of PFP programs. As shown in Figure 10-7, some programs link pay to individual performance; others link pay to group performance or to the performance of the entire organization.

In 1980, fewer than 10 percent of companies were using some form of PFP. By 1990, more than 50 percent were.[20] Companies using PFP are as different as General Motors and Burger King, Blockbuster Video and the federal government, Reebok and Federal Express. And while many early PFP plans covered only executives or sales personnel, one survey of Fortune 1000 companies found that 31 percent of these companies now have PFP programs covering all their employees.[21]

Problems with PFP Programs.   PFP programs are not without problems. To avoid conflict and negative reaction by employees, some managers may tend

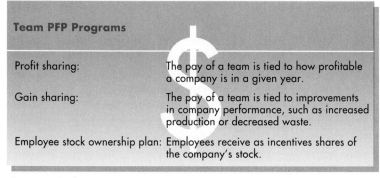

Figure 10-7   Types of Pay for Performance (PFP) Programs

either to give everyone in a unit or work group the same raise or to identify the vast majority of employees as "superior" or "outstanding." The latter situation occurred at General Motors when merit raises became automatic, regardless of performance level.[22] This left little incentive for people to perform better.

Other problems with PFP include competition among workers for higher ratings, and situations where the increase for a high performer isn't sufficient to motivate greater effort, or where there are no profits to share because of poor economic conditions. For all of these reasons, achieving the improved performance that is possible through PFP is not an easy task.

On the other hand, there are many encouraging examples. Take the very positive experience of the Lincoln Electric Company, located in Cleveland, Ohio. For more than 50 years, Lincoln Electric has operated perhaps the most unusual system of PFP in the world. The workers receive no base wage; 100 percent of what they earn is determined by performance. There are no paid holidays or sick days. The people at Lincoln Electric get paid only for what they produce. How well does PFP work at Lincoln Electric? In 1993, the average pay for a manufacturing worker was around $51,000, while the company successfully maintained its competitive advantage of being the lowest-cost producer in the industry. One of the advantages of PFP is that it can change how the worker views his or her job. According to one Lincoln Electric employee, "I don't work for Lincoln Electric; I work for myself . . . I'm an entrepreneur."[23]

PFP may not be easy to implement. Still, theory and research strongly emphasize how important incentives and rewards are for high levels of work performance. PFP gives people a clear stake in their own success and the success of the organization.

Involving Employees: Sharing Responsibility for Performance

The fourth key element in a high-performance work environment has been given several different labels: "participative management," "employee involvement," and most recently, "employee empowerment."[24] The most effective goal and incentive systems do not exist in a vacuum; almost always they are part of an overall management effort to more fully involve people in the responsibility for their own performance.

Employee Empowerment

Employee empowerment is the process of sharing with employees the responsibility for improving performance. As competitive pressures began to intensify in the 1980s at companies like Xerox, Ford, Johnson & Johnson, Harley-Davidson, GM's Saturn division, and others, managers began to share the traditional management responsibility for improving performance with their employees.

Empowerment has taken different forms in different organizations. At Johnsonville Foods of Sheboygan, Wisconsin, teams of employees share the responsibilities for hiring their own team members and for determining which employees are offered permanent employee status. Team members also do their own taste tests to determine whether the product is ready for shipping to the customer. At Xerox, employees implement their own solutions to performance problems such as how to better meet deadlines and delivery schedules, and they set their own work hours. At Harley-Davidson, workers suggested that a problem-plagued, multimillion-dollar parts storage system be shut down and replaced with their own "low-tech" system of wooden rolling storage racks. At each of these companies, employee empowerment resulted in increased levels of worker and organizational performance.

Does Empowerment Work? For a number of years there has been a steady flow of success stories about employee empowerment, ranging from the rebirth of Harley-Davidson to the triumph of the Saturn automobile. However, the early empirical research on empowerment has been somewhat less positive. Some reports question whether empowerment promises more in terms of performance improvements than it can actually deliver. One study, for example, found that some companies employing empowerment strategies were actually less efficient than companies not using empowerment. Another suggested that empowerment works best only in companies that are already achieving high levels of performance. Lower-performing companies often lack the training resources to make empowerment work.[25]

This last point suggests that the problem may not be with the empowerment strategies themselves, but with implementing them.[26] It is often difficult for managers to give up or even to share the authority and responsibility that have defined the essence of management for nearly a century. In addition, not all workers are eager to take on even part of the responsibility for the problems surrounding their work, especially when they do not feel they will be given the authority to make real changes or improvements.

To address these problems, guidelines such as those shown in Figure 10-8 might be considered for effectively involving or empowering workers.[27]

Provide a positive emotional atmosphere. Create an atmosphere of trust and achievement by staging events designed to inspire, build confidence, challenge, and encourage play.

Reward and encourage in personal ways. Publicly praise and recognize achievement. Develop events and ceremonies to celebrate groups and individuals who make important contributions.

Express confidence. Spend significant amounts of time praising people's abilities and expressing confidence in their future performance, in speeches, at meetings, and in the hallways.

Foster initiative and responsibility. Design tasks and delegate authority in ways that encourage people to take individual initiative and responsibility, to accept "ownership" of their jobs.

Build on success. Begin with small manageable tasks so that the likelihood of early success and achievement is increased. Create situations where a sense of mastery is more likely to be experienced.

Figure 10-8 What Managers Can Do to Empower Their People

The successes of empowerment at Ford, Saturn, Harley-Davidson, Xerox, and Johnson & Johnson make clear that higher levels of performance do become possible when employees are truly empowered, when management effectively shares the responsibility for performance. The challenge for management is to overcome the obstacles that exist and to genuinely involve workers in taking their own performance to the highest levels.

To summarize, then, the four essential conditions for creating a high-performance work environment are well-defined goals and standards, continuous training in high-level skills, performance-based incentives, and employee empowerment. To be effective, these conditions must be implemented through a coordinated set of systems and programs designed specifically to create and develop a high-performance workforce. These systems and programs represent a special responsibility of management known as human resource management.

HUMAN RESOURCE MANAGEMENT

The goal of *human resource management (HRM)* is to recruit, develop, and retain the highly skilled people needed for an organization to pursue and achieve its strategic goals. The most important areas or systems in HRM are shown in Figure 10-9. Effective systems in each of these areas are essential to the development and support of a high-performance workforce.

HRM Systems

In large corporations, responsibility for developing human resource management systems is often assigned to human resource professionals with expertise in such areas as job analysis, recruiting and selection, training, compensation analysis,

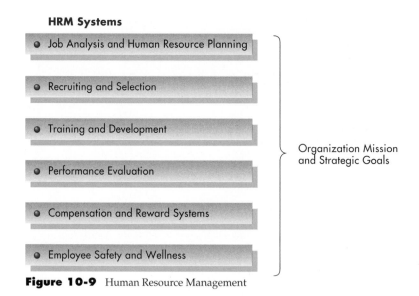

Figure 10-9 Human Resource Management

and so forth. But effective HRM systems are of vital concern to managers throughout the organization. It is only through such systems that managers at every level can be assured the skilled workers needed for high performance.

Job Analysis and Human Resource Planning

The design of effective HRM systems begins with effective job analysis. *Job analysis* is the process of describing the major tasks and responsibilities of each position in the organization, as well as the knowledge, abilities, skills, and other characteristics needed to perform them. Job analysis culminates in the development of *job descriptions,* which list the tasks, responsibilities, and skills required for each position. A sample job description is shown in Figure 10-10.

In many ways, the job description represents the keystone around which the

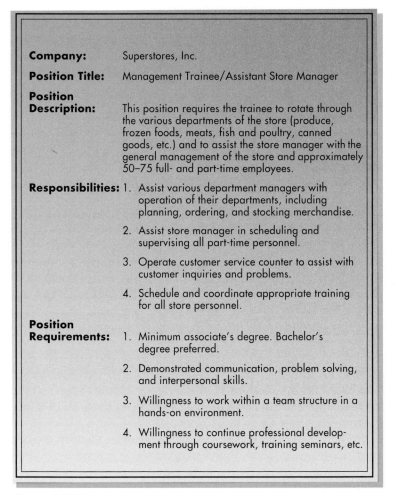

Company:	Superstores, Inc.
Position Title:	Management Trainee/Assistant Store Manager
Position Description:	This position requires the trainee to rotate through the various departments of the store (produce, frozen foods, meats, fish and poultry, canned goods, etc.) and to assist the store manager with the general management of the store and approximately 50–75 full- and part-time employees.
Responsibilities:	1. Assist various department managers with operation of their departments, including planning, ordering, and stocking merchandise.
	2. Assist store manager in scheduling and supervising all part-time personnel.
	3. Operate customer service counter to assist with customer inquiries and problems.
	4. Schedule and coordinate appropriate training for all store personnel.
Position Requirements:	1. Minimum associate's degree. Bachelor's degree preferred.
	2. Demonstrated communication, problem solving, and interpersonal skills.
	3. Willingness to work within a team structure in a hands-on environment.
	4. Willingness to continue professional development through coursework, training seminars, etc.

Figure 10-10 Sample Job Description

other HRM systems are built. The requirements listed in the job descriptions provide a starting point for determining the individuals who will be recruited and hired by the organization, the areas in which training may be needed, the wage or salary level for each position, and the criteria on which performance will be evaluated. In recent years there have been efforts to make job descriptions more general to ensure that individuals with a broader range of skills are hired. This allows organizations greater flexibility for combining positions and moving individuals from one position to another.

The importance of job analysis has been recognized for nearly a century, since the time of Frederick Taylor and scientific management. Recognition of the importance of human resource planning, however, is considerably more recent.

Human resource planning is the process of developing plans and strategies to ensure the availability and development of the human resources an organization needs to achieve its strategic goals. With the constantly changing level of competition in recent years, and the continuing development of information and other work technologies, a comprehensive plan for matching the organization's human resources to the challenges of the environment has become increasingly essential.

For example, as companies have downsized as a way to reduce expenses to meet the competition, it is often the responsibility of HRM to develop and implement plans for training and job redesign, to allow the organization to perform the same tasks with fewer workers. Similarly, an organization poised for expansion must also develop a human resource plan, in this case for recruiting and training the workforce it will need to meet its growth targets.

Recruiting and Selection

Not everyone is well suited to the demands of a high-performance work environment. Some individuals are uncomfortable with the constant training, pay for performance, and additional responsibilities associated with employee empowerment. The task of human resource management is to recruit and select people with the skills and personalities that can meet these challenges.

It is not an easy task. In one recent survey of business owners, 75 percent said that difficulty attracting and keeping skilled workers was among the most serious threats to the success of their companies.[28] Chemical Bank of New York has reported interviewing forty applicants to fill one teller position, and NYNEX tested sixty thousand applicants to fill three thousand positions. Similarly, the U.S. Labor Department projects that by the year 2000 less than 25 percent of the workforce will have the skills and education necessary to perform 60 percent of the new jobs created.[29] The other 75 percent will be chasing after the other 40 percent of the new jobs. Since the demand for high-skilled individuals appears to be much greater than the supply, organizations must learn to compete successfully for the individuals with the best skills.

It is the responsibility of human resource management to identify the best potential employees as well as the schools and programs that are the most likely sources of these potential employees. After testing and evaluating individuals' skills and other job-related characteristics, HRM is responsible for recruiting candidates with the greatest potential for success in the high-performance work environment.

Training and Development

Few employees come to work in an organization possessing all of the skills and competencies required for high performance. Employees require training in the organization's particular technologies and software, for example, or in the planning, decision-making, and teamwork skills required for effective empowerment. Managers require training in defining goals, coaching, and sharing responsibility. The need for effective training, as we discussed earlier, is continuous and continuously changing.

It is one thing to recognize the need for and importance of training; it is another to create training programs that ensure that everyone throughout the organization continues to develop the skills required for the highest levels of performance. Human resources management is responsible for determining which skills currently are critical to the organization's success and who in the organization must possess those and other skills. But this is only the beginning. Once the need has been defined, programs must be identified or developed to meet the training need. What, for example, might be the most effective way to deliver the training? Through a training consultant? Videotapes? Coworkers who already possess the skill? Self-paced computer programs? And so on.

Even after the training program has been delivered, HRM has the responsibility to assess whether the training has been effective in actually developing the targeted skills. As we pointed out earlier, the highest-performing organizations are making increasingly larger investments in employee training. It is the responsibility of human resources management to ensure that such investments pay off: to see not only that training is taking place, but that it is the right training and that it works.

Performance Evaluation

Performance evaluation is the process of measuring an individual's or team's actual performance against performance goals or standards. This process serves a number of important purposes in developing a high-performance workforce. First, performance evaluation provides individuals or teams with feedback about how well they are doing. Second, it identifies specific areas where individuals or teams need additional training to increase their effectiveness. Third, the information from the performance evaluation process becomes valuable input for decisions regarding promotion, transfer, and termination. This kind of input helps to ensure that positions throughout the organization are staffed by individuals with the greatest potential for effective performance.

Performance evaluation is particularly important in organizations utilizing pay for performance as part of their high-performance strategy. If individuals are to be paid on the basis of how well they perform, a system for measuring performance must be in place that both management and employees view as fair and accurate.

An example of such a system is shown in Figure 10-11. Lincoln Electric, mentioned earlier in the chapter, uses merit rating cards to evaluate not only the quantity and quality of worker output, but also each worker's dependability and cooperation.

Designing effective performance evaluation systems is a challenge for HRM.

Increasing Quality →

This card rates the QUALITY of work you do.

It also reflects your success in eliminating errors and in reducing scrap and waste.

QUALITY

This rating has been done jointly by your department head and the Inspection Department in the shop and with other department heads in the office and engineering.

Increasing Dependability →

This card rates how well your supervisors have been able to depend upon you to do those things that have been expected of you without supervision.

It also rates your ability to supervise yourself, including your work safety performance, your orderliness, care of equipment, and the effective use you make of your skills.

DEPENDABILITY

This rating has been done by your department head.

Increasing Ideas & Cooperation →

This card rates your COOPERATION, IDEAS and INITIATIVE.

IDEAS & COOPERATION

Increasing Output →

Days Absent

This card rates HOW MUCH PRODUCTIVE WORK you actually turn out.

It also reflects your willingness not to hold back and recognizes your attendance record.

New ideas and new methods are important to your company in our continuing effort to reduce costs, increase output, improve quality—work safely and improve our relationship with our customers. This card credits you for your ideas and initiative used to help in this direction.

It also rates your cooperation—how to work with others as a team. Such factors as your attitude toward supervision, co-workers, and the company; your efforts to share your expert knowledge with others, and your cooperation in installing new methods smoothly are considered here.

OUTPUT

This rating has been done jointly by your department head and the Production Control Department in the shop and with other department heads in the office and engineering.

It is difficult to define specific performance goals or standards for every kind of job. It is also sometimes difficult to accurately measure every aspect of an individual's work performance. For these reasons the process of performance evaluation can be an uncomfortable one both for managers and for employees. The benefits of effective performance evaluation are so significant, however, that high-performance organizations continue their efforts to improve their systems of performance evaluation and feedback.

Compensation

Compensation is the term for all of the various kinds of rewards employees receive for the work they do in organizations. It includes wages, salaries, and bonuses as well as health, disability, and unemployment insurances, and paid time away from the job for holidays, vacation, and illness.

We have emphasized the importance of providing the workforce with a stake in high performance, a reason to perform well rather than merely adequately. We have identified a number of ways in which organizations are attempting to create incentives for high-level work performance, including merit increases, bonuses, profit sharing, and employee stock ownership plans. Clearly, tying pay to performance is a key element in developing a high-performance workforce.

However, there are limits to how much compensation organizations can offer as incentives to better performance. The major limitation is that organizations cannot allow compensation levels to rise so high that the products or services they provide become too expensive for their customers. This is exactly what happened in the 1980s, when total compensation costs for workers in the United States and Europe rose so high that the Japanese and other low-labor-cost competitors were able to sell automobiles, home electronics, and other products at lower prices. With lower-labor-cost nations like Mexico, Malaysia, Korea, and China now competing globally, there is more pressure than ever before to keep tight control over labor costs and compensation.

The challenge for human resource management is to develop compensation systems that allow the organization to attract and hold on to a high-performance workforce without allowing the cost of compensation to weaken the organization's ability to compete.

Employee Safety and Wellness

Lost work time and other expenses associated with accidents and illness are one of the most serious threats to an organization's ability to operate at high performance levels. At a Senate Labor Committee hearing, it was reported that 10,000 Americans, or 40 people each working day, die each year from occupational injuries. Another 100,000 more, or 400 a day, die from occupation-related diseases.[30] Concern for the safety of employees resulted in 1970 in the creation of the federal agency known as OSHA (Occupational Safety and Health Administration). Meeting the standards established by OSHA is a major HRM responsibility.

Management, with the assistance of human resource professionals, is also responsible for employee wellness issues that impact employee performance in

Figure 10-11 (*opposite page*) Lincoln Electric Evaluation Forms

the workplace. These include alcohol and drug dependency, AIDS, and psychological problems. Referrals for professional help and rehabilitation are ways to deal with employees' psychological problems and substance dependency. State and federal laws require the development of AIDS education programs and policies ensuring reasonable accommodation of employees disabled by AIDS. All these activities relating to the wellness of employees are part of the organization's efforts to overcome some of the more difficult barriers to effective employee performance.

Equal Employment Opportunity and Affirmative Action

Beyond complying with the health and safety standards established by OSHA, organizations increasingly have been required to conform to other laws and regulations relating to human resources. The legal requirements most affecting HRM are those dealing with the issue of equal employment opportunity (EEO). EEO laws are designed to establish a discrimination-free workplace. Figure 10-12 briefly identifies major EEO laws, which have implications for hiring, recruiting, training, terminating, compensating, evaluating, and disciplining employees.

One response to EEO laws has been the development of affirmative action plans. These plans allow employers to take action to overcome the effects of past practices that have resulted in barriers to equal employment opportunity. Such actions might include setting goals to increase the percentage of members of certain groups (for example, women and minorities) within the organization or seeking to increase the number of minority-group members who receive promotions. Objections to affirmative action plans have been raised based on the charge that such goals result in unfair preferential treatment for members of these groups at the time of hiring and promotion. Defenders of affirmative action insist that the history of discrimination has left the members of these groups at a tremendous disadvantage and that affirmative action is necessary if significant progress is to be made in providing genuinely equal employment opportunity.

The Diversity Challenge

The diversity challenge goes beyond the legal requirement to create a discrimination-free workplace. The larger challenge is to develop an environment that attracts and empowers the most talented workers regardless of gender, race, age, or physical capability.

Initial efforts at creating such an environment have met with limited success. In many cases, complying with EEO laws has proved to be only a first step in meeting the diversity challenge. Many organizations have discovered that to move beyond providing equal employment opportunity to creating a work environment where all members of the organization value the differences among them can be a difficult process.

In many cases EEO requirements and, especially, affirmative action efforts have produced resentment against individuals and groups who are perceived as receiving preferential treatment in hiring and promotion. On the other hand, individuals and groups who are hired and promoted through EEO programs feel that they must constantly fight the perception that they received unfair preference.

Civil Rights Act of 1964 (Title VII) as amended by the Equal Opportunity Act of 1972

Forbids discrimination on the basis of an individual's race, color, religion, sex, or natural origin.

Age Discrimination in Employment Act of 1967 as amended in 1978

Forbids discrimination against individuals because of age.

Equal Pay Act of 1963

Forbids discrimination between employees on the basis of sex by paying wages less than the rate at which employees of the opposite sex are paid for equal work.

Rehabilitation Act of 1973

Requires certain federal contractors to employ and promote qualified handicapped individuals.

Vietnam Era Veterans' Readjustment Act of 1974

Requires affirmative action to employ and promote qualified special disabled veterans and veterans of the Vietnam era.

Pregnancy Discrimination Act of 1978

Forbids discrimination of pregnant women.

Americans with Disabilities Act of 1990 (ADA)

Requires employers to make reasonable accommodations to the known disabilities of employees or customers.

Civil Rights Act of 1991

Amends and expands the coverage of Title VII of the 1964 Civil Rights Act.

Family and Medical Leave Act of 1993 (FMLA)

Provides leave of absence for birth, adoption, serious illness of the employee or spouse, child or parent without threat of loss of employment, status or position.

Figure 10-12 Major Equal Employment Opportunity Laws

These are hardly the kinds of feelings that contribute to an environment where employee diversity is genuinely valued.

Guidelines for Managing Diversity

Fortunately, a number of organizations—Xerox, AT&T, IBM, Avon, and Levi Strauss among them—have maintained their commitment to developing a work environment that values the diversity of their employees. Some of the guidelines that have emerged from the efforts of these companies at managing diversity are discussed in the following paragraphs.[31]

Get the CEO's Commitment.   Addressing diversity issues is difficult to do well and is therefore easy to place on a back burner. When the head of the organization makes diversity a priority, everyone pays closer attention.

Set Specific Diversity Goals.   Set specific targets, such as 30 percent representation of females and minorities at all levels of the organization, especially management, by the year 2000. Measure managers' performance in terms of their contribution to these goals, and base compensation on their level of success.

Adopt a Plan for Addressing the Concerns of White Males.   White males still constitute roughly half of the overall workforce, and hold 60 percent of all management positions. Individuals from this group may feel threatened when preference is given to women and minorities in the workplace, and may view this practice as "reverse discrimination." Organizations need to acknowledge and directly address their concerns. It needs to be made clear to every member of the organization why it is in everyone's best interest to participate in the development of a diverse workforce.

Provide Training in Valuing Diversity—Carefully.   It is important, but difficult, to provide training that allows others to experience what it is like to be a minority in our culture without also seeming to point a finger of blame at nonminority participants. People often feel threatened and uncomfortable when they are required to role-play difficult diversity situations. This is sometimes not the most effective emotional state for learning. One promising approach to diversity training is to present movies such as *Thelma and Louise, Malcolm X,* or *Philadelphia* and involve participants in discussions of what they experience and feel, and how this can be applied to improve their own organization's performance in the area of diversity.

Other guidelines for creating an organization where diversity is valued include celebrating differences among workers through special events, videos, and newsletters, as well as developing strategies to identify sources of diverse workers for the organization. Even with the most effective guidelines, however, creating a diverse force of skilled and talented workers and teaching them to work together in an atmosphere of genuine teamwork remains a major challenge for HRM.

SUMMARY

This chapter focuses on the people factor and its relation to an organization's overall success. Creating a high-performance workforce has become an essential management responsibility, particularly with the increased level and intensity of global competition that is part of today's environment.

The chapter begins with a consideration of the five questions that people ask in the work environment:

1. Is the task well defined?

2. If I try, will I succeed?

3. If I succeed, will I be rewarded?

4. Is the reward something I value?

5. Is the reward fair?

Goal theory, the concept of competence motivation, reinforcement theory, needs theory, expectancy theory, and equity theory all help to clarify the issues and concerns behind these questions.

The chapter also describes the essential elements for creating a high-performance work environment. Reflecting ideas from the whole range of theories of work performance, organizations increasingly are focusing their efforts in four areas: (1) defining tasks in the most challenging and specific terms possible; (2) providing continuous training to ensure the competence and confidence required for high performance; (3) empowering employees by sharing responsibility with them for decisions and problem solving around their own performance; and (4) providing employees a stake in the success of the organization, a reason to pursue high performance.

The third major topic of the chapter is human resource management. HRM is described as a special responsibility of management to establish and maintain specific programs and systems needed to attract, develop, and support a high-performance workforce. The HRM responsibility also includes complying with legislation designed to create a discrimination-free workplace. The final HRM challenge for organizations is to go beyond the requirements of EEO and to create an environment that attracts and empowers high-performing employees regardless of race, gender, ethnic origin, or physical ability. Meeting this challenge has proved to be difficult, but the goal of valuing diversity is one to which many of the highest-performing organizations remain strongly committed.

QUESTIONS TO CHALLENGE YOUR UNDERSTANDING OF THE CHAPTER

1. Explain the effect of downsizing on worker motivation.

2. In terms of the requirements of this course, what would your response be to each of the key performance questions? Explain your answers.

3. Explain why an individual's skill level on a task can affect his or her level of effort.

4. Identify a task that you perform well. Use reinforcement theory to explain your high level of performance. Do the same for a task where your performance is not as high.

5. Using Maslow's needs theory, which needs would you say motivate college students most strongly? Explain your answer.

6. Describe how equity theory explains the level of effort people are willing to make in the work they do.

7. Select a job with which you are familiar and explain which specific PFP programs would be most effective in motivating workers on that job.

8. Define the term "empowerment" and explain how a professor might empower students in a course.

9. Discuss how an effective performance evaluation system contributes to the effectiveness of the other HRM systems.

10. Distinguish among EEO, affirmative action, and the diversity challenge.

MANAGEMENT EXERCISE

Creating a High-Performance Team of Volunteers

You are the regional manager of a group of seventeen sales and service representatives for Canolta, a distributor of plain paper copiers. Sales in your region have been growing since you were promoted to your present position two years ago, but you are convinced that they could be increasing at an even faster rate.

You are also convinced that the best way to accomplish this is to fully involve the sales and service representatives from your office in identifying and designing ways to increase sales. The problem is that almost all of your people would prefer to be in the field selling and servicing copiers. They are more concerned with achieving their goals and qualifying for bonuses, rather than working in group meetings at the office. You also recognize that most of these representatives don't have much experience working together as a team. Despite these barriers, your objective is to create a team of volunteers to tackle the challenge of improving the group's overall performance.

1. According to Maslow's needs theory, what level(s) of needs is motivating these salespeople? Explain your answer.

2. According to reinforcement theory, what might you do to encourage your people to volunteer for this team?

3. Briefly discuss any other ideas from the chapter that might be useful in helping the members of this team to succeed at their goal.

REFERENCES

1. Kenneth Labich, "Is Herb Kelleher America's Best CEO?" *Fortune,* May 2, 1994, 44–52.

2. From John A. Byrne, "The Pain of Downsizing," *Business Week,* May 9, 1994, 61.

3. Ibid., 69.

4. Ronald Henkoff, "Getting Beyond Downsizing," *Fortune,* January 10, 1994, 58.

5. Ibid.

6. Robert W. White, "Motivation Reconsidered: The Concept of Competence," *Psychological Review,* 66 (5) (1959), 297–333.

7. B. F. Skinner, *Science and Human Behavior* (New York: MacMillan, 1953); and *Beyond Freedom and Dignity* (New York: Alfred A. Knopf, 1972).

8. Tracy Kidder, *The Soul of a New Machine* (Boston: Little, Brown, 1981).

9. Abraham H. Maslow, *Motivation and Personality,* 2d ed. (New York: Harper & Row, 1970).

10. David C. McClelland, *The Achievement Motive* (New York: Halsted Press, 1976).

11. C. P. Alderfer, *Human Needs in Organizational Settings* (New York: The Free Press, 1972).

12. Victor H. Vroom, *Work and Motivation* (New York: John Wiley & Sons, 1964).

13. J. Stacy Adams, "Toward an Understanding of Inequity," *Journal of Abnormal and Social Psychology,* November, 1963, 422–36; Paul S. Goodman and A. Freedman, "An Examination of Adams' Theory of Inequity," *Administrative Science Quarterly,* December 1971, 271–88; and Michael R. Carroll and J. E. Detrich, "Equity Theory: The Recent Literature, Methodological Considerations in New Directions," *Academy of Management Review,* April 1978, 202–10.

14. J. Gordon, "Who Is Being Trained to Do What?" *Training,* 25, October 1988: 51–60. Anthony P. Carnevale and Ellen S. Carnevale, "Growth Patterns in Workplace Training," *Training and Development,* May 1994, 22–28.

15. C. Lee, "Training Budgets: Neither Boom or Bust," *Training,* 25 (10) (October 1988): 41–46.

16. D. Schaaf, "Lessons from the '100 Best,' " *Training,* 27 (February 1990): 18–20.

17. Ted Marchese, "TQM: A Time for Ideas," *Change,* 25(3), May/June 1993:13.

18. Ibid.

19. "The New World of Work," *Business Week,* October 17, 1994, 87.

20. Edward E. Lawler, *Strategic Pay* (San Francisco: Jossey Bass, 1990).

21. Labor Letter, *Wall Street Journal,* December 12, 1989, A1.

22. Jacob M. Schlesinger, "GM's New Compensation Plan Reflects General Trend Tying Pay to Performance," *Wall Street Journal,* January 26, 1988, 39.

23. Barnaby J. Feder, "Rethinking a Model Incentive Plan," *The New York Times,* September 5, 1994, 33, 36.

24. Charles C. Manz, "Self Leadership . . . The Heart of Empowerment," *Journal for Quality & Participation,* July–August 1992, 80–85; Jay A. Conger and Rabindra N. Kanungo, "The Empowerment Process: Integrating Theory and Practice," *Academy of Management Review,* July 1988, 473–74.

25. Fred R. Bleakley, "Many Companies Try Management Fads, Only to See Them Flop," *Wall Street Journal,* July 6, 1993, A1, A6; Gilbert Fuchsberg, " 'Total Quality' Is Termed Only Partial Success," *Wall Street Journal,* October 1, 1992, B1, B9.

26. Karen Mathes, "Empowerment: Fact or Fiction?" *HRfocus,* March 1992, 1, 6.

27. Jay A. Conger, "Leadership: The Art of Empowering Others," *Academy of Management Executive,* 3(1) (1989): 17–24.

28. "The Worried Rich," *Business Week,* December 5, 1994, 8.

29. Aaron Bernstein, "Where the Jobs Are Is Where the Skills Aren't," *Business Week,* September 19, 1988, 104–8.

30. Karen De Witt, "Senate Panel Hears of Human Toll in Workplace," *New York Times,* May 7, 1992, A25.

31. Faye Rice, "How to Make Diversity Pay," *Fortune,* August 8, 1994, 79–86.

CHAPTER 11
Performance Leadership

LEARNING OBJECTIVES

After studying this chapter, you should be able to:

- *Define what is meant by leadership in organizations.*

- *Explain the importance of the psychology of the leader, including the role of the leader's personality, assumptions, and expectations in effective leadership.*

- *Describe the behaviors of effective leaders using the Leadership Grid and the contingency models of leadership.*

- *Discuss transformational leadership and the behaviors common to transformational leaders.*

- *Explain the conditions necessary for effective communication in the leadership process.*

- *Describe the emerging issues in leadership that involve empowerment and leading teams.*

eadership has emerged as one of the most critical ingredients for success for organizations seeking to compete in the changing environment. In their book *Leaders,* management researchers Warren Bennis and Burt Nanus emphasize the critical importance of leadership:

> A business short on capital can borrow money, and one with a poor location can move. But a business short of leadership has little chance for survival.[1]

Leadership is critical in every kind of organization. The impact of effective leadership on performance in an educational organization is shown by the example of Jaime Escalante, a mathematics teacher at Garfield High School in East Los Angeles, California.[2] Escalante was assigned to a class that included a number of students whose behavior had gotten them into trouble at the high school. The class was considered—and considered themselves—to be a group of misfits of whom not much should be expected in terms of schoolwork in general and math in particular. The message to Escalante from these students, as well as from most of the other teachers and administrators at the high school, was "If you leave them alone, they'll leave you alone."

But Escalante had something very different in mind for these students. He established strict guidelines for classroom behavior, tested often, and demanded that homework be completed. He also entertained his students as he taught them, using games and chants to reinforce learning, and worked with them to solve some of the personal problems that were interfering with their schoolwork. By the end of the year, the students had reluctantly agreed to continue their math class right through the summer to help them prepare to eventually take the Calculus Advanced Placement test of the College Board. Not only did they all take this test, but they all received full credit for their performance on it. In less than two years, Jaime Escalante had taken a class of difficult students who had shown little if any interest in math and helped them achieve a level of math performance that only the very smallest percentage of American students ever achieve. Escalante provides dramatic evidence of the kind of performance gains possible through the efforts of an effective leader.

We define *leadership* in organizations as *the process of directing and supporting others in pursuit of the organization's mission and goals.* From this perspective, leadership is as much every team member's responsibility as it is the highest-level managers' and the CEO's. Everyone is a potential leader, capable of contributing to the direction and support of others as they pursue the mission and goals of the organization.

The question for organizations is how best to provide the kind of direction and support people need in order to be productive—in short, how to ensure effective leadership. The answer to this question is not a simple one; it has been evolving and changing as research reveals more about the leadership process, and as the nature of leadership itself has changed to meet the realities of the changing workplace. We will begin our discussion of leadership with a review of some of the early research and theories, which focused on the personality and characteristics of effective leaders.

THE PSYCHOLOGY OF THE LEADER

The early research on leadership focused on the leader as a person: on the personality traits of the effective leader, on the leader's attitudes and assumptions, and on the expectations leaders have about their followers. The underlying assumption of these early studies was that if research could determine the kind of person who would be an effective leader, organizations might become more effective in identifying and selecting people with the greatest leadership potential.

Leadership and Personality

The initial focus of leadership research was on determining whether there might be specific personality traits which were common to effective leaders. For a number of years the results from this line of research were disappointing. There seemed to be little or no evidence to support the concept of a "leadership personality." By the early 1980s, however, expanded research efforts in this area resulted in the identification of at least five personality traits consistently associated with effective leaders.[3] These are shown in Figure 11-1. The personalities of people who were considered to be effective leaders might vary in other ways—whether they were shy as opposed to outgoing, for example, or reflective versus action oriented. But most effective leaders were found to possess many of the five traits listed in Figure 11-1.

The value of recognizing the key personality characteristics of effective leaders is, as we said, that it can assist organizations in their efforts to identify potential leaders. It can aid also in efforts to develop leadership potential among employees who are not yet in leadership positions. An individual who possesses drive and initiative, for example, as well as desire to lead, honesty, and integrity might be provided specific training and assignments to improve self-confidence, which is also associated with effective leadership.

Identification of key personality traits is an important contribution to solving the leadership puzzle. Understanding the assumptions of leaders is another.

Leader Assumptions

Management researcher Douglas McGregor studied a different aspect of the leader as a person. He focused on leaders' assumptions about which factors were

- Drive: ambition, energy, tenacity, initiative
- Desire to lead
- Honesty and integrity
- Self-confidence
- Intelligence

Figure 11-1 Personality Traits of Effective Leaders

most important in motivating people at work. McGregor's research suggested to him that leaders' assumptions about worker motivation tended to fall into one of two categories, which he called Theory X and Theory Y.[4] The differences between these assumptions are shown in Figure 11-2.

One of McGregor's concerns as he considered his research findings was that Theory X might represent an inaccurate set of assumptions about what motivates most people in their work. He felt that as the educational level of the workforce continued to rise, people would become less motivated by the security needs that are the focus of Theory X and more motivated by the higher-level needs of acceptance, esteem, and self-actualization which are more consistent with Theory Y.

McGregor did suggest that in some situations Theory X assumptions may be more appropriate than Theory Y. For example, when people are being asked to perform tasks they would strongly prefer not to perform, work is not "as natural as play." In this kind of situation, the security need may become a significantly more important source of motivation, and the leader needs to realize this. From McGregor's perspective, however, an effective leader is one who recognizes that people are looking for not just security in their work (Theory X), but opportunities for growth and development as well (Theory Y). For McGregor, an effective leader might be described as a leader whose assumptions about workers' motivation accurately and fully recognizes the broad range of their needs.

The Power of Expectations

Research on the leader as a person also suggests a strong direct relationship between the leader's level of expectations and the followers' level of performance.[5] According to this research, not only must the leader's assumptions about follow-

Theory X	**Theory Y**
● Work is inherently distasteful to most people.	● Work is as natural as play, if the conditions are favorable.
● Most people are not ambitious, have little desire for responsibility, and prefer to be directed.	● Self-control is often indispensable in achieving organizational goals.
● Most people have little capacity for creativity in solving organizational problems.	● The capacity for creativity in solving organizational problems is widely distributed in the population.
● Motivation occurs only at the physiological and safety levels.	● Motivation occurs at the social, esteem, and self-actualization levels, as well as at the physiological and safety levels.
● Most people must be closely controlled and often coerced to achieve organizational objectives.	● People can be self-directed and creative at work if properly motivated.

Figure 11-2 The Difference Between Theory X and Theory Y

ers be accurate, the leader's expectations as to what the followers are capable of achieving must be as positive as possible. Jaime Escalante's attitude toward his students exemplifies this pattern. Escalante was convinced that with hard work, his students were capable of exceptional performance. And eventually their level of performance rose to the level of his expectations.

In studying the reasons for this strong direct link between leader expectations and follower performance, researchers discovered that leaders with positive expectations provide their followers with significantly more direction and support than leaders who have negative expectations about their followers. Specifically, these leaders provide their followers with greater challenge, more direction on how to complete the task, greater feedback on how to improve the task, and in general a more positive work climate. In other words, leaders with highly positive expectations provide much more *leadership* to their followers.

This pattern of effective leaders working hard to help their people succeed is an example of a *self-fulfilling prophecy*. Positive examples of this pattern can be found in every kind of organization, from schools to businesses to sports teams. The leadership lesson of the self-fulfilling prophecy is this: To positively influence the performance of their followers, leaders must expect the best of them. Only a leader with high expectations is likely to provide the amount and quality of direction and support that his or her followers need to achieve the highest levels of performance.

Research on the personality of the leader, McGregor's Theory X and Theory Y, and the concept of the self-fulfilling prophecy each contribute to our understanding of leadership. Effective leaders do tend to have in common such personality characteristics as drive, intelligence, and integrity, among others, and some of these can be developed through training and experience. Effective leaders clearly and accurately recognize the full range of needs that motivate their followers and have the highest expectations about their followers' performance potential.

LEADERSHIP BEHAVIOR

A second major focus of the research on leadership has been on the *behaviors* of the effective leader. In addition to studying the leader's personality, assumptions, and expectations, researchers have attempted to analyze and understand what the effective leader actually *does*.

In some of the initial work on leader behavior, researchers at Ohio State University and the University of Michigan suggested that leadership could be defined as a combination of two specific kinds of behavior: task behavior and relations behavior.[6] *Task behavior* is defined as leader behavior focusing on the design and completion of a specific task. It includes setting goals and establishing priorities, providing direction and instruction, and supervising and monitoring tasks to completion. In contrast, *relations behavior* focuses on satisfying the needs of the people performing the task and includes providing support and encouragement, answering questions, and problem solving with the followers. A more complete comparison of task and relations leader behaviors is shown in Figure 11-3.

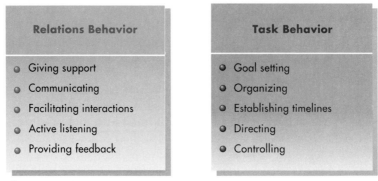

Figure 11-3 Differences between Leader Task and Leader Relations Behaviors

These studies defined leadership as various combinations of these two kinds of behaviors. The different combinations of leader behaviors are often called *leadership styles*. Defining leadership in these terms was important in that research on leadership could now concentrate on identifying which combination of leader task and relations behaviors, or which leadership style, resulted in the most effective leadership.

The Leadership Grid

Robert Blake and Jane Mouton created the "Leadership Grid" to present in graphic form the leadership styles possible from integrating task and relations behavior.[7] As shown in Figure 11-4, they call the task behavior dimension "concern for production" and the relations behavior dimension "concern for people." Based on an extensive review of the leadership research available in the early 1960s, Blake and Mouton concluded that the most effective pattern or style of leadership combined high levels of *both* concern for people and concern for production. They termed this high task/high relations approach the *team management* style of leadership, as described in Figure 11-4. According to Blake and Mouton, team management was the leadership style used in over 60 percent of situations reported in the research.

The CEO of Southwest Airlines, Herb Kelleher, has a team management style of leadership. In terms of task behavior, in the areas of controlling and monitoring expenses, for example, Kelleher is very involved personally, approving every expenditure over $1,000 and closely monitoring the cost per seat-mile to ensure that Southwest's fares remain lower than the competition's. However, concern for employees is also a top priority for Kelleher. "I feel that you have to be with your employees through all their difficulties, that you have to be interested in them personally," he notes. "They may be disappointed in their country. Even their family might not be working out the way they wish it would. But I want them to know that Southwest will always be there for them."[8] Reflecting his concern for employees, Kelleher is quick to join in as part of the team. On a crowded flight, the chairman has put ice in the glasses of passengers while the flight attendant placed drink orders; and it's not unusual to find him at 3:00 A.M. on a Sunday passing out doughnuts or putting on a pair of overalls to help clean a plane.[9]

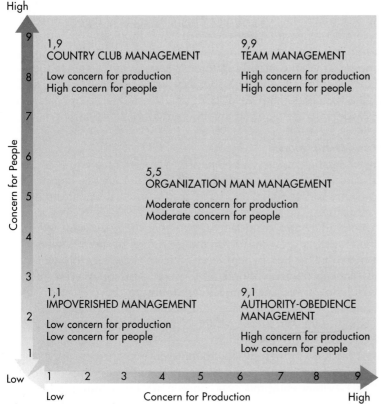

Figure 11-4 Leadership Grid

From the Blake and Mouton Leadership Grid point of view, the task of management is to ensure that leaders have the skills necessary to effectively implement the team management approach to leadership. To develop these team management skills, training is key. Individuals being prepared for leadership positions must be provided with training and work experiences that will enable them to be both high-task and high-relations in their leadership behavior.

While the work of Blake and Mouton seemed to have answered the question of which pattern of leader behaviors is effective in *most* situations, it raised an even more difficult question: How do you determine which leader behavior pattern might be most effective in a *particular* situation?

Contingency Leadership

The *contingency theory* of leadership says that there is no "one best way" to lead or influence people; that it depends on the situation. Supporters of the contingency view point out that the team management approach represents only 60 percent of the success stories in the research on leadership styles. They say that while many situations may require leaders who are high-involvement team-manager types, others may require a more directive and less personal "boss" approach, and still others may require a leader who encourages greater participation by followers in establishing goals and direction. According to the contingency theory of leadership, different leadership styles are effective in different situations.

There are a number of situational, or continency, models of leadership. We will review two models that take slightly different views of the factors that determine leader effectiveness: the situational leadership model and the leader contingency model. Unlike the Leadership Grid, both of these models emphasize that different styles of leadership are required for different kinds of situations.

The Situational Leadership Model

In the situational leadership model, developed by Paul Hersey and Ken Blanchard, the key situational variables for a leader to consider are the competency and commitment of his or her followers.[10] The leader must first determine the level of training, education, and experience of the followers (*competency*), as well as their level of motivation and confidence (*commitment*) to perform the task. These two variables together they called the *readiness level* of the followers. The leader must then match his or her style of leadership to these key follower variables. Hersey and Blanchard's four options in terms of leadership style and the matching degrees of follower readiness are shown in Figure 11-5.

Note the difference between the situational leadership model and the Leadership Grid. According to the situational leadership model, for example, a group of highly competent and highly committed professionals would probably perform better without the kind of high-involvement team-management-type leader suggested by the Leadership Grid. In fact, the situational leadership model defines the leader's role as increasing follower competency and commitment to the point where followers require less and less involvement by the leader and can be delegated ever-greater responsibility for their own tasks and performance. Although both these models emphasize the role of training in leadership development, the situational leadership model prescribes that managers be trained first to correctly diagnose the competency and commitment of their followers and then to adjust their style or pattern of leadership to provide the leader behaviors required for their followers' success.

The Leader Contingency Model

Leadership theorist and researcher Fred Fiedler developed the leader contingency model, which suggests that individual leaders may not be capable of the flexibility the situational leadership model demands.[11] In fact, there are numerous examples to support Fiedler's position that leaders rarely remain effective as situations change. Whether in sports, business, or other organizations, significant improvements in performance are usually the result of a change in who is leading the team, the group, or the organization. Fiedler argues that in view of this fact, effective leadership requires matching the personality of the leader to the needs of the situation.

The leader contingency model consists of three key situational variables that determine which type of leader is needed. These variables and the type of leader found to be most effective with each combination of factors are shown in Figure 11-6.

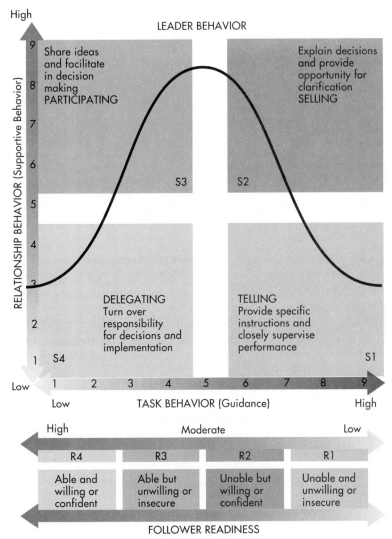

Figure 11-5 Hersey-Blanchard Situational Leadership Model®

The Leadership Grid, the situational leadership model, and the contingency leadership model all recognize the importance of the leader's behavior in influencing the performance of followers. A summary of these insights is shown in Figure 11-7.

Transformational Leadership

Most of the research on leadership, including the models described in the previous section, has focused on the leadership of small units, departments, and teams of the kind found throughout every organization. The emphasis has been on studying how department heads, unit managers, and group supervisors influence

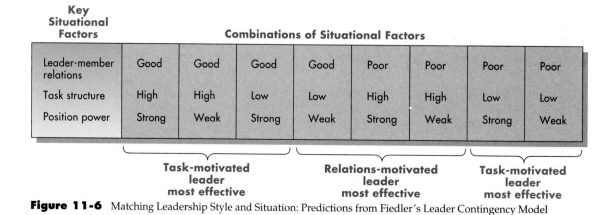

Key Situational Factors	Combinations of Situational Factors							
Leader-member relations	Good	Good	Good	Good	Poor	Poor	Poor	Poor
Task structure	High	High	Low	Low	High	High	Low	Low
Position power	Strong	Weak	Strong	Weak	Strong	Weak	Strong	Weak

Task-motivated leader most effective	Relations-motivated leader most effective	Task-motivated leader most effective

Figure 11-6 Matching Leadership Style and Situation: Predictions from Fiedler's Leader Contingency Model

subordinates to perform well. This kind of leadership has been called *transactional leadership* because the leader provides rewards, recognition, support, and direction as part of a transaction or in exchange for follower performance consistent with the organization's goals.

Several years ago, historian James McGregor Burns followed a different track in his effort to understand the essence of effective leadership. Rather than focus on leaders in traditional business units, Burns reviewed and analyzed the leadership of important political leaders from Jesus to Ghandi to Franklin Roosevelt. Based on his research, Burns coined the term "transformational leadership." In *transformational leadership,* the focus is on actually transforming or changing the beliefs, attitudes, and needs of the followers.[12] Traditional models of leadership, as we said, have been concerned with directing and supporting the performance of followers. The transformational leader, in contrast, endeavors to transform the belief system of his or her followers in order to enable them to achieve new significantly higher levels of performance capability.

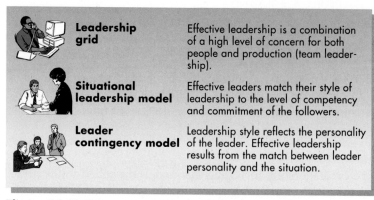

Leadership grid	Effective leadership is a combination of a high level of concern for both people and production (team leadership).
Situational leadership model	Effective leaders match their style of leadership to the level of competency and commitment of the followers.
Leader contingency model	Leadership style reflects the personality of the leader. Effective leadership results from the match between leader personality and the situation.

Figure 11-7 Behavior Models of Leadership

Former Chrysler Corporation CEO Lee Iacocca; Steven Jobs, one of the founders of Apple Computers; Patricia Carrigan, a plant manager at GM; and Jaime Escalante, Martin Luther King, Mother Theresa, and Nelson Mandela all meet Burns's definition of a transformational leader. Each has transformed the beliefs of his or her followers and led them to levels of performance that far exceed traditional expectations.

In recent years, as interest in achieving continually higher levels of performance has increased dramatically, a number of researchers and theorists have focused their efforts on identifying what the essential elements of transformational leadership might be. Researchers James Kouzes and Barry Posner identified the five behaviors shown in Figure 11-8 as common to transformational leaders.[13]

Pat Carrigan, plant manager for the General Motors parts manufacturing plant in Bay City, Michigan, is a vivid example of what it means to be a transformational leader in terms described by Kouzes and Posner. A former school psychologist who began her management career later in life, Carrigan was assigned to Bay City in what many viewed as a final effort to save a failing factory. At the time she arrived at Bay City, absenteeism was skyrocketing, the quality of the parts being produced was among the worst for GM facilities, and hundreds of worker grievances were pending against management. The status quo at Bay City was characterized by deep hostility between management and workers, and the result was poor performance on almost every measure. Forty percent of the workforce had already been laid off, and the next step would probably be to close the factory.[14]

When Pat Carrigan came to the Bay City facility, she brought a vision of what it would take to turn Bay City into a high-performance operation. Her vision was of a partnership between the workers and management to turn Bay City into one of the most productive units in the entire GM system. At this facility in which management and workers were longtime enemies, one of Carrigan's first acts was to stand outside the plant gates, shake the hand of every worker entering the factory, and offer these words: "Hi, I'm Pat Carrigan. Do you think we can make a go

1. *They inspire a shared vision.* They have a mission in which they passionately believe, and they tirelessly enlist others to share in that mission and to help make it happen.

2. *They challenge the process.* They are unwilling to accept things as they are, they push for change, and they risk mistakes to find better solutions.

3. *They enable others to act.* They emphasize cooperation and collaboration. They build teams and empower their followers.

4. *They model the way.* They live their beliefs. They communicate their vision through the consistency of their actions.

5. *They encourage the heart.* They dramatize encouragement, reward performance, and celebrate winning. They love their people, their customers, their products, and their work.

Figure 11-8 Characteristics of a Transformational Leader

of this?" Clearly, she was challenging the process. Across a gap created by decades of hard feeling between management and workers, she extended her hand to workers and asked for their help.

And Carrigan led in more than just words and gestures. She knew that new ways of doing business were needed if Bay City was to survive. She challenged workers to come up with better ways to do their work, and she challenged union leaders to join her in building a new Bay City. She shared the plant's financial and performance information with both workers and the unions. Previously, this information had always been held only by management, but Carrigan knew that if she wanted the workers to be true partners in this effort, there could be no secrets, no information withheld. Finally, she encouraged the workers to form teams to focus more effectively on the critical problems of quality and performance. The work teams were voluntary, but Carrigan challenged them to take responsibility for their own hiring and firing, their own discipline, their own quality inspection.

Thus, in a plant where both management and workers had traditionally sat back and waited for each other to fail, Pat Carrigan created an organization in which they genuinely shared responsibility for both successes and problems. In Carrigan's words, workers "owned" their jobs, and management cared about the workers. Workers said they wouldn't have even known previous plant managers if they had seen them. Not only did they know Pat Carrigan, but she knew most of them by name.

The results of Pat Carrigan's leadership were nothing less than transformational. Bay City went from having one of the worst quality records of GM manufacturing plants to having one of the best. The backlog of grievances filed by workers against management decreased from more than one hundred to less than a handful. The cost of running the Bay City operation began to fall by several million dollars a year.

Pat Carrigan is exactly what Kouzes and Posner mean by a transformational leader. She inspired a shared vision. She challenged the process. She enabled others to act. She modeled the way. She encouraged the heart.

Developing the Transformational Leader

Researchers Warren Bennis and Burt Nanus point out that most men and women in leadership positions never reach the point of involving themselves in transformational leadership.[15] In most cases they are too busy managing daily routines and crises to take the time and energy needed to engage their followers in the processes of transformation. It should also be pointed out that not every situation calls for a transformational leader. In many situations, transactional leadership is still the primary need: providing followers the rewards and recognition, the continuing direction and support that will help them to attain the goals of the organization on a day-to-day basis.

Nonetheless, the need for transformational leadership is almost certain to increase, given the increasing need for high-level performance in every kind of organization. This makes it all the more important to recognize that the essential elements of transformational leadership are leader competencies and leader behaviors. The research of Kouzes and Posner clearly shows that transformational leaders are successful not because of their charisma or personality but because of their skills in communicating a vision, challenging the system, enabling others, and so on. It is what these leaders *do* that makes them effective. This is important because it means that transformational leaders are not necessarily born that way. It means that transformational leadership rests on the skills of the leader and on how the leader communicates with his or her followers. Potentially, at least, these skills can be learned.

LEADERSHIP AND COMMUNICATION

Effective leadership requires effective communication. Virtually all of the leader behaviors, practices, and skills presented in this chapter involve communication. Every leadership task we have discussed to this point—from providing direction, support, and encouragement to providing inspiration and meaning—can be accomplished only through effective communication.

The Conditions for Effective Communication

Peter Drucker has suggested that communication is the process of making information meaningful.[16] We have all been in situations, in the classroom and elsewhere, where we are provided with a great deal of information and we find ourselves wondering just what the point is of all the information. It's not that we don't understand what we hear or see; we just don't understand what it means. Drucker's point is that the leader's responsibility is not just to provide followers the information they need to perform successfully, but to provide it in a way that is meaningful to them.

A leader can give a wonderful speech, but it will influence no one unless it is meaningful to them, unless it responds to their needs, goals, and concerns. One thing transformational leaders do well, as we said earlier, is to communicate a vision of where the organization is heading, in terms that respond to and recognize the needs of their listeners. The first condition for effective communication, then, is to understand the needs of the listeners.

Active Listening and MBWA (again)

There is only one way for a manager to understand what is meaningful to his or her followers: through listening. Drucker suggests that one of the paradoxes of management is that effective communication actually begins with effective listening, not speaking. Without the kind of understanding that only listening can provide, the leader's messages and direction, even the leader's efforts at encouragement and support, are much less certain to hit the mark.

The kind of listening that is the basis for true communication is *active*, not passive. In *active listening*, the manager is constantly interacting with his or her people, constantly seeking their views and observations, paraphrasing and asking questions to encourage them to expand and elaborate on their comments, and probing and discussing what they have to say.

Active listening lends itself very well to the practice of MBWA (management by walking around) described in Chapter 5. MBWA involves the kind of constant and consistent interaction that can provide leaders with the understanding they need to make information more meaningful to followers.

There is another advantage of active listening, beyond gaining an understanding of the listeners' needs. Stephen Covey, in his book *Principle-Centered Leadership*, points out that sincere listening creates trust. Covey suggests that when a leader genuinely listens to the concerns of followers, they are much more likely to accept his or her direction and support. When people feel they are being listened to, they feel as if someone is concerned about them and are much more willing to open themselves up to that person's influence. In short, followers are much more likely to accept *leadership* from someone who listens to them.[17]

Active listening gives a leader the level of understanding needed to provide information that is meaningful. It also contributes to building the level of trust needed for leaders to effectively influence their followers. Once understanding and trust have been developed, the leader can craft his or her messages in ways that genuinely enhance and support the performance of followers.

Communicating Meaning through Consistent Behavior

Listening and a meaningful message are not the only essential conditions for effective communication. The manager's behavior is another powerful element. Bennis and Nanus point out, for example, that leaders gain the trust of their followers through the *consistency* of what they do.[18] For communication to be effective, leaders' actions must be consistent with their words.

Take, for example, a manager's words that quality (or innovation or teamwork) is now the number one priority of the organization. If this message is to be meaningful, the manager's actions must be consistent with the message. The decisions of the manager and everything he or she does must support, encourage, and emphasize quality (or innovation or teamwork). If the manager's actions place greater emphasis on reducing costs or meeting schedules than they do on quality, the quality message becomes meaningless, no matter how often or how clearly it is repeated. If, on the other hand, the manager's actions are consistently in harmony with his or her words, there is little room for doubt about what the message means.

Communication, then, is the medium for leadership. For communication to be effective, it must begin with an understanding of the followers' needs, goals, experiences, and expectations. Active listening and MBWA are means for helping managers to achieve this understanding. And once spoken, the message must be lived by the leader—it must be reinforced by the consistency of the leader's behavior—so that there can be no confusion about its meaning.

EMERGING ISSUES IN LEADERSHIP

Empowerment and Leadership

In Chapter 10 we introduced the concept of empowerment, the process of sharing with employees the responsibility for improving performance. Empowerment is the leadership task of strengthening an individual's belief in his or her own effectiveness.[19]

According to Peter Coors, president of Coors Brewing Company, "We're trying to give employees a sense of empowerment that they haven't had before—the freedom to use their full potential. Traditionally, we've hired employees for their muscles and expected management to tell them what to do. We're beginning to realize that the employees who are intimately involved in the details of operating the company are much more capable of decision-making than we assumed. So our successes are coming from freeing up our employees to be involved in the decision-making process."[20]

In this sense, empowerment is a transformational task: to transform people's beliefs in terms of what they are capable of achieving. In Chapter 10 we also listed what managers could do to empower their people: provide a positive emotional atmosphere, reward and encourage in personal ways, foster initiative and responsibility, and so on. Such empowering leadership practices are the key to transforming followers into self-managers. When leaders are successful in empowering their followers, as Pat Carrigan was, followers begin genuinely to share in the responsibility for performance. When followers share more fully in the responsibility for performance, as the workers at Bay City did, they become self-managing. The task for leaders is to create the conditions in which followers begin to view this responsibility as their own, and to believe in their own ability to fulfill it.

Leadership and Teams

The emergence of teams has not reduced the importance of leaders. Teams still rely on leaders for support and direction. Jon Katzenbach and Douglas Smith point out that even self-managing teams, despite performing many management tasks themselves, still receive their initial direction and assignment—and in many cases their initial membership—from a leader outside the team.[21]

There is more to the team leadership responsibility than just putting the team together and pointing it in the right direction, however. Effective team leaders also recognize a motivational responsibility. Bennis and Nanus explain:[22]

> Great leaders often inspire their followers to high levels of achievement by showing them how their work contributes to worthwhile ends. It is an emotional appeal to some of the fundamental needs—the need to be important, to make a difference, to feel useful, to be part of a successful and worthwhile enterprise.

In other words, it is not enough for the leader to point a team in a direction. An effective leader inspires the team to pursue that direction by convincing them of the importance of succeeding. It is the combination of empowering team members and inspiring them to pursue important goals that together constitutes the responsibility of the team leader. Steven Jobs, in creating and directing the team that developed the Apple McIntosh computer, charged them not with building a better computer but with "changing the world." An effective team leader convinces team members not only of their own competency and their own responsibility, but of the significance and importance of the work they are doing.

Leading from Within

Interestingly, it appears that the most effective team leaders eventually work themselves out of at least part of the leadership responsibility. Katzenbach and Smith report that on highly effective teams members eventually get to the point where they rely on the leader only for feedback rather than for direction. In the highest-performing teams, the leadership responsibility is almost entirely absorbed within the group itself.[23]

> . . . [O]nce each group had become a high-performance team, leadership emerged from many members as they took whatever initiatives necessary to remove obstacles or seek opportunities . . . They still check their initiative either before or after taking it. But, and this is the essential difference, they do so primarily with other team members instead of the leader. The formal leader's comments matter. But the balance of approval is in favor of the team.

From this perspective, the ultimate achievement of the team leader is that the group eventually accepts the leadership responsibility for itself. If the task of the transformational leader is to make followers self-managing, the task of the true team leader is to make the team self-leading. At the very least, this means that the leader ensures that team members are trained in all of the skills necessary to provide the team the support and direction it needs to be successful. In the race for ever-higher levels of performance, self-leading teams are becoming more than an interesting possibility. They are becoming a powerful source of competitive advantage.

Leading "Up" and "Across"

Even when a leader succeeds in developing a self-leading team, the leadership responsibility is not complete. In supporting high-performance teams, for example, the focus of the leader's energy and activities merely shift from the team members to the organization surrounding the team. In this larger arena, the leader's task is to reduce or eliminate the barriers and interference that might hinder the team's performance and to assist the team in securing the resources it needs to achieve its goals.

Tom West was the leader of the Eagle Computer project discussed in Chapter 10. To many observers, it almost appeared that he left the Eagle team alone to manage itself. In the course of Kidder's story, however, it becomes clear that the team would never have achieved its goal unless West had secured the resources it needed in terms of equipment, personnel, work space, and time. The team never would have succeeded without West's "taking the heat" in terms of protecting the team from the criticisms and pressures from other departments and from upper management.

Thus, in the highest-performing organizations, leadership has taken new forms and is being shared more broadly than ever before. There is need for both transactional leaders and transformational leaders. Leaders are needed both by individuals and by teams. Teams need to be taught to become self-leading. And leaders must continue to manage the interface between their teams and the organization around them.

SUMMARY

Leadership is the process of directing and supporting others in pursuit of the organization's mission and goals. With the competitive pressures of the changing environment, leadership is more important than ever as organizations seek to develop high-performance workforces.

One focus of the research on leadership has been on the leader as a person, on the psychology of the leader. This research has resulted in the identification of a number of personality traits that are associated with effective leaders. Two sets of assumptions leaders have about the motivation of their followers—Theory X and Theory Y—have also been identified, which emphasizes the importance of leaders' having accurate assumptions about worker motivation. Additionally, in terms of the psychology of the leader, the importance of leader expectations has been documented.

Research has also focused on the behaviors of effective leaders. Initially the focus was on identifying the one most effective leadership style. Subsequent research resulted in the development of contingency models of leadership that emphasize the importance of matching leadership style to the needs or demands of the situation. Most recently there has been interest in the transformational leader, the leader who succeeds in changing the beliefs and attitudes of followers to enable them to achieve unprecedented levels of performance.

Communication is the tool through which the leader provides support and direction. Effective communication requires an understanding on the manager's part of followers' needs and concerns. For this reason, effective communication begins with listening and MBWA, and with consistency between the leader's words and behavior.

Finally, the trends toward empowerment and teamwork have changed the leader's role. Empowerment is a new leadership responsibility that involves encouraging followers to participate more fully in the management responsibility for work and performance. In a self-managing team, the leader's role is to provide initial direction to the team. In a self-leading team, the role of the leader is to support the team's efforts among other units in the organization and vis à vis higher levels of management.

The leadership responsibility in organizations is a critical one. In many ways, leadership represents the connection between the organization and its people. Understanding how most effectively to develop and maintain the leadership connection is a challenge, to say the least. Jaime Escalante and Pat Carrigan provide powerful evidence of the kind of performance that is possible when the leadership connection works.

QUESTIONS TO CHALLENGE YOUR UNDERSTANDING OF THE CHAPTER

1. If you were the instructor, would it be appropriate for you to have Theory X or Theory Y assumptions about the students in this course? Explain your answer.

2. Provide an example where a manager, teacher, coach, or other leader's expectations strongly influenced the performance of followers. Explain whether the leader's expectations were positive or negative and what the leader specifically did that influenced the followers' behavior.

3. Explain the difference between the leadership grid view of leadership and the contingency view.

4. Briefly explain how transformational leaders empower their followers.

5. Describe a situation from your own experience where information was provided but communication was not achieved. Why did this occur?

6. Explain why it is a problem when the leader's actions are not consistent with what he or she says. Provide an example from your own experience.

7. Identify the responsibilities of a leader in working with teams.

MANAGEMENT EXERCISE

The Assumptions of Jeffrey Robins

Jeffrey Robins has been a supervisor for Nationwide Department Stores for six months, and he is having a major problem with his department's sales staff. The sales associates have been arriving late to work and have not met their weekly sales quotas. When they arrive late, Jeffrey tries to explain how bad this looks to the rest of the employees. He has even promised to buy the employees lunch if they arrive on time for a full week. "I'm really not surprised they don't arrive on time," he said. "These sales associates don't like to work. Who does!" Jeffrey admits that some have suggested ways to improve performance in the department, but he would be happier if they just focused on meeting their individual sales quotas.

The sales associates constantly complain that the sales goals are too high, yet Jeffrey sees them taking long breaks and wasting time instead of selling merchandise. "Most of the sales associates take no initiative," he complained. "I was going to include them in the goal-setting process, but they probably prefer to avoid this responsibility. After all, they're not paid as much as I am, so why should they get involved in these activities? They really have no ambition. They just want these jobs for the insurance benefits we provide. I'm the one who's paid to manage and I guess I'll just have to keep trying to find a way to get them to do the job."

1. Does Jeffrey have Theory X or Theory Y assumptions about the sales staff? Explain.

2. What specific leader behaviors would you recommend to solve Jeffrey's problem? Cite models or concepts from this chapter to support your recommendations.

REFERENCES

1. Warren Bennis and Burt Nanus, *Leaders* (New York: Harper & Row, 1985, 20.

2. Jay Matthews. *Escalante: The Best Teacher in America* (New York: Henry Holt & Co., 1989).

3. Shelley A. Kirkpatrick and Edwin A. Locke, "Leadership: Do Traits Matter? *Academy of Management Executive* 2(5) (1991): 49.

4. Douglas T. McGregor, *The Human Side of Enterprise* (New York: McGraw-Hill, 1960).

5. John L. Single, "The Power of Expectations: Productivity and the Self-Fulfilling Prophecy," *Management World,* November 1980, 19, 37–38.

6. E. A. Fleishman, E. F. Harris, and H. E. Burtt, *Leadership and Supervision in Industry* (Columbus, Ohio: Bureau of Business Research, Ohio State University, 1955); D. Katz, N. M. Maccoby, and N. Morse, *Productivity, Supervision, and Morale in an Office Situation* (Ann Arbor, Mich.: Institute of Social Research, University of Michigan, 1950).

7. Robert R. Blake and Jane S. Mouton, *The Managerial Grid III* (Houston, Tex.: Gulf Publishing, 1985); and "How to Choose a Leadership Style," *Training and Development Journal,* February 1982, 38–45.

8. Kenneth Labich, "Is Herb Kelleher America's Best CEO?" *Fortune,* May 2, 1994, 47.

9. Bridget O'Brian, "Southwest Airlines Is a Rare Carrier: It Still Makes Money," *Wall Street Journal,* October 26, 1992, A1, A5.

10. Paul Hersey and Kenneth H. Blanchard, *Management of Organizational Behavior: Utilizing Human Resources,* 4th ed. (Englewood Cliffs, N.J.: Prentice-Hall, 1982).

11. Fred E. Fiedler, *A Theory of Leadership Effectiveness* (New York: McGraw-Hill, 1967).

12. James McGregor Burns, *Leadership* (New York: Harper & Row, 1978).

13. James M. Kouzes and Barry Z. Posner, "The Credibility Factor: What Followers Expect from Their Leaders," *Business Credit* 92 (July–August 1990): 24–28; and *The Leadership Challenge: How to Get Extraordinary Things Done in Organizations* (San Francisco: Jossey-Bass, 1987).

14. Patricia M. Carrigan, "Up from the Ashes," *OD Practitioner,* 1986, 18(1), 2–3.

15. Bennis and Nanus, *Leaders,* 217–218.

16. Peter F. Drucker, *Management: Tasks, Responsibilities, Practices* (New York: Harper & Row, 1973), chap. 38.

17. Stephen R. Covey, *Principle-Centered Leadership* (New York: Simon & Schuster, 1992), 45–46.

18. Bennis and Nanus, *Leaders,* 43–55.

19. Jay A. Conger, "Leadership: The Art of Empowering Others," *Academy of Management Executive,* February 1989, 17–24.

20. Lynne Joy McFarland, Larry E. Senn, and John R. Childress, *21st Century Leadership* (Los Angeles: The Leadership Press, 1993), 76.

21. Jon R. Katzenbach and Douglas K. Smith, *The Wisdom of Teams: Creating the High Performance Organization* (Boston: Harvard Business School Press, 1993).

22. Bennis and Nanus, *Leaders,* 93.

23. Katzenbach and Smith, *Wisdom of Teams,* 80.

FROM THE MANAGER'S E-MAIL

The Question of Merit Pay at Environmental Engineering Corp.

It's Monday morning and the team of engineers which you coordinate at Environmental Engineering Corp. is already fully involved in the week's work. You check your E-mail to see if anything has been added since Friday and find a message from the director of Human Resources. You punch it up to see what it's about.

Date:	October 16, 1995
From:	LOCALSYS (Pat Saunders, Director of Human Resources)
Subject:	The Merit Pay Program

Just a reminder: All groups choosing to participate in the merit pay program must formally notify this office no later than Wednesday, October 18. As you know, while we are encouraging as many groups as possible to convert to this program, it is still voluntary. However, if a group does choose to convert to merit pay, all members of the group will have their annual salary increase determined by this method.

If you have any questions about the program, please contact one of the compensation specialists here in the office. Please be sure to notify me of your group's decision no later than Wednesday, 5 pm.

This is a tough one. It's not that you've forgotten the deadline for notifying Human Resources; it's just that you haven't made the final decision yet. It didn't seem likely to be a difficult call when the option was first presented. Before the merit pay program was created, everyone received the same annual increase in salary. If the salary increase was 5 percent, everyone got a 5 percent raise. It didn't matter how well or poorly anyone performed during the year; if they weren't let go, everyone got the same increase.

At the time it was announced, the merit pay option definitely seemed like a step in the right direction. With merit pay, people with better-than-average performance during the year would receive a better-than-average salary increase. Paying people on the basis of how well they perform rather than just for being around another year certainly made sense to you.

The problem is, it's not that simple. You had saved the original merit pay message, and you bring it up on your screen to help you with your thinking.

Date: September 25, 1995

From: LOCALSYS (Pat Saunders, Director of Human Resources)

Subject: The Merit Pay Program

. . . With the merit pay program, your group will receive the same average increase as the rest of the company. If the company awards a 5 percent increase, for example, the members of your group will share a 5 percent average increase. The difference is that the 5 percent will be distributed among the members of your group based on their individual levels of performance, with the higher performers earning higher raises . . .

When you first read this memo you had realized that the only way some of your people could be granted above-average increases would be for other members of your group to receive below-average raises. In other words, the only way you could create winners in your company's merit pay system would be by creating losers.

You decided to ask for input from the members of your team. Pay is a sensitive issue, so you asked them to E-mail their comments to you. Based on what they said, there is no clear consensus. Consider the summary of their responses shown on the following page.

Date: October 16, 1995

From: LOCALSYS (Summary of Individuals' Comments)

Subject: Our Reaction to the Merit Pay Program

. . . We should go with the merit pay program. It's about time the people who are pulling the load around here got the recognition they deserve. Maybe some of the others will get the message . . .

. . . I think pay for performance really makes sense. My only concern is how we're going to measure performance. If we're not careful, everyone will be fighting to get the assignments they know they can succeed on. No one will want to take on the really tough projects, or the ones that might not work out right away. They'll be afraid it will hurt them on their "merit" . . .

. . . Forget the merit. I have friends from other companies where they use that system, and they say it's a joke. No managers want to give anyone on their teams a really low increase, so they end up not being able to give anyone a large increase either. If the average has to be 4 percent, they don't want to give anyone less than 3 percent, so the top performers only get 4.5 or 5 percent. Why bother killing yourself just to earn a few hundred dollars more than someone who's really taking it easy? . . .

. . . I like the idea of paying people what they deserve. There should be more to a raise than just showing up for another year. But I am a little worried about what it might do to the group. We have a lot of teamwork right now, and I'm afraid that if we go to "merit," it'll become more competitive. I just think if you're going for that above-average raise, you're a lot less likely to pitch in and help someone else look good . . .

The fact is, there are more people in your group that want the program than don't, although several who said they want it did express specific concerns. The funny thing is that they're almost all good people. You're sure almost all of them would expect an above-average increase under the new system. The problem is that the merit pay program being offered just doesn't allow a majority of any group to be rated "above average." Even if every single member of a group could be shown to be a high-level performer, the only way anyone in the group could get a higher raise is by someone getting a lower one. Still, the majority say they want it, and it does bother you that if you decide not to take the merit pay option you forgo the ability to recognize the truly outstanding performers.

1. Use a T-chart to summarize the advantages and disadvantages of choosing to participate in the merit pay program.

2. Prepare a brief memo to your department members explaining your decision on whether or not to participate in the program.

SECTION

VI

Improving Performance

A s organizations have moved through the final decades of the twentieth century, the job of managing, as we said in Chapter 1, has changed dramatically. Some of these changes have been discussed in preceding chapters. Other aspects of management represent substantially new items on the management agenda. One of these is the responsibility for continuous improvement. Another is the responsibility for managing change. In the final two chapters we will explore the development in both of these areas and consider their impact on the process of management.

Chapter 12 begins with a focus on the control responsibility of management. The process of control has been reorganized as a management responsibility from at least Henri Fayol's time. You will recall that Fayol included control among his five essential functions of the manager. In recent years, however, the concept of control has been expanded dramatically. Control is no longer merely a process of monitoring performance and finding and fixing mistakes. Increasingly, control is a process of *kaizen*, of continuously improving the organization's processes and systems. Chapter 12 reviews the processes of control and of continuous improvement, and the contribution they make to the performance of the organization.

The focus of **Chapter 13** is the process of managing change. Change in organizations is constant, and it is of major proportions. These two facts present special challenges to management. As Chapter 13 points out, organizations and the people in them do not adapt easily to the kinds of change required by the more competitive environment, the high-performance workplace, and challenging performance standards. Management's task is to overcome this resistance to change and to transform change from a barrier to effective performance into a competitive advantage.

CHAPTER 12

Control: Managing Quality and Continuous Improvement

LEARNING OBJECTIVES

After reading this chapter, you should be able to:

- *Define control and explain the steps or stages in the control process.*

- *Explain the difficulty and importance of establishing performance standards and of taking corrective action.*

- *Compare the traditional approach to control with the kaizen, or improvement-oriented, approach to control.*

- *Discuss total quality management as a process for improving performance in organizations.*

- *Describe several of the problem-solving tools used in the continuous improvement process.*

arly in 1990, NASA launched the Hubble Space Telescope and placed it in orbit 365 miles above Earth. The Hubble telescope was designed to provide astronomers a view of the universe impossible to obtain from earth-based telescopes. After a few weeks in orbit, it was clear that the Hubble didn't work. Instead of producing brilliant individual points of light from distant galaxies, quasars, and nebulae, the Hubble produced blurred, smeary images that, even with computer correction, could not be sharpened.[1]

In December of 1993, NASA successfully repaired the Hubble Space Telescope, at a cost of $629 million. Why so serious a defect was not detected well before the Hubble was ever launched into space ultimately became a management question. The answer appears to be a simple lack of what Fayol called control. Apparently, this $1.5 billion satellite that was ten years in development had never been fully tested to see if it worked. The failure of the Hubble was, from a management perspective, a failure to monitor or control performance.

One might think that after setting goals and developing strategies, after establishing structures and organizing the work, and after empowering people to pursue goals, implement strategies, and perform the work, management's responsibilities would largely be complete. The dramatic failure of the Hubble in 1990 is a graphic reminder that this is not the case. If management is responsibility for organizational performance, then management is responsibility for control. That is, management includes responsibility for monitoring performance and for ensuring that actual performance is consistent with the organization's standards or goals.

THE CONTROL PROCESS

Traditionally, control has been defined as the process of ensuring that actual performance and results are consistent with performance goals. *Control* is the process of monitoring performance to ensure that performance goals are being achieved. The steps or stages of the control process are shown in Figure 12-1. Each of these steps represents a challenge to the organization as it seeks to ensure that performance is on target.

Establish Performance Standards

Clearly defined goals of the kind described in Chapter 4 are the first step in the control process. Besides serving as a target for performance, every type of goal within the organization—from strategic to operational goals, from benchmarks and budgets to team and individual performance goals—also becomes a standard against which performance can be measured.

At computer manufacturer Unisys Corp., for example, thirteen "turnaround teams" were given the goal of generating over a billion dollars of cash by the end of 1991. Each team was assigned a different category to investigate for cash savings, from reducing costs of sales to lowering inventory levels. Specific performance standards were set in each area, and by 1992 the company had returned to profitability.[2] Much of the success of Unisys in achieving its overall goal of $1 billion in savings can be attributed to the specific standards or goals against which each turnaround team could measure its performance.

- Establish/identify performance goals or standards.
- Monitor performance.
- Compare actual performance to the standard or goal.
- Take corrective action.

Figure 12-1 Steps in the Traditional Control Process

Difficulties with Establishing Standards

The problems with establishing performance standards are the same as the problems with defining effective goals that have been discussed throughout this book. Obviously, the standards cannot be vague or general; they must be specific enough to be measurable. This presents a special challenge, as we have said, to organizations and performance units involved with providing services rather than products. What is the standard for good medical care, for example, or a good education, or good service by an insurance company?

Despite these difficulties with defining clear goals in some areas of performance, every kind of organization has seen a redoubling of effort to define specific goals and standards. The State of Connecticut provides a telling example. Like many states, Connecticut has now established standards for what students at each grade level should know. Students are tested and results are closely monitored, with corrective action taken as needed to improve performance.[3] Before these performance standards were defined, there was no real way to monitor and measure whether students statewide were actually learning what they need to know.

Establishing clear standards, then, is the first step in the control process. Without clear standards there is nothing against which to measure performance, no well-defined basis for determining whether existing levels of performance are acceptable.

Monitor Performance

Once performance standards are set, management must gather data over time to determine the actual level of performance. Management must continuously track performance so that accurate information is available about what is being accomplished.

The performance standards that are defined in the first step of the control process determine which factors or variables will be measured. If standards are set in terms of quality, cost, and speed, for example, then those are the variables that will be monitored and measured. The key decisions of the second stage of the control process involve not which areas of performance will be monitored, but when, where, and how often to inspect or monitor key performance areas. Until the 1960s, for example, most large organizations were manufacturing organizations, and in these kinds of organizations monitoring performance usually took the form of visually inspecting or testing finished products. Usually, every item—whether it was an automobile, a refrigerator, or a television set—was inspected or tested to make certain it had no major defects. Occasionally, to keep inspection costs lower, not every unit was inspected; instead, there were spot checks. Often there was no system or pattern to these spot-check inspections, so there was really no way of knowing whether they were an effective way to monitor performance.

In the early 1960s, statistical quality control, or SQC, began to emerge. Statistical quality control involves the use of statistical theory about sampling and variation to calculate how many and which items from a batch or run of products need to be inspected to determine the level of quality of the entire batch. Through statistical quality-control methods, monitoring performance has moved from the realm of guesswork to the realm of science.

In fact, through an application called *statistical process control (SPC)*, statistical theory increasingly has been used to monitor performance not just in terms of the quality of the finished product, as SQC does, but in terms of the quality of the process used to produce it. Statistical process control provides statistical information about quality from checkpoints at every stage of the production process. This allows management to monitor whether the system is operating on target without having to wait to inspect the finished product. The SPC process will be discussed more fully later in this chapter.

The form that monitoring might take and the frequency of monitoring performance can differ in ways not necessarily having to do with statistical methods. At Home Box Office (HBO), for example, performance standards are set for employees at the beginning of the year. Two reviews, one at midyear and the other at the end of the year, track employees' performance against the standards.[4] At the other extreme, Cypress Semiconductor Company generates detailed computer printouts about the status of each executive's weekly performance goals on a day-to-day basis.[5]

We repeat: Goals and standards are not enough. Systematic monitoring is needed to determine the actual level of performance. This is where the Hubble failed. As production of the telescope was rushed from stage to stage to make up for missed deadlines, time was not taken to monitor whether performance standards were being met at each stage of the process.

Compare Performance to the Standards

The third step in the control process involves an *evaluation* of actual performance against the goal or standard. Performance goals are set, performance is monitored or measured, and now it must be determined whether a significant gap exists between the goal and the reality.

An important concept in the evaluation stage is the issue of critical deviations. *Critical deviations* are any gaps or differences between goals or standards and actual performance that critically impact the success of the process. For example, suppose a community hospital sets the staffing goal or standard of 4.0 staff members per patient (which is hypothetically the national average for similar hospitals that are successful). The hospital then monitors its own actual staffing levels and discovers that it employs 4.8 staff members per patient, a rate that is 20 percent higher than the benchmark national average. This gap between the goal of 4.0 and the actual level of 4.8 represents a critical deviation in management's judgment. The 20 percent deviation suggests that the hospital may be overstaffed, which may in turn result in expenses that make it difficult for the hospital to survive in the increasingly competitive health care industry.

Defining which performance deviations are critical to the overall success of a process or to the success of the organization is an essential task for managers. Even in small organizations, there will be numerous deviations or gaps between actual performance and the goal or standard. If management attempted to respond to *every* performance deviation, there would be little time left to do anything else. The manager's task is to determine which performance deviations are genuinely *critical* and to focus on these.

One strategy for focusing management energy and attention is to identify and focus on a limited number of goals or standards. Limiting the number of critical goals not only facilitates the control process, it also tends to focus the attention and effort of everyone involved in pursuing those goals, which in turn tends to improve performance. At Texas Instruments, for example, for years there was the saying "More than two objectives is no objectives." This reflected the clear realization that performance is better when the energies of the organization are concentrated on a limited number of critical goals or standards.

Take Corrective Action

If the level of actual performance reveals that performance standards are being met, the organization knows enough to continue what it's doing, because it's working. If performance is not at a level consistent with goals, and if this gap represents a critical deviation, the organization knows that it needs to take action to improve performance. This is called *corrective action.*

The appropriate corrective action depends on the nature of the problem. At Toyota, when market share declined for three consecutive years, from 1990 to 1993, corrective action included cutting costs by $1.5 billion for 1994.[6] In nonprofit organizations, as U.S. volunteers declined 4.3 percent in 1991 from two years earlier, the corrective action was for managers to extend volunteer opportunities to nights and weekends and to broaden recruiting efforts to include minorities, retirees, and teens.[7] Regardless of the form it takes, corrective action is the action management takes to put performance back on track in terms of meeting goals and performance standards.

Problems with Corrective Action

There are two problems with corrective action. One is that is must be considered in light of today's organizations' multiple goals. The other is that corrective action may result in unintended consequences. Just as defining and measuring performance was relatively easier when the economy was dominated by manufacturing organizations, taking corrective action also was easier. Before competition became so intense and the emphasis on quality and innovation increased so dramatically, the primary goal, as we have said, was usually to deliver the product or service more or less on time. When production or delivery targets were missed, corrective action often took the form of speeding up the machines or purchasing faster ones; or speeding up the workers or hiring more of them. Production systems were simpler, goals were tangible, and corrective actions were often fairly obvious and easy to identify.

In the current environment, organizations have become infinitely more complex. Not only are goals less tangible, but there are now multiple goals. Production and speed must be balanced by concerns for quality, innovation, and social responsibility. Now, if production targets are being missed, the corrective action of speeding things up must be evaluated in terms of its impact on quality and the other changing performance standards. Downsizing in the 1990s, for example, has been a corrective action taken to help organizations meet their targets in terms of competitive costs. But, as we noted earlier, downsizing can also result in serious morale problems for the organization's workforce. Increasingly, corrective action must achieve a very difficult balance in terms of satisfying the requirements of several different goals.

In addition, our systems and organizations are so complex that corrective action sometimes has consequences that are difficult to anticipate. To correct critical deviations in terms of new car sales, for example, carmakers in the 1980s dramatically lowered the interest rates they charged on new cars, only to see sales fall even further as buyers waited to see if the rates would go any lower. In another example, in many organizations management has attempted to empower workers as part of the effort to improve performance, but many labor unions have resisted empowerment programs. They see empowerment as a threat because they fear the union will no longer be required for communicating workers' ideas to management. In both these situations, the consequence is contrary to the goal of the corrective action.

In short, managers not only must evaluate corrective action alternatives against multiple goals, but must do so under conditions where it has become increasingly difficult to anticipate what the effects of those actions will be. Where once corrective action was the solution to performance problems, more and more, identifying and evaluating corrective action options has become a problem in itself.

Defining standards, monitoring performance, comparing performance to standards, and taking corrective action—these are the steps in the control process. As we have seen, each step presents a challenge to management as it seeks to ensure that actual performance is consistent with goals.

THE PARADOX OF CONTROL

Beyond these fundamental challenges associated with the control process itself, there is another significant barrier to effective control. The more you attempt to solve performance problems by regulating and imposing direction on people, the more likely they are to resist, and in some cases even to sabotage, that effort. This pattern of resistance to control is called the *paradox of control*.[8] The paradox of control explains what happened at the Lordstown GM plant in the 1970s, when management attempted to increase the speed of the assembly line to a speed or standard that the workers felt was unreasonable. To slow down the line to a speed they found acceptable, the workers actually sabotaged the cars they were building. They sealed windshields incompletely, which resulted in leaks during final testing, and they placed empty soft-drink cans inside the car doors before final assembly, which also resulted in problems at final testing. All this was done to slow the assembly line down, to force management to set a more reasonable standard.

It appears to be human nature to resist the efforts of others to influence or even to measure our performance. Yet the need for more effective control has never been greater. The key to solving this puzzle lies in the realization that more *effective* control may not necessarily mean *more* control.

One approach for achieving more effective control lies in the concept of reciprocity of control.[9] Where *reciprocity of control* exists, management shares with workers responsibility for monitoring performance and taking corrective action. At Omni Hotel, for example, customer service improved when managers encouraged staff members to use their own judgment on how to best satisfy customer needs. Instead of creating more rules, managers encouraged the staff to bend the rules when necessary to meet the highest standards of customer service. Similarly, at Ford Motor Company, quality finally improved only when assembly-line workers were given permission to stop the production line themselves in order to correct a problem. In both cases, improvement in performance came not by imposing greater control over workers but by giving employees greater self-control.

In this sense, reciprocity of control is essentially the same as empowerment. It is by sharing responsibility for performance with workers that the paradox of control is solved and the control process is improved.

FROM QUALITY CONTROL TO CONTINUOUS IMPROVEMENT

As a result of the new competition and changing performance standards, there has been a dramatic shift in recent years in the focus and scope of the control process. It is no longer enough merely to find and fix production problems that occur. To compete effectively where quality, innovation, and service are what sells—and this is as true for nonprofit organizations as it is for business—the focus of control must extend well beyond merely monitoring performance, finding mistakes, and taking corrective action. In a world where everyone is looking for a competitive advantage, control is increasingly becoming the process not just of problem solving around critical deviations, but also of learning how to continuously improve performance even when there are no problems.

This concept of continuous improvement is called *kaizen* in Japan, where it was first adopted. The approximate meaning of *kaizen* is "to improve every day in every way possible." To understand the full meaning of the shift from control to *kaizen*, it is helpful to consider in greater detail the traditional outlook toward control.

The Traditional Approach to Control

The traditional approach to control, typical of organizations in Europe and the United States for most of this century, has three fundamental characteristics: First, it has a goal of acceptable quality; second, it is a system engineered by experts; and third, its focus is primarily on finding and fixing mistakes.

Goal of Acceptable Quality

In the traditional system of control, the emphasis is on producing goods which are only "good enough," not perfect. This philosophy began with the development of mass-production techniques in America. For nearly a century, one of the assumptions of mass production was that a product only had to be good enough for its markets, not perfect. Higher quality was often rejected as an unnecessary refinement because higher quality meant higher prices. It was General Motors' Alfred Sloan who defined the principle of *acceptable quality level (AQL)* in the 1920s. According to Sloan, a particular product did not have to be better than a competitor's; it only had to be as good. The product had to achieve an acceptable quality level and no more, since anything above the quality of competitive products only increased costs and wasted effort. In this perspective, profits come not from improving quality but from producing enough units of an acceptable quality level to be profitable.[10]

Engineered by Experts

In the traditional approach, in order to ensure a competitive quantity of acceptable-quality units, both the production process and the quality control process are designed by "experts"—by managers assisted by engineers and other specialists. This has at least two important consequences. First, because the production systems are engineered by experts, the assumption tends to be that they are designed as effectively as they can be. This in turn leads to the expectation by both management and workers that workers will focus only on doing their jobs, and certainly not on thinking about how to improve the design of the system. In other words, quality and quality control are the exclusive concerns of the engineers.

Second, because the job has been designed by experts, workers tend to view the standards that are set as "theoretical"—as targets to be worked toward but not necessarily achieved. From the workers' point of view, the "real" goal is only to come close enough to the standard to pass the work on to the next stage of the process. When each worker only comes "close enough" to the target or standard at each of the dozens of steps in the production process, the result is a final product almost guaranteed to have defects.

Focus on Finding and Fixing Mistakes

The third element of the traditional control process is a focus on mistakes. The emphasis on meeting production targets and schedules while achieving merely an acceptable quality level has led to a focus on identifying products with too many mistakes to meet the acceptable quality level. Typically, another group of experts, called *quality control inspectors,* have been responsible for this task.

The view of the worker in this system is that quality control is a process of someone *else*—the inspector—trying to catch the mistakes of the worker. Efforts to improve the quality control process tend to be viewed by the worker as an effort to increase the number of mistakes caught, and the blame that goes with them.

Thus, in this system, quality improvement efforts tend to be viewed with extreme suspicion, if not outright hostility, by front-line workers.

This is the traditional system of control: a process engineered by experts to find and fix output that does not conform to acceptable quality levels. Now compare this approach to the continuous improvement approach known as *kaizen*.

Kaizen: **The Improvement-Oriented Approach**

It should not be surprising that the Japanese have led the way in broadening the focus of the control process to include continuous improvement. After all, little more than a generation ago, "Made in Japan" was a synonym for low-quality goods, and markets everywhere were clamoring for products labeled "Made in America." In the decades following World War II, the Japanese were fully aware that their economy could grow only by improving the quality of its goods. They knew that they could not remain the low-cost, low-quality producer and at the same time develop a world-class economy.

The process of improvement that Japanese organizations developed to catch up with the United States and the European economic powers has been so effective that in a number of industries, including electronics, banking, and automobiles, not only have they caught up with the leaders, they have outstripped them. The "Made in Japan" mark now commands a respect in the marketplace that is unsurpassed by any competitor. This remarkable transformation can be attributed, as much as anything else, to *kaizen,* a system of control with three key elements: The goal is continuous improvement; responsibility for quality and improvement is shared by all members of the organization; and the focus is on improving the quality of both the product and the process.

Goal of Improvement

Because Japan started out so far behind in terms of quality, by necessity, quality control came to be viewed in Japan not so much as a process of catching mistakes as one of continuous improvement. Interestingly, this shift is actually consistent with Alfred Sloan's principle of acceptable quality level. Initially, the level of quality of most Japanese goods was not acceptable in many of the world's most important markets. It was in response to this reality that quality improvement became for the Japanese a major goal.

Japan was so open to ways of improving quality that two American quality-control experts, W. Edward Deming and J. M. Juran, convinced Japanese manufacturers to implement their specific programs for increasing quality and lowering the rate of product defects. Deming emphasized statistical controls for product improvement, and made such an impression on the Japanese that they created the annual Deming Prize, now one of the most prestigious awards a Japanese corporation can receive.

Ironically, neither Deming nor Juran could generate any real interest in quality improvement among American manufacturers. This becomes at least somewhat understandable when you realize that in the 1950s, when quality improvement was such a major concern in Japan, the quality of American goods was still relatively unchallenged. The shift to a focus on improvement then was a necessary one for Japan, just as it became a necessary shift in focus for U.S. organizations in the 1980s.

Shared Responsibility for Quality

Juran's unique contribution to the new approach to control was an emphasis on shared responsibility. In 1954 Juran taught that quality control must be the concern of all levels of both management and workers, not just the responsibility of efficiency engineers and other specialists. It was at this time, during the 1950s, that the Japanese developed the practice of viewing quality as a companywide objective shared by everyone who worked in the organization.[11]

In Japan, quality is not a "we" (workers) versus "them" (engineers and inspectors) issue. Quality is everyone's responsibility, regardless of task assignment. Because the emphasis in the Japanese approach to control was on improvement rather than on catching mistakes, quality improvement efforts became something to commit to rather than something to avoid. Individuals and teams became committed to searching for ways to improve the product and process, rather than ways to avoid the blame for defects and mistakes.

Focus on Improving the Product and the Process

Because quality is seen as everyone's responsibility, the focus of concerns in the *kaizen* system broadens significantly to include improvements not just in terms of outcomes or results, but also in terms of how they are achieved. The production process or design of the task is no longer assumed to be perfect simply because it has been designed by engineers or other experts. With *kaizen*, the existing design is only a starting place; it is always open to improvement and redesign.

Figure 12-2 summarizes the differences between the traditional approach and the improvement-oriented approach to the process of control.

Evidence of the effectiveness of the improvement-oriented approach to control is found in the quality of Japanese products, from cars to television sets and other electronic products. Does *kaizen* work, as might be claimed, only because of the extreme group orientation of Japanese culture? Apparently not; quality im-

Traditional	Improvement-Oriented
• Goal of acceptable quality; quantity over quality.	• Goal of continuous improvement.
• Quality is the responsibility of engineers and quality control experts.	• Quality is the responsibility of everyone involved in the process.
• Focus on finding and fixing mistakes in output only (since production process has been designed by experts).	• Focus on continuous improvement of both output and the production process.

Figure 12-2 Differences in the Traditional and Improvement-Oriented Approaches Toward Control

provement seems to be a product of the system rather than of the culture. Consider the case of Motorola's Chicago television set plant after it was taken over in 1974 by Matsushita, a Japanese corporation. Before the sale, Motorola was averaging 150 defects per 100 TV sets. After the sale to Matsushita, an American workforce using predominantly the same equipment and machines as before, but with a *kaizen*-style system of quality improvement, eventually achieved a defect rate of 4 per 100 TV sets.[12] In fact, in the 1990s American car manufacturers have finally begun to approach Japanese-levels of quality in their products, primarily through the adoption of continuous-improvement control techniques.

And then there is the case of the Southern Pacific Lines. This railroad was on the verge of bankruptcy in 1988 when a new owner, Philip Anshutz, chose continuous quality improvement as a turnaround strategy. By focusing on improvements to customers in such areas as pricing and service, Southern Pacific has made dramatic progress toward achieving its strategic goals.[13]

Group Involvement in Quality Improvement

An important element of the improvement-oriented *kaizen* approach, both in Japan and in the United States, has been group involvement in problem solving around quality. We mentioned earlier that it was American quality-control expert J. M. Juran who insisted that responsibility for quality should be shared by members at every level of the organization. One element of the response to Juran's challenge has been the creation of groups of production workers, called *quality circles (QCs)*, to solve problems in the area of quality and productivity improvement.

Quality circles typically consist of eight to twelve workers and often include a supervisor or manager. Groups meet for an hour or so—once or twice a month—sometimes more often—and participants are encouraged to present problems they have identified in terms of quality or productivity. The QC then works to identify solutions to these problems. It is important to note that in the improvement-oriented approach, a problem exists not just when something goes wrong or does not meet standards. Even if standards are being met, as long as there are more than zero defects or less than 100 percent efficiency, there are assumed to be problems to be worked on.

Quality circles, or *quality improvement teams*, as they are also sometimes called, are not intended to focus on major policy issues, but rather on the day-to-day problems that surface in a work area. In an example mentioned in Chapter 10, a QC group at Harley-Davidson solved a quality problem with parts by suggesting that the parts be delivered on an as-needed basis using wheeled wooden racks rather than an overhead conveyor belt parts-delivery system.

Improvement teams suggest how forms or work procedures might be redesigned, or how a work area might be rearranged. Their focus is on the hundreds of small changes that together can have a dramatic impact on quality and productivity.

Two important points need to be stressed about quality circles or improvement teams. The first is that such groups recognize the important contributions that front-line workers—whether machine operators, claims processors, or floor salespersons—are uniquely qualified to make. These individuals are the ones most familiar with the process, with whatever the problems might be, and they also possess important insights into the most effective solutions.

Second, these circles and teams also ensure that control will be a process of continuous improvement, rather than one of catching mistakes which often happen with no consistency or pattern. The existence of groups meeting regularly, specifically for the purpose of solving problems around quality and productivity, almost guarantees that control will focus less on relatively infrequent mistakes and more on the steady flow of opportunities for improvement. QCs and improvement teams place the issues of control and improvement high on the agenda of people at every level of the organization, and keep them there.

TOTAL QUALITY MANAGEMENT (TQM)

The new competition of the 1980s forced the shift to an emphasis on continuous improvement and led to the emergence of quality improvement teams. It was also as a result of this new competition that a process called total quality management, or TQM, became perhaps the most widespread improvement strategy among U.S. organizations in the 1990s.

Total quality management is the continuous process of involving employees throughout the organization in creative problem-solving to improve the quality of products and services.[14] The primary focus of TQM is on meeting and exceeding customers' expectations. By the late 1980s, TQM was being implemented in every kind of organization, including AT&T, Kodak, IBM, Xerox, Federal Express, and L. L. Bean, to name just a few.

There are many approaches to TQM, but all of them share the three characteristics of customer focus, commitment to incremental improvement, and emphasis on problem solving.

Customer Focus

The focus of TQM is the customer. The goal of TQM, as we said, is to remove all barriers to meeting or exceeding customers' expectations. When organization members become immersed in reviewing their department or company activities to develop more effective processes, they can often overlook the need for a customer or outside perspective. Yet it is difficult to effectively improve products and systems when the customer is not included as part of the process.

To ensure that customer needs are the central focus of a quality program, the TQM process often includes ways of providing customer input and feedback. For example, at Johnson & Johnson's McNeil Consumer Products subsidiary, manufacturer of Tylenol, workers who previously had no feedback from customers regarding the product can now visit a special booth in the plant to hear questions and concerns from customers.[15] Similarly, Pepsi-Cola recently surveyed ten thousand customers to develop sixteen priorities for its new TQM effort. One priority from the customer's viewpoint was the improvement of deliveries, and this became a major area designated for improvement.[16] Regardless of the form customer input takes, a true customer focus is essential for an effective TQM process. After all, quality is defined by the customer.

Incremental Improvement

The TQM process also involves improving one thing at a time, although many of these single improvements may occur simultaneously in an organization. This kind of approach is called *incremental* because it focuses on improving performance through the accumulation of single, less-than-major improvements, or "increments." A typical six-step approach to incremental improvement is described in Figure 12-3.[17]

In step 1 of the incremental improvement process, an area of improvement is chosen or identified by management or an improvement team. Examples might include reducing late shipments, reducing employee absenteeism, or improving the accuracy of a billing process. If a team has not already been organized to deal with the target area, step 2 involves forming a team. This might consist of employ-

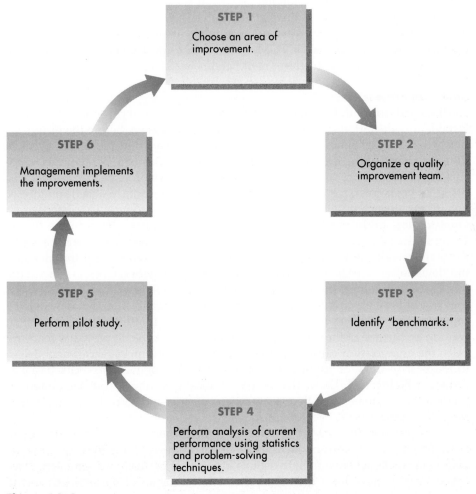

STEP 1
Choose an area of improvement.

STEP 2
Organize a quality improvement team.

STEP 3
Identify "benchmarks."

STEP 4
Perform analysis of current performance using statistics and problem-solving techniques.

STEP 5
Perform pilot study.

STEP 6
Management implements the improvements.

Figure 12-3 The Incremental Improvement Process

ees directly responsible for the work, one or more customers, suppliers, and a member of management. In step 3, the team benchmarks the best performers in the industry in the target area and identifies how much improvement is required to match their standards. Current performance is analyzed in step 4, using some of the problem-solving tools discussed below, and alternatives are identified for improving performance in the future. In step 5, a pilot study of the recommended improvement is undertaken and the results are monitored. At this point, the question becomes whether the improvement is worth the cost. If a cost-benefit study favors the change, then step 6 is full implementation. The key point is that TQM is not a program emphasizing a limited number of major changes, but a process of constant and continuing review and a steady stream of improvements to better meet customer needs and expectations.

Emphasis on Problem Solving

TQM is ultimately a problem-solving process. It is a process of identifying performance and quality problems, analyzing their causes, and developing and implementing solutions for improvement. A number of problem-solving techniques have been adopted for use in TQM. Three of the most common are statistical process control, fishbone diagrams, and Pareto charts.

Statistical Process Control

As discussed earlier in the chapter, the purpose of statistical process control (SPC) is to identify deviations in the production process or system before the product is finished. Statistical process control graphically displays deviations that occur at different stages of the production or service process. Before SPC, attempts to ensure the quality of products relied primarily on inspection after the product was made. In years past, for example, a manager might recognize a performance or quality problem only when 10 percent of the *finished* product was defective—a point too late to do much more than try to prevent this problem in the future. Using statistical process-control techniques *while the product or service is being produced* allows critical deviations to be recognized much sooner. And the causes of the deviation—such as worn tools, poor training, or worker errors—can more quickly be determined and appropriate corrective action taken.

Consider the example of a community service organization that developed a campaign for recruiting new volunteers over a three-month period. Rather than waiting for the end of the campaign to compare final results to previous years' results, the organization can use statistical data from volunteer-recruitment drives in the past to monitor its progress on a day-to-day or week-to-week basis, as shown in Figure 12-4. Using this process, critical deviations from the pattern of previous years can be identified very easily and early, and corrective action can be taken to put the process back on track.

The purpose, then, of SPC is to assist in the earliest possible identification of critical deviations in performance. For example, in the case in Figure 12-4, the deviation in weeks seven and eight signals a potential performance problem. Once key deviations have been identified, the task is to analyze the problem and to

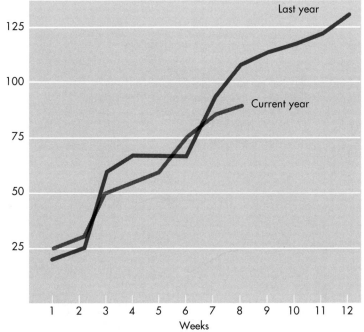

Figure 12-4 Volunteer-Recruitment Drive

identify and understand its potential causes so that the appropriate corrective action can be taken. This is the purpose of the fishbone diagram.

Fishbone Diagram

One of the simpler tools for determining the causes of problems in performance or quality is the *fishbone diagram.* As shown in Figure 12-5, this graphical technique gets its name from the fishlike shape of the diagram. The fishbone diagram is based on the assumption that performance or quality problems are caused by factors in one or a combination of four specific areas: personnel, materials, machinery, and method.

In creating a fishbone diagram, the experience and expertise of front-line workers come into play. Using techniques such as brainstorming, improvement teams made up of the individuals most familiar with the situation generate as many causes for a problem as possible in each of the four areas. From these, the most likely causes are then selected for further analysis. The value of the fishbone diagram is that it aids in organizing ideas. The four types of causes in the fishbone focus the efforts of the improvement team while at the same time encouraging systematic consideration of a broad range of possible causes. Consistent with the

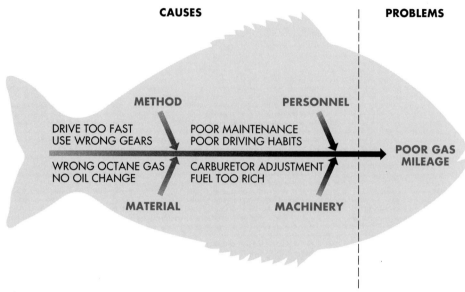

CAUSES

PROBLEMS

METHOD

PERSONNEL

DRIVE TOO FAST
USE WRONG GEARS

POOR MAINTENANCE
POOR DRIVING HABITS

WRONG OCTANE GAS
NO OIL CHANGE

CARBURETOR ADJUSTMENT
FUEL TOO RICH

**POOR GAS
MILEAGE**

MATERIAL

MACHINERY

Figure 12-5 Fishbone Diagram

decision-making process discussed in Chapter 5, the fishbone analysis prevents the group from jumping to conclusions about the cause of a problem.

Pareto Chart

Once a fishbone analysis is complete and the likely causes of a problem have been identified, a Pareto chart can be used to assess the impact of each suggested cause. Named for its creator, economist Vilfredo Pareto, a Pareto chart is a special type of bar graph that is an excellent tool for evaluating possible causes once they have been identified. For example, if a manager wanted to determine which of a number of possible causes were most responsible for late shipments of a product, a chart similar to Figure 12-6 might be constructed showing the frequency of each cause. In Figure 12-6, truck delay is the largest bar on the graph and appears to be the primary cause of late shipments. To identify reasons for the truck delay, a second-level chart could be constructed, as shown in Figure 12-7.

The Pareto chart is not the end of the problem-solving process. Once causes are determined, the improvement team still must develop and pilot potential corrective actions. The value of the Pareto chart is that it ensures that problem solving is based on real data and that solutions target the documented, actual causes of the problem.

Problems with Implementation

Despite the success of TQM at so many U.S. corporations, there are also signs of disappointment. Indeed, recent surveys reveal that two-thirds of American man-

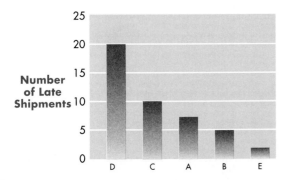

Number of Late Shipments

Reasons for Late Shipments	M	T	W	Th	F	Total
A. Late order	1	2	1	2	1	7
B. Low inventory	1	0	2	1	1	5
C. Inadequate shipping information	2	1	3	1	3	10
D. Truck delayed	4	3	4	3	6	20
E. Other	1	0	0	1	0	2

Figure 12-6 Pareto Chart for Identifying Late Shipments

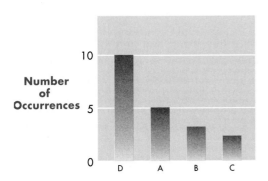

Number of Occurrences

Reasons	Week 1	Week 2	Week 3	Total
A. Truck not available	1	2	2	5
B. Driver not available	1	1	1	3
C. Truck dirty	1	0	1	2
D. Mechanical problems	4	3	3	10

Figure 12-7 Pareto Chart Reasons for Truck Delay

- The CEO must be visibly behind the total quality program. He or she must sustain the momentum through attending team sessions, chairing a steering committee for the process, and/or being part of a quality team.

- A customer focus must be maintained. Get feedback from the customer.

- Limit the total quality program to a few critical goals.

- Link changes to a clear financial payback. Demand at least some early payback from the quality effort. Look for results.

- Don't adapt a quality program off-the-shelf. Adapt it to the organization.

Figure 12-8 Guidelines for Implementing a Total Quality Program

agers think TQM has failed to achieve significant improvements in their organizations. In addition, the number of applications for the Malcolm Baldrige National Quality Award, an award given to companies achieving the highest standards of quality, has fallen off sharply since 1991.[18]

As is the case with so many management processes, the problem appears to be not with TQM itself but with how it is implemented. One survey of over five hundred companies in the United States, Canada, and Germany has suggested that different approaches to TQM work in different kinds of organizations. This study points out, for example, that lower-performing companies did best by starting with an emphasis on teamwork and training, and that only high performers were likely to have the training and other resources to take advantage of benchmarking. In general, the study concludes that TQM works best when companies start with a few highly focused practices and then build on their successes.[19]

In line with these research findings, experts suggest five guidelines for implementing an effective total-quality effort. These guidelines are shown in Figure 12-8.[20]

Simply having a TQM process is no guarantee of success. The design and implementation of the program appear to be crucial. The key is to match the elements of the TQM process to the organization's specific needs and abilities. With the right match, there is clear evidence of TQM's potential to move the organization closer to its goal of meeting and exceeding customers' expectations.

SUMMARY

Control is the process of ensuring that actual performance is consistent with the organization's goals and standards. Performance must be monitored to ensure that progress is on track, and action must be taken both to solve performance problems and to continuously improve performance. Each step in the control process is a challenge for management.

The first step involves establishing the goals, benchmarks, and budgets that are the performance targets or standards of the organization. From there, actual performance levels are monitored or measured. A number of approaches, including statistical techniques, have been developed to make this stage of the control process more meaningful. In the third step, actual performance is compared to the goal or standard. If there is a gap or deviation between performance and the goal, management must decide if it is significant or critical enough to require taking corrective action, which is the fourth step of the control process.

The control process has traditionally been characterized by emphasis on finding and fixing problems in performance. In recent years, the concept of control has been expanded to include an emphasis on quality and continuous improvement. In this new approach, called *kaizen,* the goal is no longer just to reduce defects in the product or service. The goal is now to continuously improve both the product and the process, and everyone in the organization is viewed as a partner in achieving this goal.

Total quality management is a process that reflects this improvement-oriented approach. The goal of TQM is to continuously improve performance, with a focus on meeting and exceeding the customer's expectations. Research suggests that TQM should not necessarily take the same form in every organization. Still, the successful application of TQM-type processes in a variety of U.S. and Japanese organizations suggests that control as a process of continuous improvement is here to stay.

Like the other responsibilities of management, managing quality and continuous improvement is a demanding task but one that is essential to the success of the organization. An effective control process ensures that critical deviations in performance are identified and responded to well before they threaten the organization's ability to achieve its goals and mission. An effective process of continuous improvement ensures that the organization will continue to satisfy the expectations of its customers and keep pace with the new competition.

QUESTIONS TO CHALLENGE YOUR UNDERSTANDING OF THE CHAPTER

1. List and briefly explain the steps in the control process.

2. What standards would you use to measure the effectiveness of the teaching in this course? Are there any difficulties with measuring this teaching performance?

3. Provide an example from your own experience of the "paradox of control." Suggest how reciprocity of control might have avoided the problem in this situation.

4. What are the two problems with organizations' taking corrective action? Discuss.

5. What would be involved in shifting from a traditional approach to control to the *kaizen* improvement-oriented approach? Use a business with which you are familiar to provide specific details.

6. Why is a customer focus important in TQM?

7. Use a fishbone diagram to identify the potential causes of the problem of students' not passing the first test in a course.

MANAGEMENT EXERCISE

Customer Feedback

Divide the class into groups of four or five students. Each group is assigned the task of identifying problems and recommending solutions from a "customer" perspective in terms of the following areas of the college/university:

Courses and classes

Food service

Housing and resident life

Social activities

Athletics

Clubs and organizations

For each assigned area, each group should:

1. Define the desired standard of performance (benchmarks).

2. Indicate the present level of performance.

3. Define what they would consider to be critical deviations in this area and recommend corrective action.

REFERENCES

1. Michael D. Lemonick, "Hubble Out of Trouble," *Time,* January 24, 1994, 46; Barbara Rosewicz, "Hubble Photos Show Telescope in Good Shape," *Wall Street Journal,* January 14, 1994, B8; "We Slam-Dunked It," *Newsweek,* December 20, 1993, 100–102; "Fixing a Wrinkle in Time," *U.S. News & World Report,* December 6, 1993, 28–29.

2. Dana W. Linden, "The Bean Counter as Hero," *Forbes,* October 11, 1993, 46–48.

3. Kenneth H. Bacon, "Connecticut Grades Its Schools and Holds Officials Responsible," *Wall Street Journal,* April 24, 1990, A1, A4.

4. Maryanne Coleman-Carlone, "HBO's Program for Merit Pay," *Personnel Journal,* May 1990, 86–90.

5. T. J. Rodgers, "No Excuses Management," *Harvard Business Review,* July–August 1990, 84–98.

6. William Spindle, Larry Armstrong, and James B. Treece, "Toyota Retooled," *Business Week,* April 4, 1994, 54–56.

7. Keith H. Hammonds and Sandra Jones, "Good Help Really Is Hard to Find," *Business Week*, April 4, 1994, 100–101.

8. G. W. Dalton and P. R. Lawrence, *Motivation and Control in Organizations* (Homewood, Ill.: Richard D. Irwin, 1971), 5.

9. A. S. Tannenbaum, *Control in Organizations* (New York: McGraw-Hill, 1968).

10. Jon Alston, *The American Samurai: Blending American and Japanese Managerial Practices* (New York and Berlin, Germany: W. de Gruyer, 1985), 263.

11. Ibid., 273.

12. Ibid., 267.

13. James M. Carman, "Continuous Quality Improvement as a Survival Strategy: The Southern Pacific Experience," *California Management Review*, Spring 1993, 118–32.

14. Stanley M. Cherkasky, "Total Quality for a Sustainable Competitive Advantage," *Quality*, August 1992, Q4, Q6–Q7.

15. Rahul Jacob, "TQM: More than a Dying Fad?" *Fortune*, October 18, 1993, 66.

16. Ibid.

17. Samuel C. Certo, *Modern Management*, 6th ed. (Needham Heights, Mass.: Allyn & Bacon, 1994), 563.

18. Gilbert Fuchsberg, "Quality Programs Show Shoddy Results," *Wall Street Journal*, May 14, 1992, B1, B7.

19. Gilbert Fuchsberg, "'Total Quality' Is Termed Only Partial Success," *Wall Street Journal*, October 1, 1992, B1, B9.

20. Jacob, 66–72.

CHAPTER 13

Managing Change: The Continuing Challenge

LEARNING OBJECTIVES

After reading this chapter, you should be able to:

- *Discuss how human nature and corporate culture are powerful sources of resistance to change in organizations.*

- *Explain the three stages of the organizational change process and describe the key activities for each stage.*

- *Discuss why continuous change represents a new challenge for organizations.*

- *Explain why managing change in organizations is ultimately a leadership challenge.*

n the first chapter of this book we emphasized all of the changes that have made the task of management more challenging than ever before: the new competition of the changing environment, the diverse workforce and new technology of the changing workplace, and changing performance standards. In subsequent chapters we amplified that discussion by reviewing new models of organizational structure, new job designs, new demands of empowerment and leadership, and finally the challenge of continuous improvement. Change is both the most daunting challenge confronting management and the most promising opportunity. Change threatens to overwhelm the organization, and at the same time it reveals unprecedented possibilities.

Change is also inevitable. No lesson from the past ten years is clearer than that organizations must change if they want to survive in today's environment. How important is it for organizations to manage change effectively? "To be blunt," says Louis Gerstner, Jr., of IBM, "the failure to capitalize on this sea change in our industry is the single most important mistake IBM has made in the last decade."[1]

The question is not whether to accept the challenge of change but *how* to manage change to make it as productive as possible, to make it a process for strengthening and renewing the organization. Creating such a process may be the most difficult challenge confronting management.

THE PROBLEM OF RESISTANCE

Psychology has taught us how difficult it is for individuals to change their behavior: how difficult it is, for example, to learn to eat less, to exercise more, to stop smoking or drinking, to be more assertive. Theories of personality and behavior suggest that for most of us personal change is achieved only with great effort. Over the past ten years, management has discovered that change also represents a serious obstacle for organizations.

Like individuals, organizations become accustomed to doing certain things, and to doing them in certain ways. As a result, organizations tend vigorously to resist change. Organizations view change as a threat to the status quo, and resist all efforts to modify it. This resistance to change has a number of sources. Two of the strongest are human nature and corporate culture.

The Human Response to Change

The kinds of change required for organizations to be competitive in the changing environment are not minor. People are being asked to work in teams where previously they had always worked as individuals; to learn and use technology that may not have even existed a few years earlier; to do more work, faster and with greater quality than ever before. For most people, the natural response to change of this dimension or magnitude is what is called the stress response.[2]

The *stress response* is the fight-or-flight response that prepares us for action when we are in danger. Unfortunately, most people view major change as a potential source of danger. Their natural reaction is one of stress. People become anxious about whether they can do what the change requires in terms of using new technology, doing different work than they are used to, and doing more of it, faster and with greater quality. People worry about whether there will still be a place for them in the organization. From a needs perspective, change represents a threat to people's security, and much of their natural reaction is to resist and defend against that perceived threat.

For all these reasons, the human response to change in organizations tends to be negative. Any successful change process in an organization must recognize that the natural human response to change is one of stress. To be effective, the change process must incorporate strategies for helping people to get beyond this initial response.

Corporate Culture

The other major source of resistance to change in organizations is corporate culture. *Corporate culture* is the term used to describe the set of beliefs, norms, and values that are shared by the members of an organization. These beliefs, norms, and values have to do with the way the organization operates, and what is important in that organization.

Researchers Terrence Deal and Allan Kennedy suggest that corporate culture tends to be created and communicated by the stories an organization tells about itself, by the language it uses, by whom the organization celebrates as its heroes, and by its rituals and ceremonies.[3] The following are examples of the kinds of stories, language, and rituals that communicate the beliefs and values of an organization.

- Wal-Mart refers to its employees as "associates" to emphasize the fact that everyone is a partner in the success of the organization.

- At 3M, the heroes are the individuals and teams who surmount insurmountable obstacles to come up with a successful new product.

- At Federal Express, the stories are about the incredible lengths that people have gone to in order to deliver a package on time and against all odds.

- At Southwest Airlines, the stories are about jokes that employees have played with travelers and on each other to help ensure fun in traveling.

- At Saturn automobile dealerships, the employees all gather at a ritual send-off to cheer a customer driving away with a newly purchased Saturn.

- At Apple Computer, the team initially responsible for developing the McIntosh computer raised a pirate's flag over their building to signal the values they were bringing to that task.

In a very real sense, the beliefs, norms, and values communicated through these stories, rituals, and heroes provide a mental road map to the members of an organization. They define and reinforce in people's minds what is important in the organization and "the way things are done around here."

It should not be surprising, then, that because change requires a shift in "the way things are done around here," it necessarily represents the most serious kind of threat to an organization's corporate culture. Change requires a new set of beliefs, new norms, and new values. It not only requires new heroes, new language, and new rituals; change renders the old heroes, language, and rituals obsolete.

For these reasons, it should come as no surprise that the natural reaction of the existing corporate culture is strong and determined resistance to change. It is only natural that the existing corporate culture defends itself against change, for change represents the end of the old culture's way of doing things. In 1994, Louis Gerstner admitted he was having difficulty changing IBM's culture as quickly as he felt it needed to be changed. Even after the value of IBM stock had declined and the company had eliminated more than one hundred thousand jobs, an internal survey of twelve hundred top managers showed that 40 percent still did not recognize the need for change. Employees, for example, still believed that they were entitled to their jobs. For 70 years IBM had prided itself on a no-layoff policy. The massive layoffs of the 1990s were in direct conflict with that tradition. But Gerstner was attempting to change the focus of the IBM corporate culture from an emphasis on employee job security to one of achieving results and getting things done. For Gerstner, the old IBM way of doing things was part of the problem, not part of the solution. As he said at that time, "When it comes to a results-oriented corporate culture, we're not there yet, not by a long shot."[4]

In sum, not only do people respond to change with stress at the individual level; the organization as a whole tends to strongly resist changing the shared mindset of its people about what matters and about how it should operate.

For these reasons, while the process of change in organizations may be inevitable, it is not easily achieved. As shown in Figure 13-1, for the process of change to be successful in an organization, management must recognize both the potentially intense individual human resistance to change and the intense collective resistance rising from the organization's corporate culture. The first step in managing change, therefore, is to deal with the reality of this resistance.

MANAGING THE CHANGE PROCESS

Nearly fifty years ago, social scientist Kurt Lewin studied the process of change in groups and individuals and concluded that two conditions must be met for the change process to be successful.[5] The first is that the group or individual must be ready for the change; they must be prepared to give up the existing pattern of beliefs and behaviors. The second condition is that once the change has begun, it must be supported and reinforced. According to Lewin, without support, recognition, reward, and positive feedback, even the most determined efforts at change eventually weaken and disappear.

Based on the importance of meeting these two conditions of initial preparation and ongoing support, Lewin suggested a change process with three stages: (1) the *unfreezing* stage, during which the organization addresses the problems of resistance and prepares its people for change; (2) the *change* stage, during which the new beliefs and new behaviors are communicated and modeled; and (3) the *refreezing* stage, during which the new beliefs and behaviors are supported and reinforced. Business consultant Noel M. Tichy from the University of Michigan uses

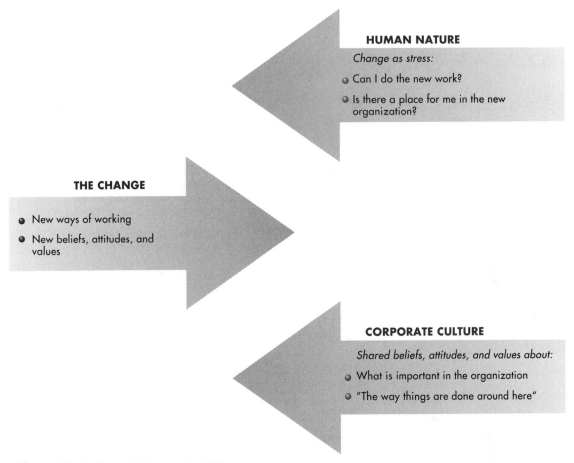

HUMAN NATURE

Change as stress:

- Can I do the new work?
- Is there a place for me in the new organization?

THE CHANGE

- New ways of working
- New beliefs, attitudes, and values

CORPORATE CULTURE

Shared beliefs, attitudes, and values about:

- What is important in the organization
- "The way things are done around here"

Figure 13-1 Forces in Organizational Change

different terms, but identifies essentially the same three stages, as shown in Figure 13-2.[6] Each stage is worth a closer look.

Stage One: Unfreezing/Awakening

Management's task in the first stage of the change process is, as we said, to reduce the resistance to change—Tichy's words, to "wake up" the organization to the need for change. Before this can begin, however, the potential sources of resistance in the particular change situation need to be identified in more detail. Lewin developed a process for identifying and analyzing the forces operating in a change situation that he called force field analysis.[7]

Force Field Analysis

Lewin suggested that in any organizational change effort, two kinds of forces will affect the effectiveness of the change: driving forces and restraining forces. Lewin defined *driving forces* as forces or factors in the situation that initiate, assist, and

	Lewin / Tichy	
Stage 1	*Unfreezing/ Awakening*	● Preparing the organization for change
		● Reducing resistance to change
		● Alerting the organization of the need for change
Stage 2	*Change/Envisioning*	● The creative process of developing a vision of the change
		● Communicating the vision through message and action
Stage 3	*Refreezing/Re-architecting*	● Reinforcing the change once it is implemented through reward, recognition, and celebration

Figure 13-2 Stages in the Change Process

support the change. Driving forces include such things as changes in the organization's environment that make change necessary or that represent an opportunity to the organization. They include key individuals and groups within the organization who are in favor of and support the change. They also include the availability of training, technology, and other resources necessary for the change to be effective. Driving forces might also include information or experiences that make clear what will happen if the organization doesn't change.

Restraining forces are forces or factors working against the change, forces generating resistance at the individual and corporate culture levels, as we have already discussed. In many ways, restraining forces are the opposite of driving forces. They include opposition from key individuals and groups within the organization, and lack of availability of training and other resources needed for the change to succeed. Restraining forces might also include negative information or experiences relative to the change.

A force field analysis for a change requiring sales representatives to transmit their orders using notebook computers is shown in Figure 13-3.

For change to be effective, managers must begin with a careful and complete force field analysis. They must first identify the driving forces in the situation and make full use of them to overcome the obstacles to change. Perhaps more importantly, managers must also correctly identify the restraining forces and develop strategies to eliminate or minimize them as the change moves forward. We have already discussed the importance of resistance as organizations attempt to change to improve performance. There are a number of strategies for overcoming resistance to change.

Strategies for Dealing with Resistance to Change

John Kotter and Leonard Schlesinger have identified a number of strategies for reducing resistance to change in organizations. Figure 13-4 shows the range of

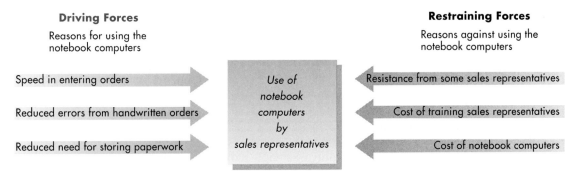

Figure 13-3 Force-Field Analysis for Increased Use of Technology

options available to management for accomplishing this essential task of unfreezing/awakening.[8]

Four of these options—education and communication, participation and involvement, facilitation and support, negotiation and agreement—could be described as people-oriented approaches to preparing people for change. These approaches have the important advantage of leaving intact the bond of trust between the organization and its employees, a bond which can have a powerful impact on workers' performance. Lawrence Bossidy, CEO of $12 billion-a-year aerospace manufacturer AlliedSignal, explains:

> You have to give people a reason to do something differently. Examples from the real world can get them motivated . . . You might want to focus on [what a major competitor is doing] to build support for improving your own performance before you're attacked. Scaring people isn't the answer. You try to appeal to them. The more they understand why you want change, the easier it is to commit to it.[9]

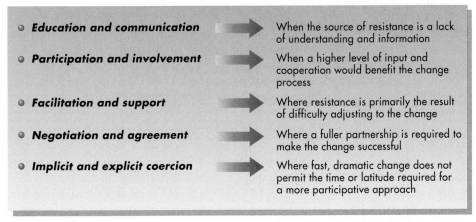

Figure 13-4 Strategies for Reducing Resistance to Change

In some change situations, however, people-oriented change simply may not be possible. For example, it is conceivable that no amount of education, participation, facilitation, or negotiation could prepare an organization for the kinds of change required in the downsizing that has become so typical in the 1990s. This brings us to Kotter and Schlesinger's fifth option for reducing resistance to change: implicit and explicit coercion.

Coercion as a Strategy

In the change situation, *coercion* is the process of imposing change on an organization. It is the process of requiring people to perform new tasks, or to perform their old tasks in new ways, or to perform in conditions that might be dramatically different from what they have been accustomed to. Coerced change is not voluntary, and it is usually not gradual.

Consider the case of Sears. Beginning in the late 1980s, Sears attempted to change itself to better compete with Wal-Mart, K-Mart, and other successful competitors. The changes were so dramatic that they met with tremendous resistance. Sears eliminated more than fifty thousand positions as it cut the number of regional offices by more than half. Former regional managers who were not terminated lost prestigious positions as well as the opportunity for promotion. Store managers lost authority and status as salespeople were reorganized to report directly to corporate headquarters. Salespeople for the first time had to sell brand-name products like GE ranges and Amana refrigerators right next to the Kenmore appliances that provided them much larger commissions.

None of this was voluntary; all these changes were required of the people of Sears. Sears was convinced that the changes could not be participatory. At the very least, there was not enough time for education, participation, and negotiation. These changes were necessary for Sears' survival. Survival became more crucial than trust, so the changes were coerced.

Some critics might argue that coercion is not a strategy for reducing resistance to change but a process of imposing change despite continuing broad-based resistance. While there is some validity to this position, there are grounds for viewing coercion as a legitimate means to reducing resistance. Twenty years ago, Harvard psychologist Jerome Bruner in his research on the relationship between feelings and behavior suggested, "You more often act yourself into feeling than feel yourself into action."[10] Applied to the change situation, this means that people may come to feel differently about a change once they have been forced to implement it. People tend to adjust their feelings to the reality of the situation, and once people have seen that they can survive new conditions and may even benefit by them, their resistance may at least be reduced, if not eliminated entirely. In this sense coercion may in fact be a viable, if difficult, approach for reducing resistance to change.

The practical experience of organizations who have actually engaged in unfreezing/awakening through coercion appears to support this conclusion. For example, Robert Frey, president of his own company in Cincinnati, Ohio, noted not long ago, "A manager has to force change. My role was to make people change at a faster pace than they would have ever chosen."[11] William Weiss, CEO of $11.2

billion-a-year Ameritech, has had the same experience, "The best way I know to get people to accept the need for change is to not give them a choice."[12]

The question about coercion is whether it results in long-term change or just short-term compliance. Some experts question whether coercion might not actually increase resistance among resentful employees over the longer term. They point out that the problem with forcing people into change is that you then find yourself meeting the global competition with a crushed and battered workforce.

Some defenders of coercion as an approach for unfreezing argue that coerced change can still be implemented in ways that respect the needs and dignity of people. Others suggest there may be no effective alternative. Given the number of companies that feel they have been forced to this approach by the demands of the changing environment and changing performance standards, the coming years will provide a useful opportunity to evaluate the ultimate effectiveness of the various degrees of the coercion option.

Stage Two: The Change/Envisioning

Once resistance to change has been reduced to the extent possible, the change itself must begin. The new behaviors, the new approach, the new priorities must be identified, preached, modeled, and practiced. Former Notre Dame president Theodore Hesburgh has suggested that in leading change, "You can't blow an uncertain trumpet."[13] In other words, you can't expect people to follow you from the old way to the new way until it is clear to them what the new way is and what it means. The three elements shown in Figure 13-5 appear to be essential to what Hesburgh might term a "clear call to change."

Vision: You Can't Get There without One

You will remember that almost forty years ago Drucker introduced the idea of vision as a critical management responsibility (It is the "first responsibility of the manager . . . to give others vision . . ."). And remember that for Drucker vision is the network of goals which alone provide the organization with its sense of purpose and direction. Finally, you will remember that for goals to be effective, they must also be challenging and specific.

Vision in the form of challenging and specific goals is never more critical than in the change situation. For change to be effective, management must de-

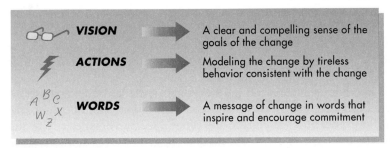

Figure 13-5 Elements of "A Clear Call to Change"

velop a vision of what the changed organization will look like that is so clear and so specific that no question or room for doubt exists as to where the change is leading. Certainty about the dimension and direction of change can itself be a powerful force for effective change.

The changing environment and changing performance standards put tremendous pressure on organizations to change. But change can finally succeed only when the manager is absolutely clear in his or her own mind on exactly how the change will look in every major dimension of the organization. Only that kind of clarity and certainty will allow managers to stay the course and not be confused by the difficult currents and challenges of change. Only that kind of clarity can minimize in the organization the kind of dangerous uncertainty that can rekindle the resistance to change.

Interestingly, "getting the vision"—what Tichy calls "envisioning"—involves not just management, but the entire organization:

> The visioning process is creative and often chaotic. A vision is a group effort. It is what the group believes to be important. It is also a work in progress, an architectural rendering that constantly gets modified. As many people as possible should be involved, thinking "out loud" and getting feedback from many different stakeholders.[14]

Bennis and Nanus come to the same conclusion:

> The leader only rarely was the one who conceived of the vision in the first place. Therefore the leader must be a superb listener, particularly to those advocating new or different images of the emerging reality . . . Successful leaders, we have found, are *great askers,* and they do pay attention.[15]

Management's responsibility, then, is to get the vision, not necessarily to create it. Once the vision is clear in the manager's mind, the next step is to communicate it clearly. Even the most inspiring vision is of little value until it is communicated. We turn now to the importance of the manager's actions and words in communicating the vision of change.

Actions Speak Louder than Words

By definition, change requires learning new behaviors, new beliefs, and new values. There is no more effective way for others to learn the "new way" than by having these behaviors modeled for them. As we pointed out in Chapter 11, all the verbal instruction in the world will not be as effective as the example of a leader in communicating new behaviors and values.

Tom Peters and Nancy Austin tell the story of a new plant manager whose vision included eliminating the divisions and bad feeling between hourly workers on the plant floor and professionals in the offices. In conversations with the hourly workers, this manager learned that these feelings had been reinforced for years by the hourly workers' having to walk a considerable distance from their parking area past the empty spaces right next to the building reserved for the office staff, who typically came to work an hour or more later than the hourlies. During his first week on the job, rather than give a speech about how everyone would be treated as equals from then on, the new manager put on a pair of coveralls, grabbed a bucket of black paint, called everyone into the parking lot, and painted over the reserved signs on the curb, beginning with his own.[16]

Words can yield a variety of interpretations in terms of the kind of behaviors people *think* they mean. But a manager's actions provide a clear model of exactly the kind of behavior that is required. In the case of change, imitation is more effective than interpretation. A manager who wants people to take a more team-based approach will almost certainly get better results by taking a more team-based approach herself rather than just by making a speech on teamwork.

The same is true for an executive who wants to see his or her managers spending less time in their offices and more time talking and working with their people. If the executive wants his or her managers out of their offices and talking with people, the best way to achieve this is to lead by example. The actions of the leader, *if they are consistent*, simply leave much less room for doubt in people's minds about the kind of new behavior required.

Words

Finally, however, there must be words. While actions do speak louder—and more clearly—than words, words are still a powerful force in focusing our attention and mobilizing our energies. Anyone who has heard Martin Luther King's "I have a dream . . ." speech, understands the power of the spoken word. When Bill Gore of Goretex talks about his people "changing the world," or when Steven Jobs, when he was with Apple Computer, spoke of his people "starting a revolution," each recognized the impact that words can have.

Change is a political process in which the forces for improvement attempt to overcome the forces of resistance and the status quo. Effective change is the result of an effective campaign, and words are a potentially powerful weapon in deciding the outcome of that campaign. Jack Welch, CEO of GE, put it this way:[17]

> Good business leaders create a vision, articulate the vision, passionately own the vision, and relentlessly drive it to completion . . . They go up, down, and around their organization to reach people. They don't stick to the established channels. They're informal. They're straight with people. They make a religion out of being accessible. They never get bored telling their story.

The three critical elements of the change or envisioning phase, then, are the change vision and the leader's actions and words. If the vision is not centered clearly on the change, or if the actions and words of management are inconsistent with the vision—or with each other—it becomes virtually impossible to hit the change target. Only when there is clarity and correctness of vision and consistency in the leader's words and actions does the change process begin to gain momentum and acceptance.

Stage Three: Refreezing/Re-architecting

Lewin termed the third and final phase of the change process "refreezing." *Refreezing* is the process of reinforcing the change to ensure that it endures over the long term. If the new patterns and the new behaviors developed in the change/envisioning phase are to genuinely take root and prosper, they must become embedded in the very fabric of the organization, and they must yield positive results. This is what Tichy means by "re-architecting": designing and building the structures and support needed to sustain the new behaviors and beliefs far into the future.

For change to endure and prosper, the new ways of doing things must become part of an overall positive experience for the people doing them. To achieve this, the refreezing/re-architecting phase requires the elements shown in Figure 13-6. In other words, successful change requires the development of an entirely new corporate culture focused on the new behaviors and the new beliefs.

Recognizing Heroes

Successful change requires heroes—individuals and groups who adopt the new behaviors and run with them. The heroism can take many forms, from the sales associate who goes miles out of her way to deliver an item on the way home from work, to the teacher who visits the homes of his students, to the machine operator who volunteers for a problem-solving task force.

Similarly, recognizing these heroes can take many forms, from a box of doughnuts, to a flag flying over the hero's section, to a sincere letter of appreciation. Tom Peters tells the story of a leader who wanted to recognize one of the heroes in his section, but when he looked for something to give him all he could find was a banana he had saved from lunch. The leader gave this hero the banana, and ever since the "Golden Banana" has been the ultimate symbol of recognition in that company.

Managers must take the time to identify and recognize heroes. In doing so, they not only clarify the direction of the change, but also reinforce the emerging value which views trying the new behaviors as nothing short of heroic.

Celebrations

Celebrations are a powerful way to emphasize and reinforce values and behaviors through a positive social experience. Celebrations are community events that dramatically enrich the experience of the group and the individual.

Until recently, celebrations by work organizations were limited largely to the

- Recognizing the heroes and champions of change
- Celebrating the successes of the change
- Rewarding commitment to change

Figure 13-6 Elements of Refreezing/Re-Architecting

award of the traditional gold watch upon retirement. It is ironic that the event most often celebrated in organizations was the individual's leaving the organization. In the more recent past, however, organizations have begun to recognize the power of celebration. Initially during this period, celebrations were organized around employee anniversaries: five years with the firm, ten years, twenty-five years, and so on. Over time, the forms of celebration multiplied from the informal Friday afternoon "beer busts" made famous by a number of Silicon Valley firms, to the slightly more formal Tupperware and Mary Kay galas that honor the most successful members of corporate sales forces. Then there is the story of Sam Walton, founder of the Wal-Mart retail chain, who danced the Hula in a grass skirt on Wall Street in the middle of winter when his employees achieved a targeted increase in profits.

The common thread in these celebrations is that they are community events marking community achievement, whether in terms of sales or service or just completing another productive week. If a change is to become a genuine part of the life of the organization, it must be celebrated as it unfolds and advances. Recognition and appreciation of the achievement of the change goals must be raised to the level of community celebration. Only very reluctantly do we give up our celebrations; so celebrations, in a sense, serve as insurance that the changes will endure.

Reward

As important as recognition and celebrations are for refreezing or reinforcing the new behaviors required by change, pay and promotion remain among the most powerful means of reinforcing behavior in organizations. The ultimate indicators of an organization's priorities are still most clearly reflected in what you get paid for and who gets promoted. Earlier we discussed pay for performance as an important element in the high-performance work environment. Basing pay and promotion decisions on progress made toward adopting the new behaviors sends a powerful signal that the organization is serious about the change.

For example, if the job of supervisor has been changed to require a greater emphasis on communication and teamwork, then some significant portion of a supervisor's compensation should be based on how well he or she has performed in those two areas. And promotion to the next level should be awarded to whichever supervisor most effectively demonstrates the new priorities of communication and teamwork.

Designing reward systems that directly reinforce the change priorities of an organization can be difficult. Resistance to change may be more strongly expressed in the areas of pay and promotion than in any others. Without reward systems that clearly reflect the change priorities, however, the organization is sending mixed messages through one of the most important channels it has for communicating what matters.

So these are the phases of the effective change process: unfreezing the existing patterns of behavior and beliefs and awakening the organization to the need for change; changing behaviors through a shared envisioning process and through ceaseless and consistent communication of that vision; and refreezing, re-architecturing the new patterns through recognition, celebrations, and reward.

MANAGING CONTINUOUS CHANGE

In the world of the 1950s, when Lewin developed his model of change, any organizational change tended to be viewed as an infrequent event that would likely be followed by a period of stability for the organization. For this reason, Lewin's change model reflects a process of moving through *a* change. In that earlier period, once the change process was complete, the organization would continue in the new direction.

As we noted in Chapter 1, in the changing environment there appear to be no periods of stability. Tichy puts it this way: "Once you have completed the three-act process [of change], it is time to start all over again."[18] Jack Welch of GE agrees:

> People always ask, "Is the change over? Can we stop now?" You've got to tell them, "No, it's just begun."[19]

The "Calm Waters" versus "White-Water Rapids" Metaphors

Management professor Peter Vaill has used the term "calm waters" to describe the conditions of the 1950s. He compares the organizations of that period to large ocean liners traveling calm waters with a crew that had made the trip together dozens of times. Under "calm waters" conditions, change is usually required only when the occasional storm appears.

As we have noted throughout this book, conditions have changed dramatically in recent years. According to Vaill, the environment is no longer one of calm waters, and organizations are no longer like large ocean liners with a veteran crew. In his words:

> The organization is more akin to a forty-foot raft than to a large ship. Rather than sailing a calm sea, this raft must traverse a raging river made up of an uninterrupted flow of permanent white-water rapids. To make things worse, the raft is manned by ten people who have never worked together, none have traveled the river below, much of the trip is in the dark, the river is dotted by unexpected turns and obstacles, the exact destination of the raft is unclear, and at irregular frequencies the raft needs to pull to shore, where new crew members are added and others leave.[20]

In many ways, Lewin's three-stage model for managing change is a model designed for calm waters. It is a model for managing a change. In the permanent white-water rapids described by Vaill, organizations need to be not merely capable of implementing an occasional change, but *built* for change, with constant change as one of their fundamental goals.

Thriving on Chaos: The Innovative Organization

Given these conditions of ceaseless change or chaos, and given the deep-rooted resistance to change typical of most organizations, it is not difficult to understand how an organization built to actually seek out and thrive upon change would have a clear competitive advantage. Tom Peters has pointed out that in a genuinely chaotic environment, an organization built to *thrive* on chaos will certainly do better than one built merely to *survive* the chaos.[21]

Peters has suggested a set of principles that typify what he calls the *innovative* organization, a blueprint for designing organizations to actually thrive on chaos. A number of Peters's principles—or "prescriptions," as he calls them—for creating such an organization are shown in Figure 13-7.[22]

According to Peters, the goal of the innovative organization is to create an organization for which the continuous "white-water rapids" are a source of competitive advantage and not a source of continuous insecurity and dread.

The Learning Organization

MIT professor Peter Senge has suggested a different prescription for prospering in this era of turbulence and change. For Senge, the key is to convert our traditional command-and-control organizations into what he calls "learning organizations."[23] The only organizations that will successfully adapt to the conditions of

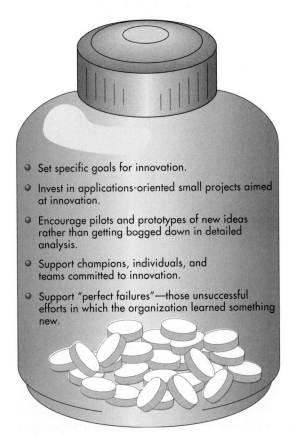

- Set specific goals for innovation.
- Invest in applications-oriented small projects aimed at innovation.
- Encourage pilots and prototypes of new ideas rather than getting bogged down in detailed analysis.
- Support champions, individuals, and teams committed to innovation.
- Support "perfect failures"—those unsuccessful efforts in which the organization learned something new.

Figure 13-7 Prescriptions for the Innovative Organization

continuous change, according to Senge, are those that constantly engage in learning from their own and others' experiences. Only organizations focused on continuous learning will be capable of the constant adjustments necessary for success in the constantly changing environment.

Significantly, while learning may be a management responsibility, according to Senge it is not exclusively—or even primarily—the task of managers. Organizations in general must become more "learningful":

> It is no longer sufficient to have one person learning for the organization, a Ford or a Sloan or a Watson. It's just not possible any longer to "figure it out" from the top, and have everyone else following the orders of the "grand strategist." The organizations that will truly excel in the future will be the organizations that discover people's commitment and capacity to learn at *all* levels in an organization.[24]

LEADERSHIP AND CHANGE

The change responsibility of management is, finally, a leadership challenge. In this chapter we have emphasized that change involves both people's beliefs and their behaviors. Whether the goal is Peters's "innovative organization" or Senge's "learning organization," people's beliefs and behaviors must change. You may recall that we defined the work of the transformational leader as changing the beliefs and values of their people to bring them to new levels of performance. In this sense, the process of managing change and the work of the transformational leader are one and the same.

You may also have noted that the key elements of the change process are defined in the same terms—compelling vision, communication through word and action, and reinforcement through recognition and celebration—as the characteristics of the transformational leader. This suggests that change in organizations should not be viewed simply as a process of moving the organization to a different set of behaviors. Rather, effective change involves actually transforming people's doubts and defensiveness in the face of change to belief in their own potential and commitment to meet its challenges.

A CLOSING COMMENT

Our final quote is from Peter Drucker: "To be sure, the fundamental task of management remains unchanged: to make people capable of joint performance through common goals, common values, the right structure, and the training and development they need to perform and respond to change."[25] Because of change, the task of management is never finished; there will never be a final set of answers to the question of how to improve organizational performance. In this sense effective management, like most human challenges, is not so much a destination as it is a journey. Responsibility for performance is now more widely shared than ever before and performance demands are more challenging. In meeting these challenges, each of us joins in the journey to more effective organizations.

SUMMARY

Change is everywhere in the world of the manager. The sources of change include the changing environment, advancing technologies, and the human diversity of the changing workplace. One of the most challenging tasks for managers is to prepare their organizations to compete in the turbulence of this constantly changing world.

One of the most significant barriers to effective change in organizations is the natural but intense resistance that comes from human nature and corporate culture. Given these forces, Kurt Lewin has suggested that any effort to change an organization must begin with a force field analysis to identify in detail the forces or factors supporting the change and the sources of resistance that must be addressed by the organization's change strategies.

Lewin also defined three stages that an effective change process must include. The first stage, unfreezing or awakening, must prepare people and awaken them to the need for change. The second stage is the change or envisioning stage. In this stage the goals of the change are defined, clarified, and communicated. The third stage, refreezing or re-architecting, requires that reward structures be created to reinforce the change as it begins to happen to ensure that it endures over time. Without the successful completion of all three stages, the process of change becomes more dubious.

But making even the most successful change is probably not enough. One of the most significant changes for management is that in today's environment change never ends. Continuous change is the new requirement. This means that management must develop organizations built for change. Tom Peters talks about the innovative organization designed to thrive on chaos. Peter Senge speaks in terms of the learning organization, in which everyone learns from their experience and makes the adjustments required by whatever change lies ahead.

Finally, change is a leadership responsibility. The challenge is to move people beyond their natural defensiveness and resistance to the point where they view change not as a threat but as an opportunity.

QUESTIONS TO CHALLENGE YOUR UNDERSTANDING
OF THE CHAPTER

1. Using the ideas discussed in this chapter, explain why there was so much resistance by bank tellers when they were first required to use computers to process customer transactions.

2. What is corporate culture and why is it a source of resistance to change in organizations?

3. Your professor has decided to base the entire grade for this course on team tests.

What does the professor need to do to unfreeze or prepare students who are not familiar with this approach?

4. Explain the meaning of the statement "Actions speak louder than words" in the change process and provide an example where someone's behavior meant more than what he or she said.

5. Briefly describe the value of celebrations and rewards in the refreezing process.

6. Compare the calm-waters versus white-water-rapids metaphors for the change environment.

7. How does Tom Peters's concept of thriving on chaos compare with Senge's learning organization?

8. How are learning organizations different from traditional command-and-control organizations?

MANAGEMENT EXERCISE

How Receptive Are You to Change?

For each of the items listed below, select the answer that best suits your degree of agreement or disagreement. When you are finished, add up your total points. Your instructor will explain the interpretation of your score.

		STRONGLY AGREE				*STRONGLY DISAGREE*
1.	*I continually like to try new things.*	1	2	3	4	5
2.	*I would prefer to have a job that forces me to learn new skills regularly.*	1	2	3	4	5
3.	*I like things just the way they are in my life.*	1	2	3	4	5
4.	*Life to me is just one new adventure after another.*	1	2	3	4	5
5.	*For the past several years, I have known exactly what I wanted to do with my life.*	1	2	3	4	5
6.	*I like to keep all of my things in their proper place.*	1	2	3	4	5
7.	*My ideal job has clear, fixed requirements that I can count on.*	1	2	3	4	5
8.	*My friends often tell me that I am adventuresome.*	1	2	3	4	5
9.	*I see myself changing jobs and careers fairly often in my life.*	1	2	3	4	5
10.	*I get bored doing the same things over and over.*	1	2	3	4	5

REFERENCES

1. Ira Sager and Amy E. Cortese, "Lou Gerstner Unveils His Battle Plan," *Business Week,* April 4, 1994, 96–98.

2. Hans Seyle, *The Stress of Life* (New York: McGraw-Hill, 1976).

3. Terrence E. Deal and Allan A. Kennedy, *Corporate Cultures: The Rites and Rituals of Corporate Life* (Reading, Mass.: Addison-Wesley, 1982).

4. Laurie Hays, "Gerstner Is Struggling as He Tries to Change Ingrained IBM Culture," *Wall Street Journal,* May 13, 1994, A1.

5. Kurt Lewin, "Frontiers in Group Dynamics: Concept, Method, and Reality in Social Science, *Human Relations,* June 1947, 5–41.

6. Noel M. Tichy, "Revolutionize Your Company," *Fortune,* December 13, 1993, 114–18.

7. Kurt Lewin, *Field Theory and Social Science: Selected Theoretical Papers* (New York: Harper & Row, 1951).

8. John P. Kotter and Leonard A. Schlesinger, "Choosing Strategies for Change," *Harvard Business Review,* March–April 1979, 109–12.

9. "A Master Class in Radical Change," *Fortune,* December 13, 1993, 84.

10. Jerome S. Bruner, *On Knowing: Essays for the Left Hand* (New York: Atheneum, 1973), 24.

11. Robert Frey, "Empowerment or Else," *Harvard Business Review,* September–October 1993, 80–94.

12. "A Master Class in Radical Change," 88.

13. Quoted in Tom Peters, *Thriving on Chaos* (New York: Harper & Row, 1987), 483.

14. Noel Tichy, "Revolutionize Your Company," *Fortune,* December 13, 1993, 118.

15. Warren Bennis and Burt Nanus, *Leaders* (New York: Harper & Row, 1985), 492.

16. Tom Peters and Nancy Austin, *A Passion for Excellence* (New York: Random House, 1985), 274.

17. Noel Tichy and Ram Charan, "Speed, Simplicity, Self-Confidence: An interview with Jack Welch," *Harvard Business Review,* September–October 1989, 113.

18. Noel M. Tichy, "Revolutionize Your Company," *Fortune,* December 13, 1993, 118.

19. "A Master Class in Radical Change," 83.

20. Peter B. Vaill, *Managing as Performing Art: New Ideas for a World of Chaotic Change* (San Francisco: Jossey-Bass, 1989).

21. Peters, *Thriving on Chaos.*

22. Ibid, 235–338.

23. Peter M. Senge, *The Fifth Discipline: The Art and Practice of the Learning Organization* (New York: Doubleday/Currency, 1990), 14.

24. Ibid., 4.

25. Peter Drucker, *The New Realities* (New York: HarperCollins, 1989), 222.

FROM THE MANAGER'S E-MAIL
Managing Change at TraveLog

You are the president and owner of TraveLog, a full-service travel agency. You assist individuals, families, and business customers in the area with designing vacations, and planning and booking travel and lodging reservations—both for recreation and business purposes. Presently, your company consists of four managers besides yourself and fourteen additional staff members organized into four separate departments: Business Travel, Recreation and Leisure Travel, Reservations, and Billing.

Your business is in trouble, with the rate of complaints from both customers and the staff increasing daily. The overall operation of your company needs improvement. Quality in terms of speed and flexibility has declined. There are times when staff members in all four departments aren't busy, but they are never the same times. During some months, Business Travel is overwhelmed and Leisure and Recreation is slow. At other times the situation is reversed, and the same is true for Reservations and Billing. You also know you can't afford to increase the size of your staff because the fierce competition in the travel industry forces you to keep expenses as low as possible. Besides, the problem isn't that you don't have enough help; it's that you never seem to have enough help where it's needed.

You've decided that you have no choice but to change the way your business is organized. You think that if you eliminate the separate departments and assign one member from each department to a customer service team, you might be able to increase the speed and efficiency of your operation. Eventually, you want every member of every team to be able to perform the work of every other team member. This would mean workers could be shifted to the area where the demand was greatest at any given time. You've asked each of your department managers for their opinion via E-mail.

Date: February 12, 1996

From: LOCALSYS (Kerry Brynes, Manager of Business Travel)

Subject: Proposed Reorganization

I like your idea. There have certainly been enough times
recently when we could have used some additional people in this
department. And I know there are times when they could use some
help in the other departments. I'm not sure my people will be
very excited about doing the work that is done in Reservations
and in Billing, especially since they really enjoy working with
our clients in developing the itineraries and plans for their
business travelers. I think you're going to have to explain that
if they don't think they are up to the change, you'll be looking
to hire new people who are.

E-mail continued on next page.

Date: February 12, 1996

From: LOCALSYS (Maria Delgado, Manager of Leisure and
            Recreation Travel)

Subject: Proposed Reorganization

Your plan makes sense. We need all the help we can get. But I
don't see how my people are ever going to have the time to
cross-train people from the other departments in what we do
here, plus receiving training in *their* work. We have our slow
days, but not *that* many.

I'm also not sure some of the staff from the other departments
will have the right temperament for dealing with our family and
individual accounts. It takes a lot more patience and hand-
holding to work with these customers. The people in Business
Travel are used to doing business on a more professional basis,
and the people in Reservations and in Billing are more
accustomed to working with computers than with people. And my
guess is that they prefer it.

Date:	February 12, 1996
From:	Ahmad Timpson, Reservations Manager
Subject:	Proposed Reorganization

Your plan makes sense to me, but I'm trying to look at this from my people's point of view. My guess is they'd be 50-50 for and against. A few of them have been complaining forever that they could do a better job than some of the staff in the Business and Leisure and Recreation departments. They say that some of the travel plans they come up with over there don't make any sense from a reservations point of view. They'd probably be all in favor of the change.

Some of the others probably wouldn't. They do a good job of processing the actual air, car, cruise, bus, and lodging reservations, and that's not easy work. In fact it's going to take a good amount of training to get anyone from outside the department to the point where they're half as good as my people. To tell you the truth, though, I just can't see some of my people dealing directly with the customers. In fact, I'm afraid some of my best people might leave before they'd agree to work in teams and do direct customer service.

E-mail continued on next page.

Date: February 12, 1996

From: LOCALSYS (Myron Winters, Billing Manager)

Subject: Proposed Reorganization

The concept of total flexibility and of everyone being able to
fill in for everyone else is great—in theory. As a practical
matter, I'm just not sure all of our people are cut out to do
everything, even if they wanted to, which I'm certain they do
not. I think we're going to lose some people over this, maybe
some of our best people. I'm not against your plan; in fact I
think it makes a lot of sense. But you may need to think about
providing some incentives along the way.

Speaking of which, I know the others won't bring this up, but I
will. All of us who are department managers are concerned about
what happens to us in this plan. We know you're going to need
help making all of this work. But we also know there aren't
going to be any departments under the new plan. Where does that
leave the managers? We'd like to help, but it will be pretty
difficult for us as managers to be enthusiastic if all we're
doing is working ourselves out of a job.

1. Based on all of the information presented above, perform a force field
   analysis of this change situation. Make a list of the driving forces and restraining forces.

2. Using Figure 13-4 from the chapter, select the strategy or strategies you feel
   would be most effective in this change situation, and explain your selection.

Index

INDEX